Harold L. Spain

*Asset Prices
in Economic Analysis*

Publications of the
Institute of Business and Economic Research
University of California

Asset Prices
in Economic Analysis

SAMUEL B. CHASE, JR.

UNIVERSITY OF CALIFORNIA PRESS
BERKELEY AND LOS ANGELES · 1963

UNIVERSITY OF CALIFORNIA PRESS
BERKELEY AND LOS ANGELES
CALIFORNIA

CAMBRIDGE UNIVERSITY PRESS
LONDON, ENGLAND

LIBRARY OF CONGRESS CATALOG CARD NUMBER: 63-10588

PRINTED IN THE UNITED STATES OF AMERICA

Foreword

The sudden death of Norman Buchanan in 1958 represented a great loss to the economics profession and to the social sciences generally. Buchanan was not only a distinguished economist in his own right—with significant contributions in economic theory, corporate organization, and economic development (in which he was a pioneer)—but he also contributed tremendously to the advancement of research in the social sciences generally. For nearly twenty years (1936–1955), he was a member of the Department of Economics at the University of California, Berkeley. In 1955, he resigned to become Director of the Social Sciences Division of the Rockefeller Foundation. He had already, while on leave from Berkeley, served with the Foundation from 1947 to 1950. He died suddenly, of a heart attack, in April, 1958, at the tragically early age of 52.

Soon after his death, Buchanan's friends and admirers—under the leadership of a committee consisting of Howard S. Ellis, Joseph H. Willits, and Philip E. Mosely, chairman—sought a fitting way of paying honor to his memory. The result was the "Norman S. Buchanan Memorial Award in Economics," to be offered approximately biennially for the best doctoral dissertation in economics submitted at the University of California, Berkeley. No prize need be given if, in the judgment of the awards committee, none of the theses submitted for the prize is sufficiently distinguished.

The first winner of the Buchanan Award is Samuel B. Chase, Jr., and the Department of Economics at Berkeley is happy to present herewith his prize-winning dissertation, *Asset Prices in*

Economic Analysis. In the author's own words, this is a study "designed to improve the treatment of assets in economic theory" —a task which, most economists will agree, badly needs to be done. Dr. Chase offers a theoretical model containing features which are usually ignored in the literature, and he provides a highly skilled analysis—but in simple, nonmathematical language —of the nature and implications of his theory of asset-price determination. His emphasis on assets and asset prices is not unprecedented, but it is unusual; and many readers will undoubtedly want to take issue with one or another aspect of his argument. To the extent that this occurs, it will merely confirm what one reader of the manuscript has referred to as the "suggestive and provocative" character of Dr. Chase's analysis.

R. A. GORDON

Preface

There is a growing feeling among economists that economic analysis has concentrated too heavily on flows to the neglect of stocks. Recent contributions have turned increasingly to asset holdings in the explanation of spending decisions, while heightened interest in economic growth has once more brought capital theory to center-stage.

This study is designed to clarify and emphasize the role of assets in economic analysis; it focuses on the asset pricing process and its interrelations with other economic phenomena. In contrast with the more usual treatment of asset markets as a kind of peripheral phenomenon, it is argued that these interrelations are crucial in the determination of general equilibrium conditions.

The problems treated are complex, or at least I have found them so. The aims of this study are modest—to make a first step toward providing a frame of reference that integrates stock and flow phenomena, with particular attention to the relatively neglected problem of asset price determination. Throughout the book, the analysis is highly abstract. A perfectly competitive pricing system is postulated. Problems of monetary and fiscal economics are discussed, but primarily for illustrative, rather than prescriptive, purposes, for although the study treats crucial monetary matters at several points, it is not primarily an excursion into monetary theory and its applications—there is, for instance, no consideration of fractional reserve banking.

I have found, nonetheless, that with proper elaboration and extension the viewpoint set forth here provides a useful framework for analyzing government financial policies, including central banking, debt management, taxation, and budget policy. An important feature of this framework is that it allows a unified and coherent view of the economic process that can embrace a wide variety of policy problems.

Chapter I sets forth a general description of the study and the problems with which it deals. The remainder of the book, except for the final chapter, is my doctoral dissertation, amended slightly.

The first year of study leading to the dissertation was financed by a Ford Foundation Doctoral Dissertation Fellowship. The dissertation was completed early in 1960, under the direction of Professor Earl R. Rolph, who first aroused my interest in stock-flow problems. His guidance, through incisive criticisms of the manuscript at various stages, through his own published works, and as a teacher, is gratefully acknowledged. Professors Howard S. Ellis and Ivan M. Lee also gave generously of their time and advice; both worked through the manuscript at its early and late stages, and their many helpful criticisms and suggestions have added much to its quality. Clarence W. Tow, Vice President and Director of Research, and D. R. Cawthorne, Senior Economist, at the Federal Reserve Bank of Kansas City, encouraged me to complete the manuscript by writing the first and final chapters. My colleagues at the bank, Lyle E. Gramley and Frederick M. Struble, provided helpful criticisms. None of these persons or the Ford Foundation is responsible for the analysis and conclusions presented here.

S. B. C., Jr.

Contents

[xi]

lationship between present values and expectations—Allowing for consumption

I

Introduction

This study is designed to improve the treatment of assets in economic theory. Although the exposition aims primarily at explaining the prices of particular assets, the subject is discussed in the setting of overall economic equilibrium. The inquiry therefore ranges over a rather broad terrain of economic analysis—we must deal not only with the interrelations among the markets for particular assets, but with the connection between assets markets and markets for consumption items.

Capital values—the prices of existing stocks of assets—have not generally been accorded a very important place in economic analysis. To be sure, a number of writers have had something to say about capital values, but the approaches commonly used have involved the supposition that, although many economic forces may affect asset prices, asset prices are not themselves an economic force and need not be integrated into economic analysis.

The commonly accepted method of explaining capital values reflects this outlook. According to this view, the price of an existing asset is to be found by capitalizing its expected returns at the going rate of interest, with perhaps some discount being allowed for uncertain expectations. The crucial analytic variable is the rate of interest, which is found by examining the equilibrium relations of various real forces (saving, investment) or monetary forces (liquidity preference), or combinations of the two.

The rate of interest is typically explained without reference to capital values, for the latter are not believed to influence the real and monetary forces involved in determining the interest rate. Thus it can be said of this common approach that prices of existing assets are treated as a kind of fortuitous residual of the working out of the monetary and real forces of liquidity preference, saving, and the expected rate of return at the margin of new investment opportunities.

The above generalization does not always hold. In several instances, authors have given considerable attention to the value of existing stocks of assets as an important economic variable. In part, this attention has been designed to improve the predictive accuracy of the Keynesian consumption function. Particularly in the light of postwar inflationary developments, which occurred in the face of reduced generation of income from governmental budgets, stock variables, mainly liquid asset holdings, merited more attention in the analysis of spending flows. This concern is evidenced in the works of Klein, Tobin, and Friedman, among others.[1]

More importantly, there has also been a fundamental concern with the methods of treating assets in economic analysis. As monetary forces have come under increasing scrutiny, logical problems have given rise to dissatisfaction with "pure flows" relationships such as the Keynesian consumption function, according to which the flow of consumption spending is determined by the flow of income. Several writers have attempted to clarify the nature of stock-flow relationships. One early landmark is "A Suggestion for Simplifying the Theory of Money," in which Hicks argues that traditional theory of choice should be used in dealing with the relationship of money stocks to aggregate expenditure flows.[2] Another contribution to this literature, Boulding's "A Liquidity Preference Theory of Market Prices," [3] and his later

---

[1] Lawrence R. Klein, "Assets, Debts, and Economic Behavior," in *Studies in Income and Wealth*, XIV (New York: National Bureau of Economic Research, 1951); James Tobin, "Asset Holdings and Spending Decisions," "Papers and Proceedings," *American Economic Review*, XLII (1951), 109–123; Milton Friedman, *A Theory of the Consumption Function* (Princeton: Princeton University Press, 1957).

[2] J. R. Hicks, "A Suggestion for Simplifying the Theory of Money," *Economica*, N.S. II (1935), 1–19. Reprinted in *Readings in Monetary Theory* (Philadelphia: Blakiston Co., 1951), pp. 13–32.

[3] K. E. Boulding, "A Liquidity Preference Theory of Market Prices," *Economica*, N.S. IX (1944), 55–63. Reprinted in *Readings in Price Theory* (Chicago: Richard D. Irwin Inc., 1952), pp. 311–328.

book, *A Reconstruction of Economics*,[4] suggest that the treatment of stock or balance sheet concepts should be given considerably more attention than is usual. Patinkin's *Money, Interest and Prices*[5] is still another example of concern for adequate treatment of stock-flow relationships. Metzler and Rolph[6] have also made important contributions to this literature.

This study is closely related in scope to the exceptionally rewarding article by Makower and Marschak, "Assets, Prices, and Monetary Theory." [7] There are important conceptual differences, however, between their treatment and the one offered here.

The viewpoint of this book is in line with the literature outlined above in the sense that assets are accorded a very important place in economic analysis. The immediate purpose is to provide a theoretical outline of the determination of asset prices. The broader objective is to suggest analytical methods that fully integrate the role of assets into economic reasoning, that is, to suggest a way of thinking about the traditional economic problems of price determination, resource allocation, and the establishment of equilibrium rates of production and spending that recognizes the importance of assets. This broader goal is pursued as a necessary by-product of reaching the immediate goal of explaining the price of any asset, since asset prices cannot be explained without reference to these broader considerations.

NATURE OF THE EARLY CHAPTERS

The first part of the book deals primarily with the nature of the choice people make when they decide between holding assets and consuming, and with the implications of the chosen theory of choice for the determination of asset prices in a very simplified setting. At this preliminary stage, the liquidity preference prob-

[4] K. E. Boulding, *A Reconstruction of Economics* (New York: John Wiley and Sons, Inc., 1950).

[5] Don Patinkin, *Money, Interest and Prices* (Evanston: Row, Peterson and Co., 1956).

[6] Lloyd A. Metzler, "Wealth, Saving, and the Rate of Interest," *Journal of Political Economy*, LIX (1951), 93–116; Earl R. Rolph, *The Theory of Fiscal Economics* (Berkeley and Los Angeles: University of California Press, 1954), Ch. V.

[7] Helen Makower and Jacob Marschak, "Assets, Prices, and Monetary Theory," *Economica*, N.S. V (1938), 261–288. Reprinted in *Readings in Price Theory* (Chicago: Richard D. Irwin Inc., 1952), pp. 283–310.

lem—the choice between holding money and nonmoney assets—
receives only superficial attention. Similarly, the complex problems of explaining the prices of assets relative to one another are
sidestepped by assuming that investors treat all nonmoney assets
as perfect substitutes for one another at prices which make their
percentage yields the same.

These simplifications serve two purposes. They allow the analysis to proceed one step at a time. The problems of liquidity preference and asset selection by uncertain investors are sufficiently complex to justify working up to them in this way. They also imple-
ment comparison of the analysis developed here with other views
of the same problem. Much of the literature on interest rates dis-
regards uncertainty and liquidity preference considerations. It is
in this way that theories of *the* interest rate, stressing real forces,
are usually derived. Comparisons with these views are made most
clearly if the level of abstraction is held constant.

In these early chapters, and throughout the rest of the study
as well, various data are taken as given, including (a) people's
tastes, (b) amounts and distribution of "inherited" assets, including both real assets and money, (c) technology of production,
(d) supplies of productive resources, and (e) competitive markets.
At several points the consequences of assuming different sets of
data are discussed, but there is no attempt to set forth a dynamic
theory which shows the effects of changing data over time.

Wealth as the source of demand

Existing stocks of assets can have value in the market only if
people attach positive utility to holding them, for a person who
holds valuable assets can always sell them and consume more.
Viewed in this way, the choice to hold assets is the obverse of the
choice to consume, and the demand for assets to hold is the mirror
image of the demand for consumption services. The relevant
choice to examine in analyzing a person's demands for assets to
hold and for consumption services is the choice he makes in allocating his entire wealth, measured by the cash value of the
assets he holds, between consumption spending and holding assets through time.

The view that cashable wealth provides the constraint on a

person's demands for all things is conceptually different from the more usual practice of specifying that people spend out of incomes. Rather than holding that people allocate income flows to saving and consuming, the approach adopted here specifies that demands arise out of the allocation of existing stocks of wealth, either to dissipation on current consumption or to holding assets through time. The stock-of-wealth concept of constraint on a person's demands seems superior to the income-flow concept in important respects, for it appears that the final limitation upon a person's dollar demands for all things, including real and financial assets, money balances, and consumption services, is in fact his cashable wealth.

The consumption budget, which in discussions of consumer demand is traditionally taken to be income, or some portion thereof, is more correctly viewed as that part of his cashable wealth which a person decides to devote to consumption spending. People can, and often do, spend more than their incomes. A person's investment budget—his total dollar demand for assets to hold—is that part of his cashable wealth which he decides to devote to holding assets rather than to dissipate on consumption. All currently available wealth is either expended on consumption, or devoted to holding old assets, including cash, or to producing new real assets. Thus the decision to use wealth for consumption is the mirror image of the decision to hold or acquire assets.

The identification of cashable wealth as the ultimate constraint on and source of any person's demands can be contrasted with three forms of the income-demand relationship often employed. When income is thought of as *recent* income, the income and cashable wealth notions of the constraint on demands are similar in that they both postulate, in fact, stock-flow relationships. This income is really a stock of wealth—albeit marginal in that it includes only wealth that has been recently acquired. When such a recent income viewpoint is used, the demand for assets to hold, including money balances, is also viewed in a marginal sense. Marginal demand for assets to hold is considered as *saving*, that part of recent income not dissipated on consumption. Implicit is the assumption that old assets (wealth which was held through the period when the recent income accrued) are held through a given period so long as net saving is positive, but are sold off, at least in part, when saving is negative (consumption exceeds income).

The notion of constraint used here is broader than the recent income view. All wealth, including both old wealth and recently accrued income, is treated identically, for the distinction based on timing of receipt is artificial and cumbersome. Nonetheless, everything said in the following chapters could be translated algebraically into a recent income-demand view without encountering any insuperable logical barriers. But the two approaches involve important differences in emphasis.

The concept of total wealth as the objective limit on any person's demands is more fundamentally at odds with the interpretation that current demands are financed out of current incomes. Often, the writer who uses such a relationship is merely seeking a short cut to a Keynesian equilibrium solution. But the consequences of taking such a short cut would be very serious for the present study. Since an act of spending by one person raises the income of someone else, to say that present spending is financed by present income is to say that, for a group, current spending finances itself. If this were in fact true, there could be no objectively determined limitation on spending.

This kind of analysis, a form of Say's Law, is not applicable to a money economy. Spending is a process that involves the exchange of money for goods and services. Such a process takes time, and before it can occur, spenders must possess spending power (money stocks in a money economy). Since the same money cannot simultaneously finance a number of different expenditures, the notion that current receipts provide for current expenditures is rejected in favor of the notion that money must be held before it is spent.

Still another view rejected here is the idea that people can spend their future incomes. Interpreted literally, this notion cannot be accepted, since it postulates an impossibility. People can, to be sure, borrow money on the security of their earning power. But selling a claim based on earning capacity is fundamentally like selling any other asset. The salability of an IOU, like the salability of any other asset, requires that there be a market for it—there must be some investor willing to use part of his limited wealth to acquire the IOU as opposed to holding other assets or spending on consumption. The constraint on demands financed out of sales of IOU's is to be found in the markets for debts, where the prices of IOU's are established. In the absence of sufficiently expansionary central banking policies, attempts to raise the rate at which personal debts are sold lead to financial pressures in the form of a reduction in their value (rise in interest rates), reflecting the fact that the process of borrowing is merely one form of the process of shifting assets, not a process that somehow allows a group of people to realize flows of income in advance.

Choice between consumption and thrift

The cashable wealth notion of the constraint on an individual's total demands for all things, including old assets, consumption outlays, and acquisitions of newly produced assets, is used in the early chapters in the formulation of principles regulating the division of total demands between consumption and holding assets. From these principles demand schedules for assets and for consumption services are derived.

Traditionally, much of the literature on the subject of consumption and thrift has turned on the proposition that all economic satisfactions stem from taking final consumption services. If this is true, holding assets is simply an instrument for redistributing consumption through time, and a willingness to abstain from taking present satisfactions must be explained by *time preference*. Under such an interpretation of the division of demands between consumption spending and holding assets, the rate of interest at the margin of investment opportunities becomes an important factor in consumption decisions. It sets the terms of abstinence whereby future satisfactions can be exchanged for present satisfactions.

For reasons set forth in Chapter II, the time-preference theory is not used here. An alternative theory is offered which makes the crucial objective variable involved in the determination of a person's consumption his *real consumption potential*, or his total command over consumption services. This theory of consumption is at the same time a theory of demand for assets to hold, since people must either dissipate their wealth on consumption or use it to hold assets. This should not be taken to mean that demands for assets are in any sense residual; the choice between consumption and thrift is viewed as a choice between two desirable alternatives.

Specification of the nature of the constraints on demands and the establishment of a theory of choice between consumption and thrift make it possible to derive demand curves for consumption items and for assets to hold. Supply considerations can then be introduced to round out the explanation of equilibrium prices in both assets and consumption markets. Examination of the interrelation between the two markets on the demand sides and the supply sides permits analysis of the conditions necessary to equilibrate both markets simultaneously. When this step has been taken, the proposed theory of asset prices in its most simplified form is complete. This simplified theory is set forth in Chapter III. In the following chapter, it is compared with alternative formulations that employ roughly the same degrees of abstraction. This comparison focuses particularly on savings-investment theories of interest and on the role of supplies of new real assets in the determination of the prices of old ones.

EQUILIBRIUM WITHIN THE ASSETS MARKETS

The second section of this book, Chapters V through VIII, is concerned not so much with amending traditional viewpoints as with exploring problems that have received relatively little attention. The simplifying assumption of investor certainty and the mechanical view of liquidity preference are dropped. Removing these assumptions makes it necessary to formulate principles to be used in analyzing the interrelations among assets markets, and to show how these principles can be employed to explain the emergence of thoroughgoing equilibrium in the markets for all assets taken together.

The first task is to develop a way of looking at the demand for a single asset when all other asset prices, as well as the prices of consumption services, are given. The method used here is an adaptation of the theory of consumer demand, in the form it has been given by Hicks. Investors' tastes are portrayed by indifference maps showing equally desirable combinations of assets. The investment budget is then introduced, and the tangency solution indicates the number of units of any asset a person will wish to hold at a given price. A demand schedule for the asset is generated by observing variations in quantity held as price is varied.

However, the technical features of indifference maps and of budget constraints where assets are involved differ from those applicable to consumers' services, and considerable spadework is necessary if the comparatively simple concepts so useful in consumption and production theory are to be applied to the case of assets. For one thing, the possession of an asset makes an owner wealthy, and his wealth depends, in part, on the price of the asset. This means that variations in price affect the dollar value of the owner's investment budget, as well as the terms on which the asset can be acquired. When a person already owns some of an asset, it is useful to distinguish between the *wealth effects* and the *price effects* of a change in its price on the amount he chooses to hold in the future. This distinction is not analogous to that between the "income" and "substitution" effects Hicks uses in *Value and Capital*.

A second problem involved in adapting the familiar tools of consumption analysis to the demand for assets arises out of the relationship between the present price of an asset and its expected future prices. As Hicks pointed out, indifference curves as he develops them are applicable only to the case of goods or services whose desirability is unaffected by changes in price. In consumption theory, this qualification gives little trouble except for snob goods. But in investment theory, it applies whenever people's expectations about future prices of assets hinge partly on their present prices.

Postulating some systematic connection between present prices and expectations as to future prices offers a solution. Hicks's concept of "elasticity of expectations" is often used in this connection. But the meaning of the elasticity concept is not clear when it is applied to any assets whose characteristics change over time, such as maturing bonds, ripening wheat fields, or depreciating houses. The problem of providing an alternative treatment of the connection between present and expected prices is taken up in Chapter V. The case of nonspeculative demand for assets—a neutral-expectations case—is used. This nonspeculative view is in line with a great deal of the work that has been done on interest rates and capital values generally. It differs significantly from Keynes's view in the *General Theory,* however. Keynes holds that expectations as to future prices of bonds are invariant with present prices. In that case, indifference maps for assets are independent of present prices, and Hicks's reservation does not apply.

It is, of course, possible to postulate any kind of a relationship between the present state of affairs and expected future states. The justification for the neutral-expectations assumption used here is not that it is universally applicable, but that it concentrates attention on forces that are thought to be more basic and pervasive than the vagaries of investor speculation. Nothing prevents the use of other assumptions, however, although the results may be quite different.

When the two problems of interdependence—that between investors' wealth and the prices of assets they own and that between present and expected prices of assets—have been met, it is possible to proceed with the determination of equilibrium conditions in the market for any one asset and in markets for all assets, including cash balances, taken together. In the process, problems arising on the supply side must be treated, particularly those revolving around the distinctions between existing stocks of assets and forthcoming production flows of assets. Consumption markets are then brought back into the picture and reconsideration of the interdependence between asset markets and consumption markets is undertaken.

GOVERNMENT FINANCE AND PRIVATE DEMAND

The importance assigned to stocks of wealth as the source of individuals' demands for all things—including consumption, non-money assets, and cash balances to hold—is relevant to the analysis of the determination of demands for new output as they vary in response to government policies that affect private asset holdings. In Chapter IX, the effects of government debt operations are discussed to clarify the workings of the equilibrium system of prices as it is envisaged in this book. This discussion of government debt also sets the background for Chapter X, in which several implications of government financial policies for the level of aggregate demands for new goods and services are elaborated. This treatment of government financial policies establishes various differences between the analysis proposed here and the more commonly employed formulations based on Keynesian relationships.

II

The Desire to Hold Assets

People like to hold assets, stocks of things with exchange value. According to most treatments, it is not necessary that people expect a positive rate of return from their asset holdings, although the prospect of income from investment *may* affect the intensity of the desire to own property. A desire to hold assets is perfectly consistent with zero, or even negative, rates of return.

Each decision-making unit in an economy is continually involved in the process of accumulating and dissipating wealth. We will take this decision between dissipating wealth on consumption and maintaining it as our starting point, examining it in a highly simplified setting. For the moment, we evade the problem of asset prices by postulating that there is but one asset, money, available to hold. This assumption reduces the complications involved in discussing the fundamental nature of the choice between consuming and maintaining assets, and it is not incompatible with the usual explanations of this choice.

Imagine a society where the only scarce resources are human beings, that is, where the only scarce productive services are labor services. No ways of producing other valuable resources (capital) are known, and those resources that are endowed by nature are in sufficient supply to be free goods. To avoid problems of barter, which are not central to the investigation, assume further that this economy is a pure money economy. There can be no exchange without money being passed in payment. No securities

[12]

can be sold, so that money is the only possible store of value and therefore the sole form which accumulation may take.

People will wish to hold this sole form of wealth at least for the purpose of being able to participate in exchange. It is easily seen that in a pure money economy the objective source of all exchange demand is the asset money. The constraint on a person's spending during any period of time is the money he has at his disposal during that period. We can define a period as short as we please, even one so short that no money earned during the period can be spent in the time span. This short period is akin to the Robertsonian "day." [1] Since the expenditure power for any individual during a "day" is limited by the stock of money he holds at the outset, all flows of spending during a "day" can be traced to, and are limited by, preëxisting stocks of money. The flow of spending is simply a movement of the stock of money. (Service flows, too, can be traced to preëxisting stocks of resources in which the potential flows are embodied.)

Since no real assets can be produced, the scarce services of human beings must be final, or consumption, services. To take these services, a person must hold cash, and the choice he must continually make is how much of his potential consumption he wishes to take, or, to put it another way, to what extent he is to dissipate his cash. Consumption involves giving up assets and holding assets involves giving up consumption.[2] The problem here is to decide how to treat the maintenance of wealth, or the failure to consume all that it is possible to consume.

---

[1] D. H. Robertson, "Saving and Hoarding," *Economic Journal*, XLIII (1933), 399–413, assumes "the existence of a period of time which is finite but nevertheless so short that the income which a man receives on a given day cannot be allocated during its course to any particular use." Robertson uses the same concept in *Banking Policy and the Price Level* (New York: Augustus M. Kelley, 1949), Ch. V.

[2] People may choose to take leisure, which can be defined loosely as a person's use of himself in such a way that the money payments he realizes by the sale of his services are lower than the maximum possible amount. In this case, the producer and the consumer are one and, as in the Crusoe economy, there is no need to distinguish between the producer and the taker of products. A person need not hold money to take leisure, although leisure-taking involves a sacrifice of potential money receipts; the market is bypassed in this case since there is no exchange involved. The problem created by the bypass of exchange when leisure is taken is dealt with here by assuming that market supplies of resource services are perfectly inelastic, so that the ratio of total production to production for exchange is constant.

THE TIME-PREFERENCE THEORY

Economists generally take the desire to consume as a datum not susceptible to economic "explanation." But the desire to hold assets has been subjected to some highly painstaking explanations. It is widely believed that holding assets is not, on the face of it, rational. The propensity to theorize about the roots of the desire to hold assets stems from the widely accepted proposition that economic satisfaction can arise only from the taking of consumption services. Those who accept this proposition usually explain accumulation in terms of time-preference theory. Irving Fisher presents a particularly lucid and, in general, internally consistent version of this doctrine.[3]

According to Fisher, people will hold accumulated assets if the present value of the gain in future consumption satisfactions made possible by "abstention" is sufficient to compensate for the reduced present consumption satisfactions. He maintains that present consumption is typically valued more highly than is an equal amount of future consumption. The difference in value is explained by time-preference, or the impatience to consume. Discounting future consumption satisfactions by the rate of time-preference reveals their equivalents in present consumption satisfactions.[4] However, because of the postulate of diminishing marginal utility of consumption taken in any period, a person, even though impatient, may accumulate if he expects his earnings to be lower in the future than they are at present, for the consumption that can be obtained with lower future earnings will have a higher marginal utility (when it is taken) than will present consumption equal to the higher present income. Thus if cash is the only asset available, persons who expect their incomes to decline

---

[3] In *The Theory of Interest* (New York: Macmillan Co., 1930), and *The Nature of Capital and Income* (New York: Macmillan Co., 1906).

[4] In *The Theory of Interest*, Fisher says (p. 62, n. 2): "We obtain the rate of time-preference for a present dollar over a dollar one year hence by the following process:

(a) take the present want for one more dollar; and

(b) the present want for one more dollar one year hence; and then,

(c) subtract (b) from (a); and finally

(d) measure the result (c) as a percentage of (b)."

will typically hold idle money balances sufficient to equalize the discounted marginal utility of consumption over all periods. Those persons (rare in Fisher's view) who do not discount future consumption satisfactions to express impatience might postpone consumption even though they expected their incomes to be constant, or rising, through time.

Thus, the time-preference theory explains a desire to hold assets through time even if there are no opportunities to earn an objective return on assets. Holding assets (money in this case) is simply the instrument for redistributing consumption, or satisfactions, through time. For saving[5] to occur, a person must feel he can raise his lifetime satisfactions from consuming, viewed from the point of time in question, by allocating some part of his income to holding cash balances. Objective consumption (real bundles, or money values, assuming constant price-levels) need not be raised by this process; it is expected merely that satisfactions, properly discounted, will be raised.

Individual saving does not require the opportunity for social saving, or investment. For the individual to refrain from taking all the consumption he can, given the assets he has available for dissipation, society need not refrain from taking all current output in the form of consumption services. In our example, the idle balances a person holds measure the amount of current consumption that he is prepared to forego so that he may consume more later. Summing the idle balances for all individuals, a figure is obtained that tells us how much the group wishes to hold in the form of accumulated assets. But there is no social accumulation in the form of greater productive potential for later consumption. Although every individual who holds cash balances will be in a position to take more consumption services in the future than he could take in the absence of accumulations of money, the potential consumption of the entire group is not increased by the accumulation of idle balances.

---

[5] The term "saving" is taken to mean adding to idle balances in such a way that they increase from one period to the next. The difficulties surrounding the use of this term are well illustrated by the Keynes-Robertson-Hawtrey discussion of 1933. See "Mr. Robertson on Saving and Hoarding," *Economic Journal*, XLIII (1933), 701–712. Here the concept will be avoided wherever possible, and attention will be centered, rather, on wealth preservation as an indication of thriftiness.

THE SIMPLE TASTE APPROACH TO ACCUMULATION

A number of writers have taken exception to the time-preference theory. The central issue is the assertion that rational behavior consists entirely of trying to maximize consumption satisfactions. Only if this view is accepted is it necessary to explain how accumulation contributes to raising consumption satisfactions. The basic dispute does not revolve around the alleged process of discounting future consumption to express impatience; even if the time-preference theorists discarded the impatience notion and did not discount future satisfactions, the central issue would remain so long as consumption is viewed as the only form of economic satisfaction.

Objections to the time-preference theory fall into at least two categories. Pigou contends that time-preference theories offer a useful but incomplete explanation of accumulation. In his celebrated "Economic Progress in a Stable Environment," he writes that "people are led to save in part by a desire actually to hold wealth for the amenity, so to speak, from holding it." [6] Thus, people hold accumulated wealth for two reasons, time-preference and "amenity." Holding assets in and of itself yields satisfactions. Thus, "a thorough-going equilibrium requires, not that the rate of interest in terms of consumption goods shall be equal to the rate of time-preference, but that it shall be less than the rate of time-preference by some quantity that represents the rate of amenity return from marginal saving." [7]

Pigou believes that this new consideration is necessary to explain why people, whom he views as being typically myopic, may save even if the rate of return on investment is zero.[8] According to Pigou, it is the existence of saving at zero rates of interest that can explain the arrival, at least temporarily, of Keynes's "Day of Judgment," a position of short-term unemployment equilibrium.

---

[6] A. C. Pigou, "Economic Progress in a Stable Environment," *Economica*, N.S. XIV (1947), 180–188. Reprinted in *Readings in Monetary Theory* (New York: Blakiston Co., 1951), pp. 241–251. Quoted from p. 246.

[7] *Ibid.*, p. 247.

[8] This is a departure from Pigou's earlier position in *The Economics of Welfare* (London: Macmillan and Co., Ltd., 1920) that time preference alone explains saving, so that people typically "undersave" because they are myopic.

For our purposes, the important point about Pigou's view is its implication that saving is carried farther than can be explained by the time-preference theory. The amenity value is not derived from the increased later consumption made possible by present abstention; it is derived from asset owning *per se*. This notion contrasts sharply with Fisher's position that the satisfaction, or desirable result, achieved by abstaining from present consumption is achieved only in the future when the assets are dissipated on final consumption services. Pigou's amenity yields are not consumption yields; they do not involve consumption-taking. They cannot be taken apart from the ownership of assets through time, and they disappear when wealth is dissipated, whereas Fisher's exclusive yields appear only as wealth is dissipated to finance additional consumption expenditures.

When consumption is defined as the act of taking final services at the sacrifice of wealth, the admission of Pigou's assertion involves a rejection of the doctrine that all economic satisfactions derive from consumption-taking. It is a long way from the position that a person directs all of his economic activity toward maximizing his satisfaction from consuming to the position that he maximizes his satisfactions by adjusting his consumption-taking and asset holdings so as to obtain the most desirable combination of the two. According to the latter position, consumer behavior is only a subfield of economics, not the exclusive core.

The second category of criticism, found in the writings of Henry Simons and F. H. Knight, involves the complete rejection of the time-preference notion. Simons contends that:

Time-preference theories are . . . interesting for their emphasis upon consumption as the unique end of all economic behavior. The discounting process is conceived in terms of choices between present and future consumption goods, as though all saving were intended as a redistribution of consumption through time. Now the observable fact is that many people save instead of consuming, just as some smoke pipes instead of cigarettes; that it seems reasonable to hold that the choices are of the same order in the two cases. . . . There is raised here a most difficult problem of social psychology and culture history; and it hardly becomes the economist to make a pretense of competence by resort to verbal legerdemain. To assume that all economic behavior is motivated by desire for consumption goods, present and future, is to introduce a teleology which is both useless and false. . . . In a world where capital accumulation proceeds as it does now, there is something sadly inadequate about the idea of saving as postponed consumption.[9]

While Simons's point is telling, it does not absolutely disprove the time-preference theory. Progressive accumulation could, for example, be due to a growing population, where the younger savers always outnumber the older dissavers, or to a secular fall in rates of time-preference. These explanations may seem farfetched, but the crucial issue is, not whether societies accumulate progressively, but whether individuals do in fact try to maximize their consumption satisfactions during their lifetimes. If they do, it should be possible to prove it by observation. People who concentrate on maximizing consumption satisfactions will prefer to die with zero wealth. Valuable estates are only mistakes, presumably due to imperfect foresight. Assets left behind are, in this view, sheer waste, a "loss."

Annuity programs insure against such losses, and, in view of the usual human aversion to risk, we should expect these programs to be very popular if consumption is the only form of economic satisfaction. The fact is that they are considerably less popular than life insurance, which would seem to be of no value to a person who gets his only satisfaction from consuming.[10] Students of insurance describe this relative unpopularity of annuity programs as being due to a desire to leave something to one's heirs.[11] Time-preference theorists do not deny this motivation, nor do they dismiss it as unimportant. Fisher contended that people will leave wealth to their heirs if the discounted marginal satisfaction of augmented consumption by the heirs exceeds the marginal satisfaction of present consumption to the individual making the

[9] Henry Simons, *Personal Income Taxation* (Chicago: The University of Chicago Press, 1938), pp. 94–99. F. H. Knight's view is similar. See his "Capital and Interest," *Encyclopædia Britannica*, IV (1946) 779–801. Reprinted in *Readings in the Theory of Income Distribution* (Philadelphia: Blakiston Co., 1946), pp. 384–417.

[10] In 1958, life insurance premiums in the United States amounted to $10.8 billion. Individual and group annuity premiums totaled only $1.4 billion. From *Life Insurance Fact Book* (New York: Institute of Life Insurance, 1959).

[11] See Robert L. Mehr and Robert W. Osler, *Modern Life Insurance* (revised edition; New York: Macmillan Co., 1956), p. 83.

choice.[12] This view must mean that the benefactors do not expect to experience satisfactions as a result of their own savings during their own lifetimes. To the extent that they leave wealth when they die, either they expect to be able to participate, somehow, in the deferred consuming of the heirs at the time the heirs consume, or they do what they really would rather not do, that is, abstain from taking the desirable course, the one that yields consumption satisfaction to themselves.

This latter position is either untenable or else the notion of people acting on their preferences breaks down. As V. C. Walsh has argued:

As the words "preference" and "indifference" are ordinarily used, and presumably as they are used by economists, we can correctly be said to observe people's preferences and to notice that they are indifferent. . . . Preferences are not hidden happenings, primarily because they are not happenings at all. . . . The theory of consumer choice is about *economic* relations with which we are all familiar, and it is inappropriate to make it look like a psychological story about mental "goings on" . . . as we ordinarily use "prefer," it is distinctly odd, if not meaningless, to say that someone does not choose to do what he most prefers.[13]

This leaves us with the proposition that people who intentionally bequeath valuable estates expect to be able to join in taking the satisfaction from the consumption provided by the legacy, perhaps in heaven. If this is the case, the objection Pigou elaborates in *The Economics of Welfare,* that future consumption is undervalued and that welfare can be raised by a greater degree of

---

[12] In *The Theory of Interest,* p. 85, Fisher contends that "whereas the shortness and uncertainty of life tend to increase impatience, their effect is greatly mitigated by the . . . solicitude for the welfare of one's heirs. Probably the *most powerful* cause tending to reduce the rate of interest is the love for one's children and the desire to provide for their good." Life insurance "represents, for the most part, an investment of the present generation in the next." (Italics supplied.) Pigou, in *The Economics of Welfare,* p. 20, holds that "our desire for future satisfaction would often be less intense than for present satisfaction, because it is very likely that the future satisfaction will not be our own." Knut Wicksell, too, states that heirs may do the consuming. See *Lectures on Political Economy* I (London: Routledge and Kegan Paul, 1951), 207–211.

[13] V. C. Walsh, "On Descriptions of Consumers' Behavior," *Economica,* N.S. XXI (1954), 244–249.

postponement of consumption, is reinforced, for now we have the consumption yielding satisfaction not only to the living consumers but to their ancestors who provided it. The whole notion may sound somewhat preposterous, but it is the logical consequence of a theory which holds that all economic satisfactions stem from consuming, that people do what they prefer to do, and that it is consistent that people wish to leave wealth behind them when they die.

Unscientific as the satisfactions-after-death proposition may seem, even if it is accepted the time-preference theory becomes meaningless. Once no limits are set on an individual's useful life for consuming, it is entirely consistent that estates be enlarged generation after generation. The chain leading to ultimate consumption may be endless, and the necessity of ultimate consumption fails to impose any limit upon the amount of abstention or accumulation. The doctrine of time-preference becomes, in effect, indistinguishable from the notion that people save because they like to be wealthy and consume because they like to consume, their choices depending upon the relative attractions of the two alternatives.

Thus, as Simons contends, the order of choice between consuming and maintaining wealth seems no different than that of the choice between pipes and cigarettes, or any other possible disposition of assets. The freedom to consume later may be a factor in a person's decision not to dissipate all of his wealth immediately, just as a supposed superiority of the nutritional qualities of bread could influence him to spend more on bread than on potatoes. One can say that a person who purposely abstains from consuming in order to leave something when he dies does so out of a desire to feel he can influence the future course of events.[14] But it is the present desire to have that feeling which influences him rather than a hope that he can participate in the world which he influences. People act on the basis of present states of mind; the satisfactions under consideration are present ones, always in

---

[14] In *The Hidden Persuaders* (New York: David McKay Co., Inc., 1957), pp. 81–82, Vance Packard tells of a "study in depth" of hidden attitudes toward life insurance which found that one of the prime movers behind the purchase of policies is the promise of immortality to the insured, not only in that he *provides* for his survivors, but that he *controls* their destinies. This section of Packard's book is labeled "Selling Immortality."

some way influenced by expectations. We could list a long set of "explanations" of accumulation just as we could draw up a long list of "reasons" why people like bread, but the possible inter-actions of the desires and the simultaneous emergence of different "classes" of satisfactions can hardly be said to lie within the realm of analytical economics. Motivational research is a growing field, and apparently not a simple one.

Thus it appears that the notion of time-preference is not suf-ficient as an explanation of the accumulation of assets through time. The widespread use of the term time-preference to encom-pass the demand for assets to hold indicates either that a significant part of the economics profession regards this theory as an adequate explanation of the process of accumulation, or else, possibly, that it has become habitual to substitute the term time-preference for what might more properly be called the desire to be wealthy. To the extent that the former is true, the facts do not bear out the theory. If it is amended so as to encompass observable behavior, the theory loses its meaning and it becomes apparent that the term is not a suitable description of the notion intended.

Attempts such as Pigou's to attribute to time-preference theory a partial explanation of saving entail the disadvantage of being based on an unconfirmed and perhaps naïve view of the mental process. The assumption that people assign a unique present value to the future consumption to be derived from present asset hold-ings and add to this an amenity return from being wealthy, thus getting a total satisfaction to be balanced against the satisfactions of present consumption, is quite possibly an incorrect elaboration on the fact that people like to be wealthy. What is important for economic analysis is that people have tastes regarding choices be-tween alternatives, and that by exercising choices according to their tastes they influence the economic process. It is the influence of tastes, rather than the explanation of them, that is amenable to economic analysis.

III

The Determination of the Level of Asset Prices

When the complexities of uncertainty are brushed aside, the prices of assets relative to one another depend upon the ratios of their discounted future incomes. Given some rate of interest, it is simple to find the price a particular asset will obtain in the market.[1] But the discounting process explains only the relative prices of assets in as much as the level of asset prices is assumed when the interest rate is taken as given. Typically, discussions of the prices of assets where uncertainty is assumed away involve solving for the capitalization rate by the use of schedules relating the amounts of spending on new real assets which would be profitable at various interest rates (the demand for investment funds), and of amounts people would be willing to provide for new investment spending at each rate (the supply of investment funds). The latter schedule is held to be unpredictable as to slope, even if constructed upon the time-preference theory.

The equilibrium rate of interest is the one at which the funds seeking investment (savings) equal the amount of investment profitable. Prices of existing assets are found by discounting their anticipated incomes at this rate, and the flow of saving turns out to be identical with the rate of spending on new investment goods.

[1] See, for example, George J. Stigler, *The Theory of Price* (New York: Macmillan Co., 1947), pp. 322–324.

Here, the determination of the absolute level of asset prices is analyzed without reference to any saving concept. The theory makes the prices of inherited assets, rather than their expected yields, a crucial factor in the determination of the demand for assets in general, including both the inherited stock of assets and flows of currently produced assets. Asset prices are explained directly, by using supply and demand schedules, without reference to either saving or interest.[2]

As in the previous chapter, the choice, continually confronting an individual, between dissipating his wealth on consumption and maintaining it by holding assets, is our center of attention. We shall now, however, take into account the presence of existing stocks of nonhuman productive resources capable of being bought, sold, and produced. The problem is to determine the prices of these real assets along with the prices of consumption services. For the sake of simplicity, it is assumed that no securities, including personal debt instruments, can be sold. (The determination of securities prices is taken up briefly in subsequent chapters.)

THE PROPOSED THEORY OF ASSET PRICES

Suppose that all people know, or think they know, the income to be earned by every real asset over its entire life, and that all individuals agree in their predictions. This is equivalent to the perfect foresight assumption. It follows that all assets are perfect substitutes for each other for ownership purposes at price ratios which equalize rates of return per dollar of value. The assumption that all individuals make identical unique-valued forecasts as to incomes disposes of the problem of solving for relative prices of assets. If the assets have different maturities, however, relative prices may change as the absolute level of prices changes. Therefore, we also assume that all assets are perpetuities. We can then express the quantities in terms of their equivalent to some asset arbitrarily chosen as numeraire. For purposes of analyzing asset

---

[2] In this respect the proposed analysis is similar to that of Helen Makower and Jacob Marschak. They, however, employ a time-preference theory to derive people's demands for assets to hold, specifying that assets are held as a means of transforming present "yields" (consumption) into future "yields." See "Assets, Prices, and Monetary Theory," *Economica*, N.S. V (1938), 261–288. Reprinted in *Readings in Price Theory* (Chicago: Richard D. Irwin, Inc., 1952), pp. 283–310.

prices, we have the equivalent of one asset, even though the services of the assets, which give rise to their incomes, may be quite diverse. It must be kept clearly in mind that the subject under consideration is the determination of asset prices, or capital values, and that the relevant demand is for assets to hold. The demand for and the pricing of the productive services of real assets is quite another matter.

In a pure money economy, a person's consumption-taking over any period is limited by the amount of money he can raise to spend on consumption.[3] For a sufficiently short period, which we call a "day," this limit is given by the total money value of the assets he possesses at the beginning of the day, or the sum of his holdings of cash and the money value of the real assets he owns. This differs from the common identification of income as the constraint on a person's consumption spending.[4] Presumably the objective constraint upon a person's spending is a matter of fact, and is not connected with his tastes or expectations. His buying power traces to his wealth, which is a stock, not to his income, which is a flow.

The position sometimes taken, that expected income imposes the constraint, seems strange, for under this condition a person could spend whatever he thought he could spend. It is often said that people spend expected income by borrowing against it. But the fact that a person can sell debt instruments to someone who has faith in his earning power does not mean that he can spend the

---

[3] Because of the assumption that no securities can be issued there can be no "barter" of personal debt in exchange for consumption services.

[4] See, for example, J. R. Hicks, *Value and Capital* (2d ed.; London: Oxford University Press, 1946), p. 16; Eugen E. Slutsky, "On the Theory of the Budget of the Consumer," *Giornale degli Economisti*, II (1915), 1–26. Translated by Olga Ragusa and reprinted in *Readings in Price Theory* (Chicago: Richard D. Irwin Inc., 1952), pp. 27–56; George J. Stigler, *op. cit.*, p. 63; I. M. D. Little, *A Critique of Welfare Economics* (London: Oxford University Press, 1950), p. 33; Milton Friedman, "The Welfare Effects of an Income Tax and an Excise Tax," *Journal of Political Economy*, LVII (February, 1952), 25–33. Marshall, however, in *Principles of Economics* (8th ed.; London: Macmillan and Co., Ltd., 1947), p. 838, considers the constraint on the consumer to be "the amount of money or general purchasing power at a person's disposal at any time." Earl R. Rolph and George F. Break adopt a similar position in "The Welfare Aspects of Excise Taxes," *Journal of Political Economy*, LVII (February, 1949), 25–54. Rolph, in *The Theory of Fiscal Economics* (Berkeley and Los Angeles: University of California Press, 1954), develops the exact notion of the constraint that is to be used here.

expected income itself. It means that he has an asset, his earning power, that he can sell to someone who prefers holding this asset to consuming. Even though we will for the present abstract from such sales of securities, their later introduction does not upset the notion that wealth is the constraint upon consumption spending.

At any date the stocks of real assets and money held by all persons in the group are legacies of the past and are, along with their distribution among individuals, taken as given. For any person at a date, his money holdings (m) and the number of units of real assets he holds (a) being given, his wealth (v) measured in dollars is given by

$$(1) \qquad\qquad v = m + aP_A$$

where P_A is the price of a unit of real assets. This sets the upper limit on the dollar value of consumption he can take over the next day, and, alternatively, it sets the upper limit upon the value of assets he can elect to hold over the day.

Considering consumption-taking in terms of fixed-composition bundles of consumption services, a person can choose to dissipate some, all, or none of his money wealth on consumption-taking. The alternative to consuming is holding real assets or money. The maximum number of units of real assets a person can hold is given by v/P_A, while the maximum number of composite units of consumption he can take equals v/P_C, where P_C is the price per unit. He can also hold a cash balance (b) whose maximum possible value is also v, his total wealth. The set of possible combinations of the three uses of his inherited wealth is given by

$$(2) \qquad\qquad v = xP_A + yP_C + b$$

where x represents the number of units of real assets he chooses to hold over the day, y the number of units of consumption he takes, and b, his cash balance. It should be noted that v is not independent of P_A if the person has inherited any real assets.

Equation (1) defines the objective constraint upon the individual's choice—the conditions beyond his control which limit him; equation (2) defines the possible dispositions of his wealth. *His potential demands for real assets, cash, and consumption together are clearly traceable to stocks of assets, including money, inherited from the past.*

Behavior: consuming versus thrifting

We shall call the behavior of a person who does not dissipate all of his wealth on consumption over any day "thrifting." Denoting v/P_C, the maximum number of composite units of consumption he can take, as his real consumption potential, thrifting, measured in real terms, is the difference between real consumption potential and the amount of consumption he chooses to take. Thus, t, the number of units of thrifting, plus y, the number of composite units of consumption taken, equals v/P_C, the real consumption potential. All of the real consumption potential is either dissipated or thrifted.

Our theory of consumption is as follows: A person will both consume more and thrift more the greater is his real consumption potential. However, as his real consumption potential increases, his thrifting will increase relatively more than his consumption-taking, so that the rise in consumption is less than proportionate, and the rise in thrifting is more than proportionate, to the rise in real consumption potential.

The notion that both consumption and thrifting rise with a rise in real consumption potential is consistent with the ordinary theory of choice, according to which, if a person can have more of two things he likes (consumption and wealth holdings), he will ordinarily take more of both. This theory, like the view of objective constraint, is taken from Rolph. He states, in *The Theory of Fiscal Economics,* that

The amount of a person's consumption expenditures depends upon the value of his asset holding, including cash. The greater his asset holding, the more he spends on consumption, but the smaller is the proportion of these expenditures to his asset holding. . . . This hypothesis is offered as a statistical generalization in the sense of applying to groups on the average, or to "typical" persons, rather than to every person.[5]

The theory offered here is an adaptation of Rolph's theory, being stated in real terms after making the simplification of treating

---

[5] *Ibid.*, p. 90. Rolph calls attention to the paucity of empirical findings on this point, but points out (p. 91) that the available data appear consistent with his hypothesis.

consumption-taking in terms of fixed-composition bundles. Studies of Keynesian consumption function provide indirect support for Rolph's theory.

Klein, although arguing that income is the primary determinant of consumption, finds in material from the Survey of Consumer Finances a positive correlation between liquid assets and consumption spending.[6] Tobin's view of the relationships between the value of assets owned by a household, the prices of consumption items, and consumption spending is similar to the one adopted here, except that he also includes income as a determinant of consumption.[7] Friedman argues that a change in permanent income causes a greater change in consumption spending than does an equal change in transient (windfall) income.[8] This idea fits in very nicely with Rolph's notion, since a permanent rise in an individual's earning power brings about a more or less proportionate rise in his ability to borrow on his earning capacity, or the value of the assets (including his own IOU's) he can sell for cash, while a windfall gain does not. Friedman also includes nonhuman wealth as a variable affecting consumption.

The demand for consumption, asset price given

Since a person's consumption depends upon his real consumption potential, the relevant objective determinants are his money wealth, on the one hand, and the price of a composite unit of consumption, on the other. Given P_A, the price of a unit of real assets, variations in P_C, the price of a composite unit of consumption services, produce inversely proportional changes in a person's real consumption potential, v/P_C. We can construct a demand curve for consumption, measured in composite units, by finding how real consumption varies as P_C changes.

Since a fall in P_C produces proportional rise in real consumption potential, it causes consumption-taking to increase. The demand curve for consumption has a negative slope due en-

[6] Lawrence R. Klein, "Assets, Debts, and Economic Behavior," *Studies in Income and Wealth, XIV* (New York: National Bureau of Economic Research, 1951), pp. 195–227.

[7] James Tobin, "Asset Holdings and Spending Decisions," "Papers and Proceedings," *American Economic Review,* XLVII (1951), 109–123.

[8] Milton Friedman, *A Theory of the Consumption Function* (Princeton: Princeton University Press, 1947).

tirely to the effect of a decline in P_C upon real consumption potential. (If a person's wealth were to fall proportionately with the
decline in P_C, his consumption-taking would remain unchanged.)
However, since consumption-taking typically varies less than proportionately with real consumption potential, the demand curve
for consumption is inelastic. The market demand curve for consumption services, given P_A, is downward sloping and inelastic,

Fig. III-1

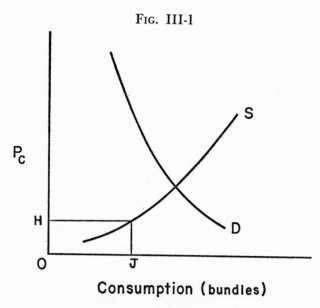

Consumption (bundles)

reflecting the typical individual's inelastic demand curve for consumption. D in Figure III-1 is a market demand curve for
consumption services, in composite units.

The supply of consumption services, asset prices given
Productive resources can be used to produce either consumption
services or new real assets. Figure III-2 shows the production possibilities or transformation curve for the economy. Consumption
services are measured in composite units on the horizontal axis,
while net production of new real assets is measured on the vertical
axis. The transformation curve is drawn concave to the origin on
the assumptions that there are no returns to scale in either industry, that the two production functions are not identical, and that
resources are not perfect substitutes for one another in either ac-

tivity. Real assets can be both produced currently and used up currently in the production of consumption services. If no consumption services are produced, so that all resources are used to produce real assets, OR units of real assets can be added to the existing stock over the day. If, on the other hand, the entire productive effort of the community is devoted to producing consumption services, SN units can be produced, involving a net disinvest-

FIG. III-2

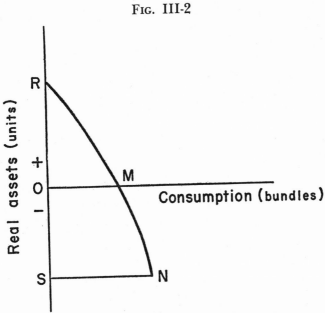

ment of OS units of real assets. Points on the transformation curve intermediate between R and N represent situations in which resources are used to produce both new real assets and consumption services. OM is the greatest amount of consumption possible if there is to be no net disinvestment during the day. Any further increases in consumption involve capital consumption over and above the amount of new real assets that can be produced.

Resources will be used to produce consumption services as long as their earnings in that use are equal to or exceed their earnings when used to produce new real assets. Given the production possibilities or transformation relationship, competitive equilibrium requires that the production of consumption services be carried up to the point where the marginal rate of transformation of consumption services for real assets is equal to the price of consumption services relative to the price of real assets, or P_C/P_A.[9] Because the marginal rate of transformation increases moving from R toward N (Figure III-2), the consumption supply curve defined for any given P_A is upward sloping, indicating that only as P_C increases does it pay the owners of resources to move them into the consumption industry.[10] This relationship is shown by S in Figure III-1. At $P_C = OH$, OJ units of consumption services are produced, while at higher prices more are produced as owners are induced to move additional resources into the consumption industry until the marginal cost of consumption in terms of real assets has again reached P_C/P_A.

For any given price of real assets, the equilibrium price in the consumption market is given by the intersection of the demand and supply curves. The thriftier people are, the lower will be the demand curve and the lower will be the price (and the rate of production) of consumption services.

Effect of a change in the price of assets

The fundamental relationship of the equilibrium price of consumption services to the price of assets can be demonstrated by assuming a change in P_A. If, for example, P_A is doubled, any person holding real assets experiences an increase in his wealth, measured in dollars. If he holds only real assets, and no money, his wealth is doubled, and so is his real consumption potential given any P_C. With P_C constant, he consumes more as P_A is doubled; but

---

[9] See Paul A. Samuelson, *The Foundations of Economic Analysis* (Cambridge, Mass.: Harvard University Press, 1947), Ch. VIII.

[10] However, if resources are perfect substitutes for one another in the two uses, or if the production functions are identical, the transformation curve will be a straight line and the supply of consumption services, given P_A, will be a horizontal straight line. Only by coincidence would the two production functions be identical. Perfect substitutability of resource services is unlikely for a short period situation such as the one in question, resource specialization being widespread. See Joan Robinson's "Rising Supply Price" in *Readings in Price Theory* (Chicago: Richard D. Irwin Inc., 1952) pp. 233–241. F. H. Knight appears, at times, to feel that constant costs prevail even over very short periods. See, for example, his article "Interest," in the *Encyclopedia of the Social Sciences*. However, in "Interest" in the *Encyclopædia Britannica* (1946), he states that it is long-run, or "normal," costs that are likely to be constant, so that one is left with the distinct impression that even Knight would grant that both supply and demand enter into the determination of prices at any moment.

he does not double his consumption, for consumption rises less than proportionately to the increase in real consumption potential. To generalize, the consumption demand curve of a person who holds only real assets shifts rightward as P_A rises, but the rightward shift is less than proportional to the rise in P_A.

For a person who holds money along with real assets, the effect of an increase in P_A is less pronounced, because his total wealth does not increase by as much, relatively, as P_A increases. The smaller his holding of real assets relative to his holding of money, the less will be the rightward shift of his consumption demand curve induced by a rise in P_A. In the limiting case, a person who holds only money finds his wealth, and hence his consumption demand, unaffected by changes in the price of real assets.

It should be kept in mind that P_A enters into the determination of a person's consumption only through its influence on his real consumption potential. This contrasts with the time-preference theory, which holds that consumption depends on the rate of interest and hence may vary as asset prices vary, even for people who hold no stocks of real assets.

As long as some people hold stocks of real assets, a rise in P_A will induce an upward shift in the market demand curve for consumption services. Measured vertically, the rise is less than proportionate to the increase in P_A, since, if P_A and P_C rise equally, any people holding money balances find their real consumption potentials reduced, and therefore reduce their real consumption-taking. Thus suppose that, in Figure III-3, D_1 is the demand curve for consumption when $P_A = \$1$. A rise in P_A to \$2 would increase the money wealth of anyone holding real assets, raising his consumption demand. The vertical rise of the market demand curve to D_2 is less than proportionate to the increase in P_A because of the real balance effect; a doubling of both prices reduces the real consumption potential of anyone holding money. Thus, if at $P_C = \$2$ people take OR units of consumption when $P_A = \$1$, they will take less (shown by OQ) at $P_C = \$4$ when $P_A = \$2$ as long as they hold any cash.

The supply of consumption services depends exclusively on the relative prices of real assets and consumption services, given the transformation function, so that a change in P_A induces a proportionate vertical shift in the consumption supply curve. In our example, when P_A is raised from $1 to $2, the P_C at which any given amount of consumption services is forthcoming is doubled. This is illustrated by the shift from S_1 to S_2 in Figure III-3.

Since both the demand curve and the supply curve shift upward as P_A is raised, the equilibrium P_C is higher as P_A is higher. But the demand curve shifts upward relatively less than does the sup-

FIG. III-3

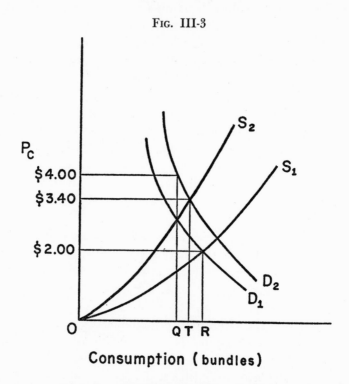

Consumption (bundles)

ply curve, so that the equilibrium price of consumption services falls relative to P_A. In Figure III-3, P_C rises from $2 to $3.40 as P_A is assumed to increase from $1 to $2.

The rate of production of consumption services falls (from OR to OT in Figure III-3) as P_C falls relative to P_A. Only if the supply curve is vertical, indicating a complete lack of mobility of resources between the production of consumption services and real assets, will a rise in P_A fail to reduce the real rate of production of consumption services.

The relationship between the equilibrium P_C and the price of real assets can be shown graphically. In Figure III-4, XX' traces a set of such prices. As P_A rises, the equilibrium P_C always rises, but less than proportionately. The elasticity of XX', measured by

$$\frac{\Delta P_C}{P_C} \Big/ \frac{\Delta P_A}{P_A},$$

is less than one throughout.

We turn now to the determination of P_A, the equilibrium price of a unit of real assets. Just as the equilibrium P_C depends in part upon the level of P_A, so, it will be seen, the equilibrium P_A de-

FIG. III-4

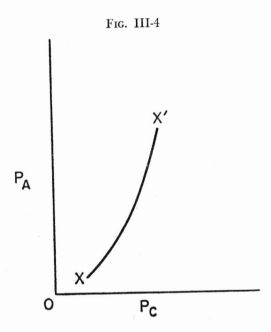

pends in part upon P_C. Ultimately we will want to solve for both prices simultaneously, but first we must see how P_A is determined when P_C is given.

The demand for real assets to hold, P_C given

The number of units of real assets a person will wish to hold may be thought of as involving three things: (1) his dollar demand for assets in general, including both real assets and cash; (2) the division of this total demand between real assets and cash; and (3) the price of a unit of real assets. The question of the division of his total demand for assets to hold between cash balances and real assets will not detain us much at this point. Under the perfect foresight assumption, people will always be sure of a positive yield from real assets, unless they expect their prices to decline. Ruling out this possibility by assuming that they take present prices as the best indicator of future prices, they will hold cash balances through time only for transactions purposes.

We shall assume that people always wish to hold transactions balances equal to some fixed proportion of their total dollar demand for assets, denoting the proportion by k. (This simplified treatment of liquidity preference is amended in later chapters where we take up the problems raised by investor uncertainty.) From $v/P_C = y + t$, the identity showing that all of a person's real consumption potential is either dissipated or thrifted, we obtain $v = yP_C + tP_C$, the financial counterpart. All money wealth is dissipated or maintained, yP_C being spent on consumption and tP_C representing the total dollar demand for assets to hold or the money value of thrifting. The demand for real assets is given by

$$(3) \qquad\qquad x = \frac{tP_C(1 - k)}{P_A}$$

where x is the number of units of real assets demanded, and k is the fraction of the total dollar demand for assets devoted to holding cash balances. Taking P_C as given, the demand schedule for real assets is found by seeing what happens to x as P_A changes.

Suppose a person comes into the day holding, as his inheritance from the past, only cash. His real consumption potential is unaffected by changes in P_A, and his thrifting does not vary as P_A changes. Therefore, in equation (3), x, the amount of real assets he holds varies in inverse proportion with P_A, and the demand curve for real assets is a rectangular hyperbola. If no one held inherited stocks of real assets, this would be the whole story concerning the elasticity of demand for real assets to hold given P_C; everyone's demand curve would be a rectangular hyperbola.

The role of existing stocks in determining demand

As soon as existing stocks are introduced, matters become more complex. Suppose a person inherits from the past only real assets and no money. Then his real consumption potential varies directly and proportionately with P_A. According to the theory of consumption used here, his thrifting varies more than proportionately with his real consumption potential; the numerator in equation (3) increases relatively faster than P_A. Therefore x increases as P_A rises; the demand curve for real assets to hold has a positive slope.

It is important to examine this case carefully. Consider a person who inherits OA units of real assets, measured along the horizontal axis in Figure III-5, and no money. Suppose that at $P_A = OF$ his real consumption potential is such that he divides his total wealth

FIG. III-5

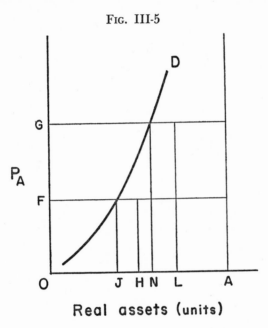

Real assets (units)

equally between consumption and holding assets. Then his total dollar demand for assets to hold, or tP_C, is given by the area OF(OH) where $OH = \frac{1}{2}(OA)$. If k, the fraction of this total he wishes to keep in cash balances, is $\frac{1}{4}$, his total dollar demand for real assets is OF(OJ), JH being equal to $\frac{1}{4}OH$, and he holds OJ units of real assets.

An increase in P_A to OG increases his money wealth and his real consumption potential proportionately, to OG(OA). But his consumption rises less than proportionately to this increase in his wealth, so that he now needs to dispose of less real assets to finance consumption. His total dollar demand for assets to hold rises relatively faster than does P_A, as is shown by the increase from OF(OH) to OL(OG). Since k is constant, his dollar demand for real assets to hold rises by the same proportion as his total dollar demand for all assets, or to ON(OG). He holds ON units of real assets. Curve D denotes his demand curve for real assets to hold, given P_C.

If we reverse our point of view, looking at point A as the origin, D becomes the person's selling curve, indicating the number of units of real assets, measured leftward from A, he is willing to sell at each P_A. Although he sells less of his holdings as P_A rises, he will never cut his sales to zero, since this would imply that his consumption spending and cash balances fall to zero as his wealth increases, whereas in fact they both increase. D lies to the left of point A over its entire range, and the total *value* of real assets sold increases as P_A increases.

In the intermediate case, a person who inherits both real assets and cash finds that his wealth varies directly with, but proportionately less than, changes in P_A. His money wealth is given by $aP_A + m$, where a is the number of units of real assets he inherits and m is his inheritance of money. The real asset component of this total becomes relatively more significant as P_A rises, so that the percentage change in his total wealth accompanying a given percentage change in P_A becomes greater as P_A rises. Since his thrifting rises relatively faster than does his money wealth, it may, at sufficiently high levels of P_A, also rise relatively faster than does P_A. Referring to equation (3), this would mean that x rises as P_A rises, and the slope of the demand curve is positive.

Starting at a price where the slope of the demand curve is positive, successive equal percentage reductions in P_A are accompanied by successively smaller percentage reductions in the investor's real wealth and tend to induce successively smaller percentage reductions in his thrifting. At some sufficiently low P_A, thrifting may cease to decline relatively faster than P_A, and the demand curve will take on a negative slope. This is illustrated in Figure III-6. At $P_A = OG$, the demand curve is vertical; at all higher prices it has a positive slope and at all lower prices the slope is negative. The differences are due to the increasing relative significance of changes in P_A as its absolute value rises.

Over the negatively sloped portion, the elasticity of demand will always be less than one, for the investor's thrifting, and hence his dollar demand for real assets to hold $tP_C(1-k)$, always fall as reductions in P_A lower his wealth.

There will be some price of real assets low enough so that an investor who inherits a mixed bundle of real assets and cash will wish to hold just the amount of real assets he has inherited from the past. At this price he devotes all of his inherited cash either to consumption spending or to cash balances to hold over the next

FIG. III-6

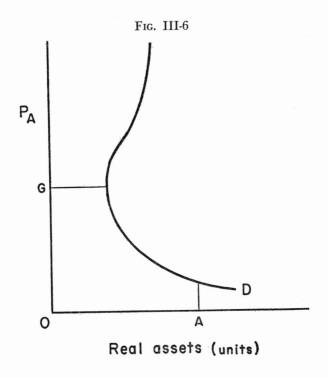

Real assets (units)

day. If P_A falls from this level, he reduces both his consumption spending and his demand for cash balances because his wealth is reduced. The diverted cash is used to acquire more real assets. Therefore his demand curve must be downward sloping at $x = OA$, where OA is the inherited stock of real assets.

An interesting and important thing about the demand for real assets is that existing stocks of real assets always create a part of their own demand, since owners of the stocks are wealthier, and therefore more willing and able to thrift, for owning them.

The market demand curve

The market demand curve for real assets to hold, obtained by
summing the individual demand curves horizontally, reflects the
general characteristics of the demand curve for a person who holds
a mixed bundle of real assets and money. Over lower ranges of
P_A, it is negatively sloped, while it may be positively sloped over
the upper ranges. Curve D in Figure III-7 is a market demand

FIG. III-7

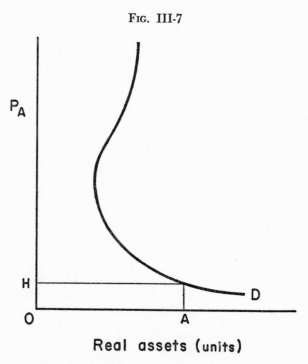

Real assets (units)

curve showing the number of units of real assets the group is
willing to hold at any price. It incorporates the demands of those
who do and those who do not already own real assets as an inheritance from the past. An important feature of the market demand curve for real assets is that it is not independent of the
amount and distribution of inherited real assets. Because there can
be no such thing as a stock of services, a parallel complication does
not arise in the case of the consumption demand curve.

If no additional supplies of assets to hold are available from
outside sources and none can be sold by the group to outsiders,

the inherited stock (OA in Figure III-7) constitutes the entire supply of assets available to be held through the day. The equilibrium price is the one at which the group is willing to hold just this inherited stock; it is shown in Figure III-7 by the intersection of the vertical stock supply curve erected at A with the demand curve D.

This equilibrium price is by definition the one that equates the number of units of real assets that buyers (those who are adding to their inherited stocks) wish to buy and that sellers (those who are divesting themselves of some of their inherited stocks) wish to sell. As Wicksteed has argued, a division of the group into buyers and sellers for the purpose of drawing the demand schedules of the former and the supply schedules of the latter tends to confuse the fundamental forces involved in the determination of equilibrium.[11] For the present problem, the supply of assets available to hold is a fact, and is not a function of anything; the relevant functional relationship is between the amounts people wish to hold, regardless of whether they are buying or selling, and P_A, the price per unit of the stock. The trading involved in establishing the equilibrium price is incidental to the fundamental determination of the price; its importance lies only in helping to explain how the equilibrating mechanism works.

It might be asked if there could be two equilibrium prices for real assets, since the market demand curve may turn back on itself and become positively sloped at sufficiently high levels of P_A. If the demand curve were to intersect the vertical stock supply curve over its positively sloped range, the equilibrium indicated by the intersection would be unstable.

Such an unstable equilibrium is impossible, as can be seen by thinking of the equilibrium in terms of buyers and sellers. Starting from any equilibrium price, where buying and selling are matched, the equilibrium would be unstable if, in response to a decline in the price, sellers increased the amounts of real assets they wished to sell more than buyers increased the amounts they wished to buy, if, that is, the total demand of both buyers and sellers for assets to hold were to fall.

Buyers are, by definition, using a part of their holdings of cash

[11] Philip H. Wicksteed, *The Common Sense of Political Economy*, Vol. II (New York: Augustus M. Kelley, 1950), Book II, Ch. IV.

to acquire real assets, and are dividing the rest of their cash holdings between consumption spending and cash balances to be held over. Buyers who hold any real assets will reduce their consumption spending and their cash balances as P_A falls because of the reduction in their wealth; at the same time they increase their total outlays for additional real assets, so that the number of units they buy increases more, in percentage terms, than P_A falls. Buyers who have inherited no real assets do not experience a wealth effect as P_A falls, and hence do not change their consumption spending, their demands for cash balances to hold, or their total outlays for real assets. The number of units of real assets they buy increases in proportion to the decline in P_A. Lumping both classes of buyers together, as a group they will wish to increase the amounts they buy at least proportionately to the fall in P_A, and more than proportionately if any of them holds real assets so that he experiences a decline in his wealth as P_A falls.

Sellers, on the other hand, are divesting themselves of a part of their real asset holdings to raise cash either to hold or to spend for consumption. As P_A falls, they will, since their wealth declines, reduce both their consumption spending and their demand for cash balances. They therefore will wish to raise less cash, and, while they may sell more real assets as P_A falls, the increase in the amounts they sell will be less than proportionate to the fall in P_A.

Since at the starting equilibrium price the buyers wish to buy just the amount sellers wish to sell, and since a reduction in price leads buyers to increase the amounts they wish to buy more than proportionately to the fall in P_A while sellers will increase their sales less than proportionately, the fall in P_A produces an excess demand, and the equilibrium from which we started is stable. The demand curve must be negatively sloped where it crosses the vertical stock supply curve.

The effect of changes in the inherited stock

It is essential to recognize that the demand curve is defined only for the given size and distribution of the inherited stock of real assets. Any change in the inherited stock will produce a change in the demand curve.

To demonstrate this point, we shall consider what happens to a person's demand curve if his inherited stock of real assets is doubled. Suppose D_1 in Figure III-8 is the demand curve for real assets to hold of a person who has inherited from the past OA units of real assets. The schedule is drawn on the assumption of some given P_C and shows that he is willing to hold just his inherited stock OA at $P_A = OG$.

FIG. III-8

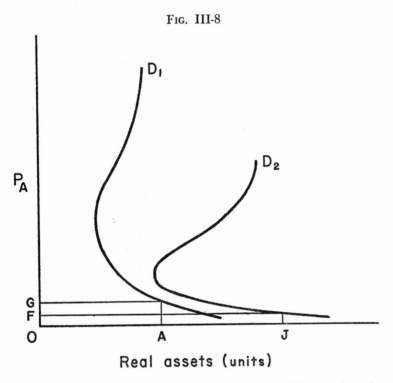

Real assets (units)

Now suppose instead that he inherits $OJ = 2(OA)$ units of real assets. At any given price such as OG, he will find himself wealthier so that, given P_C, his real consumption potential is increased. He will devote a part of the increase in his real consumption potential to increased consumption and the remainder to increased thrifting. Equation (3),

$$x = \frac{tP_C(1 - k)}{P_A},$$

shows that the number of units of real assets he will hold at any given pair of P_C and P_A increases as his thrifting rises. Therefore we know that an increase in inherited holdings of real assets causes a person's demand curve for assets to hold to shift rightward.

The percentage of the rightward shift of the demand curve depends on three factors. It will be greater the greater is the proportion of the investor's wealth deriving from inherited holdings of real assets as opposed to cash, the smaller is k, the proportion of his wealth he devotes to holding cash through the current period, and the greater is his propensity to thrift, rather than to consume, as his real consumption potential is raised. These are also the factors that determine the shape of his demand curve for any given inheritance of real assets, and there is a precise relation between D_1, and the demand curve defined for inheritance OA, and D_2, the demand curve defined for an inheritance of $OJ = 2(OA)$ units of real assets.

Starting at any particular P_A, and continuing to hold P_C constant, the investor's dollar wealth can be kept unchanged if we halve P_A at the same time that we double his inherited stock of real assets. In that case, his real consumption potential would be unaffected and therefore his thrifting would not change. In equation (3), the numerator, $tP_C(1 - k)$, is unaffected since thrifting does not change, while the denominator (P_A) has been halved, so that the amount of real assets the investor will wish to hold is doubled. This rule holds regardless of the P_A from which we start. D_2, defined for OJ units of inherited real assets lies to the right of D_1, defined for an inheritance of OA units, and shows that the price at which the investor will wish to hold any given quantity of real assets when he inherits OJ units is half the price at which he would wish to hold half as many units when he inherits only OA units. Thus, if he will hold his entire inherited stock of OA units at price OG, he will hold an inherited stock of OJ units at price OF, where $OJ = 2(OA)$ and $OF = \frac{1}{2}(OG)$. More generally, the price at which an investor will wish to hold just his inherited stock of real assets varies inversely with the size of his inherited stock. For the group, we can say that doubling everyone's inherited supply of assets while holding their inherited cash balances and the price of consumption services constant would halve the price at which the group would be willing to hold just the inherited stock through the next day.

Changes in the stock over time: flow supply

Two opposing flows, capital consumption and new production, work to change the size of an existing stock of real assets over time. The treatment of these flows is crucial in the analysis of asset prices. The role of flow supply is distinctly different from the role of (inherited) stock supply.

The transformation curve shown earlier in connection with the supply of consumption services is reproduced in Figure III-9.

FIG. III-9

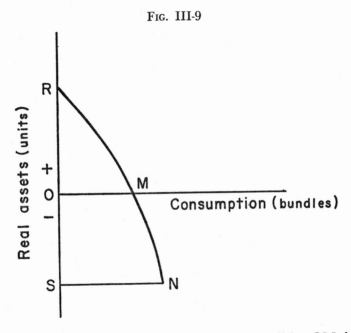

OR is the maximum net real investment possible, OM is the amount of consumption services that can be produced without net disinvestment, and SN is the maximum consumption that can be taken over the day. Maximizing consumption involves a net disinvestment of SO units of real assets.

Starting from R, as consumption increases, net investment must decline because of the increased capital consumption involved in the production of more consumption services and the transfer of resources out of the production of new real assets and into the production of consumption services. Just as knowing the transformation function enabled us to draw a competitive supply curve for consumption services when P_A was given, so it enables us to draw a net flow supply curve for real assets, given P_C. This curve is defined by the condition that net production of real assets is carried up to the point where the marginal rate of transformation of real assets for consumption services is equal to the ratio of P_A to P_C. SS' in Figure III-10 is a net flow supply curve. It

FIG. III-10

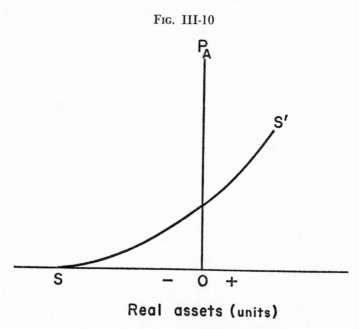

Real assets (units)

shows, for each P_A, the sum of capital consumption in the consumption services industry (a negative amount) and the output of new assets net of any capital consumption in the investment industry.

The stock-flow equilibrium

The role of the net flow supply in the determination of P_A can be seen most easily by first thinking of its components separately.

Capital consumption involves a *flow demand* for the existing stock of real assets as opposed to a demand to hold them. Because the consumption industry acquires some of the existing stock for consumption over the next moment, the supply of real assets available to hold is lower than is the inherited supply. The flow demand of capital consumption is an additional demand over and above the stock demand, and it tends to drive up P_A; alternatively, it can be thought of as a reduction in the supply of real assets available to hold.

The effect of this flow demand in reducing the supply of assets available to hold is fundamentally different than would be that of a reduction in the inherited stock. If the inherited stock is reduced, there is a simultaneous reduction in the source of demand for all things, including consumption services, cash balances, and real assets, since the people who experience the reduction are made poorer by it. At any given P_A, the demands for consumption, for cash balances to hold, and for real assets to hold are lowered.

Capital consumption, on the other hand, affects only the supply of assets available to hold. People's wealth is not affected, given any P_A, by changes in the amount of capital consumption to take place over the next moment, because prospective capital consumption does not affect the amount of assets they inherit. The demand for assets to hold is defined independently of the capital consumption demand.

New investment flows are similar to capital consumption in that they affect the supply of real assets available to hold without simultaneously affecting the stock demand. Investment in new real assets is a substitute for holding old ones. It is, like holding old real assets, made possible only by thrifting. Thrifters will invest in new real assets whenever the return to be earned on the investment exceeds or is equal to the return to be earned by holding old real assets. Whenever the cost of producing new real assets is lower than the price at which the group would be willing to hold just the inherited stock less any capital consumption, there is an incentive to produce new real assets, for no one will wish to hold old real assets at prices that exceed the marginal cost of producing new ones.

To see this more clearly, consider Figure III-11. D, taken with reference to O as the origin, is the market demand curve for real assets to hold. It is defined for the inherited stock whose amount is measured by the distance OO′ along the horizontal axis. OG, measured along the vertical axis, is the price at which the group would wish to hold just the inherited stock, and SS′ is the net

flow supply schedule drawn with reference to O′ as the origin. It
shows, for every P_A, the amount of production of new assets less
capital consumption.

At price OG it is profitable for thrifters to invest in the production of new real assets in excess of capital consumption. But
new investment spending cannot be financed by holding less real
assets at $P_A = OG$, because the entire supply of money is being
used for consumption spending and cash balance holdings at

FIG. III-11

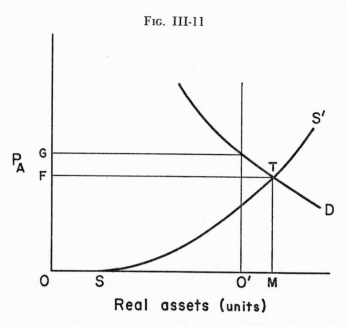

Real assets (units)

this price. P_A must fall, since people prefer investing in new assets to holding old ones at $P_A = OG$. As P_A falls, owners of inherited stocks experience a reduction in their wealth, inducing
them to reduce their consumption spending and cash balances
and to increase their holdings of real assets. P_A must fall until the
group is willing to add to its inherited stock, through new investment, just the amount of new real assets it is profitable to produce in excess of capital consumption. This equilibrium price is
indicated by the intersection of D and SS′ at point T in Figure
III-11. At $P_A = OF$, the group is willing to hold OO′, the inherited stock, plus O′M, the net new investment profitable at this
price.

Demand curve D defines the demand for the entire net stock flow supply, including both inherited real assets and new ones. The stock flow supply is given by SS', measuring from O (rather than O') as the origin. It shows the total amount of real assets available to hold plus the amount of profitable new investment as a function of P_A. Curve D, which is the demand for both old and new real assets, is independent of the net flow supply but it is not independent of the stock (inherited) supply. Whereas pre-existing stocks provide a source of demand for real assets, new investment spending cannot simultaneously provide a source of demand for anything because the new real assets being produced are not simultaneously a source of disposable wealth to producers.

New investment opportunities make room for themselves by competing with old assets. By forcing the prices of old assets down, the new investment opportunities induce the group to add to its inherited holdings of real assets. A lowering of the cost of producing new assets (which involves a change in the trans-formation function) would be reflected in a downward shift of the net flow supply function. P_A would fall until the group again became willing to add to its inherited stock of assets all that can be profitably produced in excess of capital consumption.

Effect of a change in the price of consumption

A change in P_C would induce a shift in the demand curve for real assets by changing people's real consumption potential. As P_C falls by some given percentage, given any P_A, people experience an equal percentage rise in their real consumption potentials. They respond by consuming more and thrifting more. Since thrifting (t) increases more, proportionately, than the real consumption potential, people devote a greater part of their wealth to holding assets and reduce their consumption spending. In the equation for the demand for real assets

$$(3) \qquad x = \frac{tP_C(1 - k)}{P_A}$$

x rises as P_C falls and P_A is held constant.

On the supply side, the inherited stock of real assets is unaf-fected by changes in P_C. The net flow supply curve moves in the same direction and by the same proportion as the change in P_C,

since net flow supply is determined exclusively by the price of
assets relative to the price of consumption services. A halving of
P_C leads to a halving of the price of real assets at which any given
net flow of new real assets is forthcoming.

Since the supply and demand curves move in opposite directions, the net effect of a decline in P_C might be either to raise or
to lower the equilibrium P_A shown by their intersection. P_A will

FIG. III-12

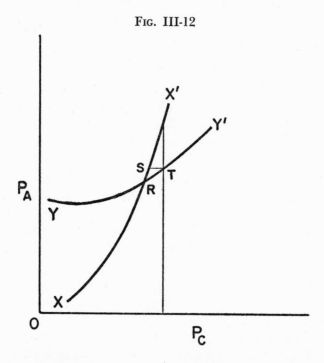

rise if the transformation function is sufficiently convex; in the
limiting case of absolute immobility of resources P_A must rise as
P_C falls since the net flow supply does not change as demand increases. At the other extreme, if the transformation function is a
straight line (constant costs), P_A must fall proportionately with P_C.

Except in the limiting case of constant costs, then, a fall in the
assumed level of P_C causes P_A to rise relative to P_C. Plotting
equilibrium prices in the assets market as functions of assumed
P_C's, we obtain a curve such as YY' in Figure III-12. It shows that
the equilibrium P_A rises, relative to P_C, as P_C falls. Over the lower
ranges of P_C, YY' is drawn with a negative slope on the assumption

that resources become less and less perfect substitutes for one another as asset production is increased in response to successive increases in P_A/P_C. However, the only necessary specification is that P_A/P_C declines as P_C rises. The YY' curve could have a positive slope throughout its range as long as its elasticity, measured by

$$\frac{\Delta P_C}{P_C} \Bigg/ \frac{\Delta P_A}{P_A},$$

is greater than one throughout.

The XX' curve, taken from Figure III-4, shows the prices at which the consumption market is brought into equilibrium for each possible price of real assets. It will be recalled that the elasticity of XX' is less than one throughout; an increase in the assumed level of P_A brings about a less than proportional increase in the equilibrium P_C. The intersection of XX' and YY' at R denotes the pair of prices at which the two markets are simultaneously in equilibrium. There can be only one such intersection, since the XX' curve is inelastic throughout and the YY' curve is elastic throughout. However, if costs are constant, the two curves will coincide, and the analysis must be modified to find which particular pair of prices satisfies the general equilibrium condition.

The equilibrium is stable because XX' cuts YY' from below. A rise in P_C above the equilibrium level would raise the price at which the real assets market is equilibrated to a point T on YY'. At this higher level of P_A the consumption market would be equilibrated at the price represented by point S on XX', a lower price than the one from which we started. The forces set to work by a rise in P_C above the general equilibrium level tend to restore the general equilibrium.[12]

---

[12] This treatment of the general equilibrium prices is from Hicks, who uses it in *Value and Capital*, Ch. V, to discuss complementarity and substitutability of goods. Of course, since only two commodities are considered here, they are substitutes according to Hicks's criterion.

IV

The Level of Asset Prices:
An Elaboration

The significance of the theory set forth in Chapter III becomes more evident when we compare its implications with those of other theories that have been developed to handle the same class of phenomena. The present chapter will explore a number of these specific relationships.

INVESTMENT SPENDING, INTEREST, AND CAPITAL VALUES

Given the expected incomes of both old and new assets, and knowing the prices of real assets, the rate of interest is computed by finding that rate of time discount which when applied to the future income of any asset equates it with the market price of the asset. Nowhere in the analysis does the rate of interest have significance as a determinant of anything; it is a derived figure.

Suppose we are told that the rate of interest is, in fact, 5 per cent. We explain the rate by arguing that the expected income of a unit of real assets is such that at the equilibrium P_A the computed annual yield is 5 per cent. The proposed analysis explains only P_A, the price for real assets that makes the amounts people wish to hold equal to the total of the inherited stock plus all the new assets, over and above the rate of capital consumption, it is profitable to produce at that price, with the further provision that the price of a unit of consumption equilibrates the consumption markets simultaneously.

The price of a unit of real assets is independent of the expected income per unit, for supply and demand for real assets to hold are defined independently of the magnitude of expected income per unit. To demonstrate this, suppose a uniform 50 per cent tax were levied upon the earnings of real assets. The existing stock of real assets is unaffected by the tax. The net flow supply, which depends exclusively on the ratio P_A/P_C, is also unaffected. The demand for real assets to hold depends on (1) the size and distribution of the inherited stock, (2) the price of consumption services, (3) the money supply and its distribution, and (4) the ratio k, the fraction of their total wealth people hold in cash. None of these is related to the expected rate of return from real assets, so that demand, too, is unaffected by the tax. Therefore, the equilibrium P_A does not change when a uniform tax is levied on the income from real assets.

This must mean that the rate of investment in new assets, equal to the physical volume of new investment times P_A, is also unchanged. The rate of interest, net of tax, is the only thing changed by the tax. It is halved by a 50 per cent tax.

Rolph reaches a similar conclusion.[1] Basing his argument on the assertion that savings, all of which are invested under conditions of perfect foresight, are unaffected by changes in the yield on new investment, he points out that the marginal efficiency of capital, after tax, is reduced by the full amount of the tax. The prices of existing assets, found by capitalizing their after-tax earnings at the lowered marginal after-tax yield on new investment opportunities, are therefore unaffected.

This argument is interpreted graphically in Figure IV-1. MEI_1 is the schedule of the marginal efficiency of investment before the tax is imposed. OS is the given rate of saving and SN is the equilibrium marginal efficiency of investment. The prices of old assets are found by capitalizing their anticipated incomes at this rate.

The imposition of a 50 per cent tax on the earnings of all assets causes a 50 per cent downward shift in the schedule of the marginal efficiency of investment. MEI_2, the after-tax schedule,

---

[1] Earl R. Rolph, *The Theory of Fiscal Economics* (Berkeley and Los Angeles: University of California Press, 1954), Ch. II.

cuts the vertical savings "schedule" at M; SM ($= \frac{1}{2}$ SN) is the after-tax rate of return on new investment. The anticipated incomes from existing assets are discounted at the new after-tax rate of return on new investment SM, so that their prices are not changed by the tax. There is no capitalization of a uniform tax on the earnings of all real assets.

Rolph's finding depends on the lack of a functional relationship between saving and the rate of interest. If saving is a positive

Fig. IV-1

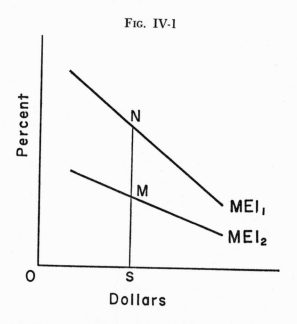

function of interest, as Marshall and other time-preference theorists contend, lowering the schedule of the marginal efficiency of investment induces people to save less and consume more. In this case, as investment spending falls, the marginal efficiency of investment taken before tax is raised, so that the equilibrium after-tax yield on new investment is more than half as great as the yield that would obtain in equilibrium without the tax. This is shown in Figure IV-2, where a shift in the schedule of the marginal efficiency of investment from MEI_1 to MEI_2 brought about by the imposition of the tax results in an equilibrium after-tax rate of return of GN as the pretax yield rises to GL.

According to this view, the prices of old assets fall as a result of the tax, since their after-tax earnings fall relative to the rate of return at the margin of new investment. The prices of old assets and identical new ones are uniformly lowered as a consequence of the tax-induced reduction in new investment spending. Only if the cost of producing new assets were constant, making the schedule of the marginal efficiency of investment a horizontal straight line, could the after-tax yield fall by the full percentage of the tax. In this case, since the cost of new assets is not lowered

FIG. IV-2

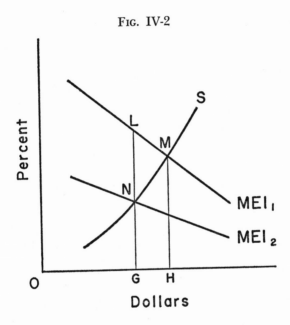

by reduced investment, neither is the price of old ones, and the discount rate falls by the same percentage as does the expected after-tax income from existing assets.

The Marshallian view is not compatible with the theory proposed here. It makes the demand for new assets depend on their expected yields. Only if the rate of spending on new assets is changed by the tax can their cost and the prices of old assets be changed. The theory proposed here agrees, in its implications, with the constant-savings hypothesis, as applied by Rolph, because it does not relate the rate of investment spending to the yield on new investments.

However, the fact that both our approach and Rolph's reject

the time-preference notion does not mean they will always agree in their implications; nor does the different theory of capital formation set forth by time-preference theorists always differ, in its implications, from the one proposed here. This can be illustrated by a further pursuit of the tax-capitalization question.

Suppose a tax of 50 per cent is levied on the earnings of new real assets only, existing stocks of assets being exempted from any tax liability. Regardless of the theory of asset prices used, the prices of old assets must rise relative to the cost of producing new ones subject to the tax liability. If the rate of tax is 50 per cent, it will take twice as many physical units of any new real asset to substitute for ownership of one physical unit of an existing one if the units are identical in all respects except the tax liability. The crucial matter is the effect of the tax on the rate of investment spending and the levels of old and new asset prices.

From the savings-investment viewpoint, the effect of the tax may again be thought of as a reduction in the marginal efficiency of investment. According to Rolph, the equilibrium rate of investment is unchanged by the reduction in yield, so the equilibrium marginal efficiency of investment, after tax, is halved. In this respect, his conclusion is the same as for the case of a uniform 50 per cent tax on the income from all assets, both old and new. However, because existing stocks of assets escape the tax liability, their prices rise; the capitalization rate is halved while their prospective earnings are unaffected. Rolph calls the increase in the prices of old assets negative tax capitalization; holders of the existing stock of assets are made wealthier because of the tax.

The theory proposed here has different implications. The constant-savings approach involves the implicit assumption that the prices of existing assets have nothing to do with the rates of consumption and investment spending. The dollar amount of new investment spending, which is by definition equal to the total dollar demand for assets to hold less the dollar value of existing stock, remains unchanged in the face of a rise in the prices of old assets only if the total dollar demand for assets to hold rises by the full amount of any increase in their value, only, that is, if people who hold real assets devote all of the increase in their wealth to additional thrifting.

According to the proposed theory, however, people who experience an increase in their wealth respond by both thrifting more *and* consuming more. As the dollar value of the inherited stock of assets rises, the holders of it do not devote all of the increased wealth to thrifting, so the total dollar demand for assets to hold rises by less than the increase in the value of the existing stock. Investment spending, the difference between the total dollar demand for assets to hold and the value of the existing stock, declines as the prices of old assets rise. As the demand for new real assets declines, marginal cost falls along with the rate of production, tending to reduce the upward pressure on prices of old assets. In equilibrium with the tax, the prices of old assets are higher than they would be in the absence of the tax, but they are not higher by the full proportion of the tax. The costs of producing new assets are lower than they would be in the absence of the tax, and after-tax yield is lower by less than 50 per cent.

The Marshallian approach yields similar results but because of a different mechanism. According to this view, the tax on new real asset earnings discourages saving by reducing the yield on new investment. The after-tax rate of return falls by less than the full proportion of the tax (Figure IV-2). Old asset prices rise, but by less than under the constant-savings hypothesis, for the discount applied to their earnings falls by less than 50 per cent. The results are similar to ours because according to both approaches in this case the tax reduces investment spending.

For a third problem in tax capitalization, the implications of the theory proposed here differ from those of both the constant-savings approach and the Marshallian approach. Suppose a 50 per cent tax is levied upon the earnings of existing assets only, all assets produced after a certain date being free of tax liability. According to both theories, the prices of old assets fall; the tax is fully capitalized. The net earnings of existing assets are reduced by the full amount of the tax while the marginal yield on new investment, used to discount the earnings of old assets, is unaffected. Neither the schedule of the marginal efficiency of investment nor the savings schedule is influenced by a tax that exempts the earnings of new assets.

The implication of both savings-investment approaches is that the holders of old assets maintain their consumption in the face of reductions in their wealth. The total dollar demand for assets to hold is presumed to fall equally with the dollar value of existing assets so that the excess of total dollar demand for assets to hold over the dollar value of the existing stock is unaffected. The proposed theory, on the other hand, leads to the conclusion that this excess, or investment spending, is increased as people who hold old assets experience a reduction in their wealth; their total dollar demand for assets to hold falls by less than the fall in the dollar value of their inherited holdings as they reduce their consumption spending. The tax on the earnings of old real assets is not fully capitalized because the cost of producing new real assets is raised as investment spending increases. In terms of the savings-investment approach, the marginal efficiency of investment is lowered, so that the prices of old assets fall by less than 50 per cent.

The difference in implications stems directly from the differing identifications of the determinants of investment demand. Since the tax affects the wealth of the holders of existing real assets, it will affect the rate of investment spending as long as consumption spending depends on wealth.

Marginal Costs and Capital Values

Marginal costs are of crucial importance in the determination of asset prices. In terms of the proposed theory, marginal costs help to determine the net flow supply of new assets. Any change in the costs of producing new real assets shifts the net flow supply function and thereby changes the equilibrium level of asset prices.

Suppose that the cost of producing new real assets declines, causing the combined stock-flow supply curve in Figure IV-3 to shift from SS_1 to SS_2. The equilibrium price of a unit of real assets falls from OG to OH, eliminating the excess supply generated by the reduced cost of production.

Similarly, the savings-investment approach recognizes the relation of marginal costs to asset prices through the influence of costs on the schedule of the marginal efficiency of investment. A reduction in costs increases the marginal efficiency of investment, causing the prices of existing assets to fall sufficiently to keep their yields equal to the marginal efficiency of investment.

But the literature on asset prices does not always recognize the crucial role of marginal costs in the pricing of stocks. There is a time-honored custom of holding that the price of any particular asset is independent of its current cost of reproduction. This line of thought traces back at least to Marshall's *Principles* where, in a chapter entitled "Marginal Cost in Relation to Values," it is argued that cost influences the price of a stock of assets only in the long run.[2]

FIG. IV-3

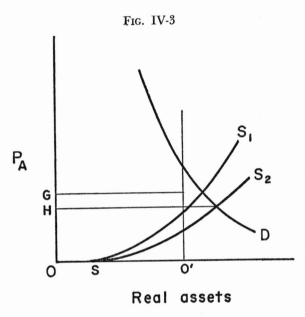

Real assets

To demonstrate his point, Marshall asks the reader to suppose a meteoric shower of large stones, harder than diamonds, having industrial uses. Assuming that some of the stones can be picked up at will, so that they are immediately available for use, their price is found by capitalizing their anticipated earnings. If a search will turn up more stones, the cost of searching determines the cost of producing new stones, given the expectation of success. According to Marshall, this cost of production has no influence whatever on the current value of the stones already available for use. However, if the current price of stones exceeds their

[2] Alfred Marshall, *Principles of Economics,* 8th Ed. (London: Macmillan and Co., Ltd., 1947), Book V, Ch. IX.

cost of production, there is an incentive to "produce" new ones. Through time, as additional stones enlarge the stock, the marginal productivity of stones will fall, reducing net income per stone. The process continues until the capital value of a stone is lowered to equality with the cost of production. The adjustment of cost to price is thought to occur only through a reduction in the net income per stone, and is therefore a long-run phenomenon. If, after a long-run equalization of cost and price, the cost were suddenly to be cut in half by an innovation in the searching process, the prices of existing stones would be unaffected for the moment. The influence of the reduced cost would be felt only through time as the size of the stock increased again. Marshall concludes, then, that the price of an asset is always independent of its current cost of production, though it may be influenced by historical cost because the present size of the stock is determined by past relationships of price to cost.

Although Marshall's logic is correct, given the assumptions, the failure of the change in the cost of producing an asset to affect its current price is due entirely to the *ceteris paribus* assumption of a given capitalization rate. F. H. Knight takes a quite opposite position. Using the assumption of constant costs, Knight argues that costs exclusively determine the prices of reproducible assets, since no one would be willing to pay more for an asset than it costs to produce it, and the rate of capitalization is determined by the return on newly produced assets where costs are given.[3]

More generally, in terms of the savings-investment approach, a reduction in the cost of producing any asset raises the marginal efficiency of investment, lowering the prices of all real assets. This is true even if marginal costs are increasing. Thus, as long as new assets can be produced, cost enters into the determination of all asset prices.

The theory proposed here recognizes the influence of production costs on prices by incorporating flow supply into the total supply of assets available to investors. For equilibrium to be established, the price of real assets must be such that investors are willing not only to hold the inherited stock but in addition to add to their holdings the amount it pays to produce currently.

---

[3] See "Interest," *Encyclopedia of the Social Sciences*, VIII, 131–144.

A decline in the costs of producing new real assets causes asset prices to fall. As was shown in Figure IV-3, the flow supply curve moves downward and to the right, and asset prices decline to the level which makes investors willing to absorb the increased supply. The increased spending on new real assets induced by a rightward shift of the flow supply curve is made possible by the reductions in consumption and cash holdings which are induced by the decline in wealth of real asset holders as the value of inherited stock of asset falls.

ALLOWING FOR PERSONAL DEBT

The assumption that no one can issue securities based upon his own earning power has made it possible to simplify the analysis of asset prices and investment, but completeness requires that we now remove the assumption.

Human beings are resources and it is conceivable to find their values by capitalizing their earnings. Modern societies do not tolerate the institution of slavery. But although no one may own anyone else, it is possible, in societies of the advanced capitalistic type such as the present-day United States, for people to sell partial claims to their earning power. Those claims must compete with all other assets in the assets markets, and under conditions of perfect foresight the value of any specific claim to the income of a person relative to the values of other claims is such that the percentage yield is equivalent to the yields on real assets. When claims to earning power are included, a person's total wealth is equal to the sum of (1) his money holdings, (2) the value of the real assets he owns, (3) the value of unissued claims against his own earning power, and (4) the value of any claims he holds on others. At any given level of asset prices, his wealth and his real consumption potential are raised by the inclusion of unissued debt; personal earning power is a source of personal wealth. People who are mortgaged to the hilt have exhausted this source of wealth, but it has not disappeared, since the persons who hold the claims are wealthier for them. The total value of all the claims is independent of its distribution in the sense that the claim to all human earning power is all held by someone. Therefore, at any P_A, the money wealth of the community is greater by the value of these claims. It is to be expected that those who hold them consume more because of the additional source of wealth.

The effect of introducing these claims is formally equivalent to the effect of increasing the inherited stock of real assets. At any P_A the total money demand for earning assets, including these claims, is raised, but by less than the increase in the existing supply, so that excess demand is reduced at all prices. New in-

FIG. IV-4

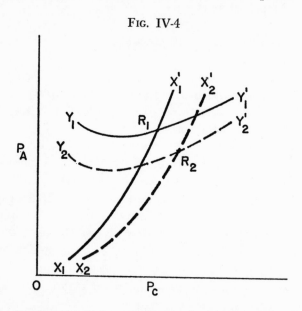

vestment spending is discouraged, as we would expect; adding to people's ability to consume adds to their consumption.

In terms of the general equilibrium system, the addition of borrowing power tends to shift the XX′ curve to the right as the demand for consumption services rises, given any P_A, and to shift the YY′ curve downward as the demand for assets to hold rises by less than does the value of people's asset holdings, including their newly added borrowing power. As is shown in Figure IV-4, the shifts from $X_1X'_1$ to $X_2X'_2$ and from $Y_1Y'_1$ to $Y_2Y'_2$ move the intersection of the curves to the southwest, from R_1 to R_2, indicating that P_C rises relative to P_A.

V

The Tastes of Uncertain Investors

In the previous chapters, we have analyzed the determination of the level of asset prices with a minimum of complication by assuming that all investors were perfectly certain and all assets perfect substitutes for one another for ownership purposes.

Although theories of the level of asset prices (theories of *the* interest rate) are helpful, they cannot be used to treat the interesting and often crucial problems relating to the pattern of particular asset prices (the structure of interest rates). By considering the implications of uncertainty for investors' preferences, this chapter lays the foundation for a treatment of particular asset prices.

THE TREATMENT OF UNCERTAIN EXPECTATIONS

The orthodox view of the uncertain investor treats his expectations in terms of subjective frequency distributions of possible outcomes for each line of investment open to him.[1] Various sta-

[1] See, for example, E. Domar and R. A. Musgrave, "Proportional Income Taxation and Risk-taking," *Quarterly Journal of Economics,* LVIII (May, 1944), 381–422; William Fellner, *Monetary Policies and Full Employment* (2d ed.; Berkeley and Los Angeles: University of California Press, 1947), pp. 152–156; Irving Fisher, *The Nature of Capital and Income* (New York: Macmillan Co., 1906); J. R. Hicks, *Value and Capital* (2d ed.; London: Oxford University Press, 1946), p. 125; O. Lange, *Price Flexibility and Full Employment* (Bloomington, Indiana: The Principia Press, 1944), p. 30; Friederich and Vera Lutz, *The Theory of Investment of the Firm* (Princeton: Princeton University Press, 1951), Ch. XV; Helen Makower and Jacob

[61]

tistical measures derived from these frequency distributions are used to characterize the complete distributions; for example, the arithmetic mean is most often used to indicate the magnitude of the prospective return, while the standard deviation is used to measure the uncertainty surrounding this projection.[2] Although this orthodoxy has never seemed quite adequate to many students of the problem, and has, upon occasion, come under heavy attack, several features of investor behavior cannot be rationalized in any other manner yet developed.[3] The subjective frequency approach is used here, with results that turn out to be at least consistent with observable behavior.

Our aim is to clarify the determination of particular asset prices by treating the demand for them in a manner similar to that developed for analyzing the demands for consumption services and for resource services. The first step is to demonstrate that investors' tastes can be portrayed by indifference curves similar to those used to show consumers' tastes.

Alternative treatments of investors' tastes

The economic attraction of holding an asset lies in its promise to make the owner wealthy. No one will wish to hold an asset that promises to be worth nothing and to earn no income. We shall call the amount of a person's wealth that can be traced to his holding a particular asset the contribution of the asset. In consumption theory, the parallel feature is the satisfaction derived from consuming a particular item. In making decisions, the investor weighs the possible contributions of alternative asset

---

Marschak, "Assets, Prices, and Monetary Theory," *Economica*, N.S. V (1938), 261–288; Gunnar Myrdal, *Monetary Equilibrium* (London: W. Hodge & Co., Ltd., 1939), pp. 58–59; A. C. Pigou, *The Economics of Welfare* (4th ed.; London: Macmillan and Co., 1932), Appendix 1.

[2] There is no orthodoxy concerning the statistical measures used. For example, Fellner uses the mode to describe the prospect of gain against which the risk is weighed, Lange uses a percentile deviation to describe the risk, and Domar and Musgrave use the mathematical expectations of gain and loss to describe the two properties. The most common measures are the ones used here, the actuarial value and the standard deviation.

[3] G. L. S. Shackle is particularly critical of the use of probability notions as applied to the behavior of uncertain investors. His objections, expressed in *Expectation in Economics* (Cambridge: Cambridge University Press, 1952), are taken up at the end of this chapter.

holdings, just as consumers weigh the prospective satisfactions of various lines of consumption open to them.

Suppose an investor is interested in holding, over the current moment, two assets, A and B, both of which can be traded without costs in perfect markets. For each of these he entertains a frequency distribution of possible contributions to his wealth as of the beginning of the *next* short moment. The contribution of an asset may take the form either of a market value at the beginning of the next short moment or of gross income (separated from capital values) accruing over the current moment. Or, it may be a combination of the two forms. An uncertain investor envisages a number of possible contributions for any particular asset he considers holding over the current short moment. To each of these possible contributions he attaches some relative frequency or probability.

The simplest treatment of the investor's preferences would have him rank all bundles of A and B in ascending order of their actuarial contributions, implying that his object is to maximize his prospective wealth in actuarial terms. In this case, the investor is willing to substitute A for B at the rate that keeps the actuarial value of the bundle he holds constant. The actuarial value of a joint-frequency distribution is given by the sum of the actuarial values of the component distributions. Denoting by m_A and m_B the actuarial contributions of units of A and B respectively, μ, the actuarial contribution of a bundle of A and B together is given by $\mu_{x+y} = x m_A + y m_B$ where x and y are the numbers of units of A and B included in the bundle. If one unit of A is taken from any bundle of A and B, the investor will require m_A/m_B units of B to compensate him. Since m_A/m_B is the same for all bundles, the investor's indifference curves are parallel straight lines, as shown in Figure V-1.

Reactions to uncertainty

Observation suggests that matters are not really this simple. Most investors hold more than one asset, which implies that they do not consider assets to be perfect substitutes for one another. The advantage of diversified asset holdings lies in the possibility of spreading risk, or reducing the dispersion of the estimated contribution. Investors are usually concerned, not only with the magnitude of the prospective contribution of a bundle of assets, but also with its predictability.

The most common treatment of the reaction to uncertainty involves discounting for it. It is sometimes contended that an investor discounts the actuarial contribution of a particular asset for dispersion, thus determining its certainty-equivalent contribution.[4] The adjustment brings the actuarial contribution down to

FIG. V-1

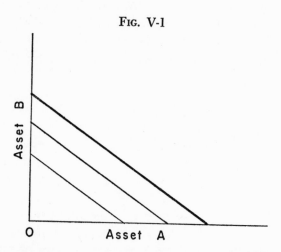

an amount which, if it could be expected with certainty, would be just as attractive as is the uncertain contribution in question. Assets are then compared on the basis of their certainty-equivalent contributions. According to this view, the marginal rate of substitution of A for B is given by the ratio of the discounted, or certainty-equivalent, contributions of A and B. Again, indifference curves are straight lines, and the appeal of diversification is not explained.

Statistical fallacy of the certainty-equivalent approach

Certainty-equivalent reasoning of the type outlined above involves the implicit assumption that the relevant characteristics of the prospective contribution of a mixed bundle of A and B are simple weighted sums of the characteristics of the components. Although

---

[4] Fisher, Keynes, and all others who treat the demand for new investment goods in terms of "the" rate of interest without specifying perfect certainty are users of certainty equivalents.

this reasoning is correct with reference to the actuarial value, it is incorrect in the case of the standard deviation for the bundle unless the performances of A and B are thought to be completely interdependent.[5] So long as any independence of outcome is envisaged, the standard deviation of the joint-frequency distribution of possible contributions for a mixed bundle of A and B is less than the weighted sum of the standard deviations for A and B considered alone.

If the outcomes for the two assets are thought to be entirely independent of one another, the standard deviation about the actuarial contribution of a mixed bundle of A and B is given by

$$(1) \qquad \qquad \sigma_{x+y} = \sqrt{x^2 s_A{}^2 + y^2 s^2{}_B}$$

where x and y denote the numbers of units of A and B included in the bundle, and s_A and s_B represent the standard deviations about m_A and m_B, respectively. So long as both x and y are greater than zero, the standard deviation for the bundle as given in this equation is less than the weighted sum $x s_A + y s_B$ implicitly assumed by the certainty-equivalent formulation. It is in this sense that asset diversification reduces dispersion.

By failing to recognize the laws of joint probabilities, the certainty-equivalent approach misses the most interesting feature of mixed bundles of assets. Assigning an asset a unique expected contribution by the certainty-equivalent method is comparable to assigning shoelaces an independent utility in consumption theory, without any regard for the availability of shoes. Just as a consumer considers shoes and shoelaces together, so an investor who is at all concerned with dispersion considers complete bundles of assets. His ultimate interest is in his financial prospects viewed in their entirety and the features of a particular asset are of interest only insofar as they influence this entire picture.

The investor may not, of course, consider the outcomes for A and B to be entirely independent. The earning powers of two assets may rest on closely related bases.[6] But only in the special

---

[5] See Harry Markowitz, "Portfolio Selection," *Journal of Finance,* VII (March, 1952) 77–91. What follows in this chapter is an adaptation of the ideas set forth by Markowitz. Makower and Marschak also recognize this point explicitly, but do not treat it at length.

[6] Markowitz takes up the role of the covariance systematically.

case of complete interdependence would the characteristics of an asset considered in isolation correctly describe its contribution in a mixed bundle of assets. In all but this special case of complete interdependence the dispersion for a mixed bundle of A and B is lower than the certainty-equivalent approach indicates. For this reason, the certainty-equivalent approach underestimates the attraction of mixed bundles of assets. Since both methods give the same results for pure stocks of one asset, while the straight-line indifference curves derived by the certainty-equivalent method underestimate the investor's valuation of mixed bundles, the correct indifference curves, based on the joint-frequency approach, are apparently convex to the origin. This can be demonstrated mathematically.

The investor is willing to substitute A for B at a rate which leaves the discounted actuarial value of his bundle of assets constant. Adding one unit of asset A to a bundle increases its actuarial value by m_A, the actuarial contribution of A. It increases the discounted actuarial value of the bundle by m_A minus the product obtained by multiplying the change in the standard deviation for the bundle resulting from the addition of a unit of A, which we call the marginal dispersion of A, by the investor's rate of discount for dispersion.

The marginal dispersion of A is given by the first derivative of equation (1) with respect to x, or

$$(2) \qquad \frac{\partial \sigma_{x+y}}{\partial x} = \frac{x s^2_A}{\sqrt{x^2 s^2_A + y^2 s^2_B}}$$

and the discounted marginal contribution of A is equal to

$$(3) \qquad m_A - \frac{\partial \sigma_{x+y}}{\partial x} d$$

where d is the rate of discount applied for dispersion.

Similarly, the discounted marginal contribution of B is given by

$$(4) \qquad m_B - \frac{\partial \sigma_{x+y}}{\partial x} d$$

where

$$(5) \qquad \frac{\partial_{x+y}}{\partial y} = \frac{y s^2_B}{\sqrt{x^2 s^2_A + y^2 s^2_B}}.$$

The marginal rate of substitution of A for B is such that, as A is substituted for B, the discounted actuarial value of the bundle is left unchanged. It is therefore equal to the ratio of the discounted marginal contribution of A to the discounted marginal contribution of B, or

(6)
$$\frac{m_A - \dfrac{\partial \sigma_{x+y}}{\partial x}\, d}{m_B - \dfrac{\partial \sigma_{x+y}}{\partial y}\, d}.$$

Consider (2). Given any value of y, $\dfrac{\partial \sigma_{x+y}}{\partial x}$, the marginal dispersion of asset A, is greater as x is greater. Given any x, the marginal dispersion of A is greater as y is smaller. It follows that the marginal dispersion of A is greater as x/y is greater. Similar reasoning when applied to equation (5) shows that the marginal

FIG. V-2

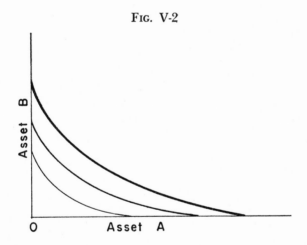

dispersion of B is smaller the greater is x/y. As x/y increases, the discounted marginal contribution of A falls and the discounted marginal contribution of B rises. The marginal rate of substitution, given by equation (6), declines as successive substitutions of A for B are made. Indifference curves tracing bundles of A and B with the same discounted actuarial values are convex to the origin, as shown in Figure V-2.

Factors behind the shapes of indifference curves

The indifference curves would be less sharply convex if the investor envisaged a positive correlation between the possible outcomes in the two cases, and more sharply convex if he contemplated a negative correlation, which would raise the possibility that a disappointing outcome for one asset would be offset by a better outcome for the second. Their configuration also depends upon the disutility the investor attaches to dispersion. A lesser dislike for dispersion would, for any combination of assets A and B, change the marginal rate of substitution in favor of the asset whose marginal dispersion was the smaller, relative to its actuarial contribution, making the curves less sharply convex. For adventurous investors who prefer "long shots," the indifference curves would be concave, reflecting the desirability of the increased marginal dispersion of one asset as its proportion in the bundle is increased.

The relative importance of dispersion, measured by the rate used to discount for it, may not be independent of the absolute magnitudes of the actuarial contribution and dispersion being considered. As these magnitudes vary along an indifference curve, any accompanying change in the rate of discount for dispersion will affect the shape of the curve. For example, if the marginal disutility of dispersion is a rising function of total dispersion, as Domar and Musgrave[7] and Lutz and Lutz[8] assume, the increasing marginal dispersion resulting from greater concentration of one asset in a bundle is all the more significant, accentuating the convexity of indifference curves.

According to Friedman and Savage,[9] who rationalize investors' choices wholly in terms of maximizing the expected (actuarial) utility of income, dispersion affects an investor's tastes only if the marginal utility of income is not constant. Their hypothesis, that the marginal utility of income (which is comparable to wealth in our analysis) falls over some ranges and rises over others, implies that indifference curves might be convex over some ranges

---

[7] *Op. cit.*

[8] *Op. cit.*

[9] Milton Friedman and L. J. Savage, "The Utility Analysis of Choices Involving Risk," *Journal of Political Economy*, LVI (1948) 297–304. Reprinted in *Readings in Price Theory* (Chicago: Richard D. Irwin, Inc., 1952), pp. 57–96.

and concave over others as the changes in actuarial value involved in movements from one point to another make the investor alternately cautious and adventurous.

Evidence suggests that most people are cautious in the management of their financial affairs, and give diversification a positive value that is reflected in convex indifference curves. Rather than treating the typical aversion to "putting all the eggs in one basket" as a refinement to be tacked onto a certainty-equivalent approach, the indifference curve method presented here integrates it fully into the determination of preferences.

The case of many assets

The problem becomes more complex when more than two assets are involved. However, if a technique is borrowed from the analysis of consumption, the graphical representation of an investor's tastes as they relate to some particular asset can be confined to two dimensions by measuring the amount of the asset in question along the horizontal axis and all other assets lumped together, in terms of their dollar value, along the other.[10] Movement along an indifference curve then represents the substitution of the particular asset in question for money, which signifies general command over all other assets. This procedure is applicable as long as the prices of all other assets are given, defining the value of a dollar in its alternative uses.

We need to know whether the general conclusions as to the shape of indifference curves must be modified when the analysis is extended in this way. A mathematical investigation into this question would be complex (and possibly tiresome) because of the large number of variables involved when many assets are considered. Fortunately, it can be shown without further mathematics that the general shape of the indifference curves for bundles of a particular asset combined with all other assets lumped together is the same as for the two asset case.

Suppose an investor is given OR dollars to invest as he sees fit in any assets other than asset A. Given the prices of these other assets, he will select among all possible bundles he can afford the one which has the highest discounted prospective contribution. Representing this bundle by point R in Figure V-3, where dol-

---

[10] See J. R. Hicks, *op. cit.*, pp. 33–34.

lars' worth of assets other than A are measured along the vertical axis, the problem is to discover the configuration of the indifference curve terminating at R.

The difference between the present problem and the two-assets case is that the investor is free to vary the relative proportions of his other asset holdings as he substitutes asset A into his bundle. For example, as his holdings of A increase, he might also increase

FIG. V-3

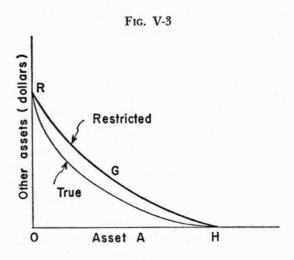

his holdings of some asset C whose outcome he expects to vary inversely with that of A, even though he is reducing the total dollar value of his holdings of other assets. Because the characteristics of the other assets component can change as the amount of A in the bundle is varied, we would not be justified in treating the other assets component as the equivalent of one asset.

However, if the investor is required to maintain the relative proportions of his holdings of other assets constant, the other assets component becomes the analytical equivalent of a single asset. For cautious investors who dislike dispersion, indifference curves drawn on this restricted-choice basis will be convex to the origin. Curve RGH in Figure V-3 is drawn for the restricted-choice assumption; the proportions the investor would choose if he invested OR dollars in other assets only are frozen as A is substituted for other assets.

Since investors do not actually labor under the restriction of having to maintain any fixed relative proportions among their assets, the true indifference curve passing through R may differ from RGH. However, because bundle H is a pure stock of asset A, its discounted prospective contribution is not affected by the restriction on the composition of his holdings of other assets. Therefore, point H also lies on the true indifference curve passing through R.

Over the rest of its range, the true indifference curve may lie below RGH. It can never lie above RGH because the investor can always do at least as well when he is completely free to determine the composition of his holdings of other assets as he can when he is restricted. For a cautious investor, the true indifference curve is therefore generally convex in the sense that it must lie entirely within the boundary set by the convex restrictive curve, and its intercepts with the axes must coincide with those of the restrictive curve. The natural presumption is that the marginal rate of substitution declines continuously as successive substitutions of A for all other assets are made.

This makes sense in the light of the logic of portfolio management. Because the investor is free to reshuffle the composition of his holdings of other assets, he is willing to give up more of them in return for a unit of A than he would be if he were required to maintain the relative proportions of his holdings of other assets constant. Starting at point R, the marginal rate of substitution of A for other assets is higher than it would be in the restrictive case. But as successive substitutions are made, the investor's declining holdings of other assets leave him less and less room to maneuver, so that he becomes less and less willing to give up other assets in return for a unit of A. There is no reason to expect that this tendency for the marginal rate of substitution to decline would not operate more or less continuously over the entire range of an indifference curve.

Similar conclusions follow for adventurous investors who attach positive utility to dispersion. The restrictive indifference curve is concave to the origin because of the increasing marginal contribution associated with increasing concentration on a single asset. Lifting the restriction can work only in the direction of lowering the indifference curve at all points other than R and H, where the restriction is not relevant. But the concavity will not be upset,

since successive substitutions of A for other assets will still raise
its discounted marginal contribution.

The one other possibility mentioned above, in connection with
the Friedman-Savage argument, is that the restrictive or two-asset
indifference curve will inflect as substitutions change the actuarial
contribution of the bundle of assets held because the investor
changes from a cautious to an adventurous approach. In this case,
too, the restrictive indifference curve forms the boundary for the
true one, which may also inflect.

Asset Selection

Cautious investors

The amount of any particular asset a cautious investor will hold
is shown by the tangency of his constraint with an indifference
curve defined for bundles of that asset combined with all other
assets lumped together. He allocates his investible resources in
such a way that the ratio of the discounted marginal contribution
to price is the same for all of the assets he holds. He may not hold
some assets at all, there being no guarantee that the discounted
marginal contribution of any particular asset, even if held in small
amounts, will be as great as could be obtained from other assets.

Investors probably tend to favor some assets over others simply
because they consider themselves more expert at predicting their
outcomes. Knowledge, as it relates to some particular asset, may
reduce the dispersion in the investor's estimate of its outcome,
thereby increasing its discounted marginal contribution. But investors who are seriously concerned about dispersion probably
inform themselves about more than one asset so that they can
diversify intelligently. There is no reason to suppose, therefore,
that greater knowledge must work against diversification.

Adventurous investors

An adventurous investor will hold only one asset. His indifference
curves are concave for every asset because he likes dispersion. Substitution among assets is, in his case, "more than perfect." Because
the indifference curves are concave the tangency solution is inap-
plicable. Instead, the point where the constraint touches the highest
possible indifference curve will lie on one of the axes—the other

assets axis for all assets but one. He chooses the asset whose actuarial contribution plus the positive discount for dispersion is highest. It seems likely that it will be an asset whose outcome is considered quite uncertain, one that is shunned by more cautious investors who discount it heavily. For this reason adventurous investors are better off in a world of timid souls than they would be in one where everyone concentrated on taking long shots. Although there may be significant exceptions, observation suggests that most investors are cautious. Our later analysis will be concentrated on cautious investors.

SHACKLE'S OBJECTION CONSIDERED

G. L. S. Shackle offers an objection to the kind of analysis used here. He contends:

The theory of probability, in the form which has been given to it by mathematicians and actuaries, is adapted to discovering the tendencies of a *given* system under *indefinitely repeated* trials or experiments. In any set of such trials, each trial is, for the purpose of discovering such a tendency, given equal weight with all the others. No individual trial is considered to have any importance in itself for its own sake, and any tendency which may be inductively discovered or predicted, *a priori*, for the system, tells us NOTHING about any single individual trial which we may propose to make in the future.[11]

Since indefinite trials can never be made, Shackle's argument is that probability reasoning, of the frequency type, can never fully rationalize investor behavior correctly.

   In constructing his alternative theory, Shackle is careful to avoid violating his rule that "the power of *mutually exclusive* hypotheses of success to afford enjoyment is *not additive,* and . . . therefore the power of the entire set of hypotheses of success associated with any given course of action to afford enjoyment by imagination is simply that of one alone among these." [12] Shackle contends that to each possible course of action (investment program) the investor attaches a focus-gain and a focus-loss. The investor then selects that course of action whose combination of focus-gain and focus-loss he prefers to all other available combinations of the two.

---

[11] *Op. cit.,* p. 5.
[12] *Ibid.,* p. 17.

In this regard, Shackle's argument is unconvincing. The "therefore" in the passage quoted above seems uncalled for. By ending up with two values relevant for choice, the focus-gain and the focus-loss, Shackle has simply eliminated a large number of other possibilities; but saying that investors concentrate on two from among all the possible outcomes seems no more inherently correct than saying they concentrate on three or ten—or even on one, the ultimate reduction.

The most serious shortcoming of Shackle's theory from the standpoint of asset selection is that it offers no systematic treatment of diverse bundles of assets as compared with pure stocks of one asset. He says, "the idea that a collection of assets can be assigned a *lower focus-loss* than would result from adding up the focus-losses of the assets when each is looked on as an isolated individual is familiar from the practice of insurance, of which, from the policyholder's point of view, it is the basis." [13] But this is all he says on this subject, giving us no idea as to just how the reduction of the focus-loss comes about. He goes on to show that his theory can handle the problem of the individual who, even when fair games are available, will choose to take a long shot. But the probability approach can do as well on this question, either on the Friedman-Savage basis, or on the assumption that the person likes to gamble (prefers uncertainty for its own sake), or a combination of both. Similarly, Shackle offers no treatment of liquidity problems (which are taken up in Chapter VII below), so that one very important asset people choose to hold is entirely left out of the picture.[14]

It is, I believe, perfectly permissible to be uneasy, along with Shackle, about the use of frequency distribution reasoning, and still to prefer it to Shackle's theory, for it provides reasonable results in handling problems that Shackle's theory does not cover.

---

[13] *Ibid.*, p. 90.

[14] *Ibid.*, p. 93.

VI

The Demand for a Particular Asset

The analysis of investors' tastes presented in the last chapter lays the foundation for a theory of the demand for a particular asset, the material of this chapter. The treatment conforms, in most respects, with that used in the theory of consumer demand. In determining how an investor reacts to changes in the price of a particular asset, all other prices are taken as given. However, two inherent differences between stocks (assets) and flows (final services, in the case of consumption) make the analysis of asset demand somewhat more complicated than the theory of consumer demand.

THE INTERDEPENDENCE OF WEALTH AND ASSET PRICES

The first of these complications, and the easier one to handle, arises on the constraint side. The two objective factors combining to limit a person's holdings of any asset are its price and his money wealth. In consumption theory, the prices involved are those of forthcoming consumption services, and the dollar constraint on a person's spending is unrelated to the current prices of the things he can buy. But in the theory of asset demand, the prices involved relate not just to flows of newly produced assets but also to stocks of existing assets. People who hold the existing stock of an asset experience a wealth effect every time its price changes. The dollar magnitude of the wealth effect is the change in the value of the stock brought about by the change in price.

[75]

Because a person's holdings of an asset depend partly on his wealth, the wealth effect must be considered in the analysis of demand. Also involved is a price effect resulting from the change in the relationship of the price of one asset to all others, given the investor's wealth. Thus, to anticipate the argument, an increase in the price of an asset might be expected to cause present owners of it to choose to hold more in view of the wealth effect, but to hold less because of the price effect. In later chapters we will show that both effects, are involved, although in different ways, in the establishment of overall equilibrium in the assets markets. We turn first to an examination of these two influences on the demand for a particular asset.

The wealth-investment relationship

Suppose an investor has OM_1 dollars to allocate between asset A and all other assets lumped together, given all prices, including that of A. He picks bundle D_1, where the constraint M_1N_1 is tangent to indifference curve I, as shown in Figure VI-1. An increase

Fig. VI-1

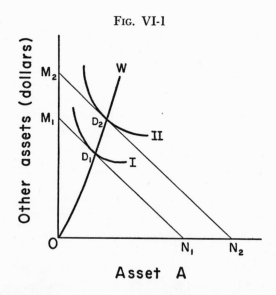

Asset A

in his wealth to OM_2 moves the constraint outward to M_2N_2, making it possible for him to hold more of A and more of all other assets lumped together. He now selects bundle D_2, where M_2N_2 is tangent to indifference curve II. There is such a point of tangency for every possible level of his money wealth, and the movement of these points as his wealth increases traces a *wealth-investment curve*, OW.

The wealth-investment curve could be a straight line extending outward from the origin, indicating that the investor always increases his holdings of A proportionately with the increases in his wealth. However, the relative attractiveness of a particular asset might well depend on the scale of a person's investment program, making the wealth-investment curve nonlinear. As increasing wealth allows an investor to hold bundles of assets with greater actuarial values, he may become more willing to countenance dispersion, comforted by the larger total "cushion" against his wealth declining to some critical minimum level. As his rate of discount for dispersion falls, the marginal rate of substitution shifts in favor of relatively risky assets and his holdings of them rise faster, relatively, than his wealth. Or, the opposite reaction to increasing actuarial values might lead the investor to reduce his holdings of risky assets relative to safer ones as his wealth increases. In either event, the wealth-investment curve is not a straight line through the origin.

It is possible for the wealth-investment curve to have a negative slope, indicating that A is an inferior asset. This would require that the marginal rate of substitution of A for all other assets lumped together rise as the amount of other assets held with a given amount of A is reduced; the tendency for the marginal rate of substitution to fall as x/y, the ratio of A to other assets, rises, would have to be more than offset by the changing rate of discount for dispersion due to changes in the magnitude of the investment program contemplated.

In the two-assets case, the marginal rate of substitution of A for B is given by

$$\frac{m_A - \dfrac{\partial \sigma_{x+y}}{\partial x}\, d}{m_B - \dfrac{\partial \sigma_{x+y}}{\partial y}\, d},$$

as shown in Chapter V. A decline in the amount of asset B held with a given amount of asset A would cause $\partial \sigma_{x+y}/\partial x$ to rise, $\partial \sigma_{x+y}/\partial y$ to fall. For the marginal rate of substitution to rise, making A an inferior asset, d would have to fall sufficiently to offset the influence of the changing marginal dispersions. This can happen only if the relative marginal dispersions are unequal, meaning that

$$\frac{\dfrac{\partial \sigma_{x+y}}{\partial x}}{m_A} \neq \frac{\dfrac{\partial \sigma_{x+y}}{\partial y}}{m_B}.$$

The likelihood that d could change sufficiently to offset the changes in marginal dispersion varies directly with the difference between the relative marginal dispersions of the two assets. Inferior assets can be considered the exception rather than the rule.

THE RELATIONSHIP BETWEEN PRESENT VALUES AND EXPECTATIONS

We come now to the second complication peculiar to the demand for stocks. In addition to the difference on the constraint side discussed above, the theory of the demand for an asset differs from consumption theory in the matter of expectations. In both cases expectations guide a person, but the satisfactions one expects to derive from consumption are generally independent of the prices of the consumption items in question. Exceptions, such as snob goods, are not considered very important.

The opposite is the case with asset preference. As Hicks has properly pointed out, the indifference curve approach he uses to analyze consumer choice is suitable for describing an investor's tastes only if his expectations of future asset prices are independent of their present prices.[1] Only if people ignore the present prices of assets in predicting their future prices, will the expected contribution of an asset be independent of its present price.

An alternative assumption is that investors entertain neutral expectations concerning future asset prices. In the literature on the subject, the assumption is often made, although not always explicitly, that investors take going asset values as the best indication of their future prices.[2] Assigning expectations of future asset prices

---

[1] *Value and Capital* (2d ed.; London: Oxford University Press, 1946), p. 56.

[2] This is a special case of Hicks's unit elasticity of expectations.

a passive role permits analysis uncluttered by problems of specula-tion. Although speculation may have important effects on asset prices, this study is confined to the nonspeculative aspects of the problem. A nonspeculative theory is a useful approximation be-cause it focuses on the most basic aspects of investor choice, aspects that are important enough, and complex enough, to warrant special treatment with a minimum of outside complication. The neutral-expectations assumption allows such a treatment, although it will soon become apparent that not even neutrality of expectations is a simple concept.

Under the assumption of neutral expectations, where present prices are taken to be the best indicators of future prices, indif-ference curves are generally defined only for one present price of an asset. Any change in the present price generally causes the investor to revise his estimate of "tomorrow's" price, which must mean that his estimate of the asset's contribution to his wealth one day hence changes.

There is a third dimension, price, in the utility system that ranks bundles of assets according to their discounted actuarial values. Boulding has shown that a price dimension can be repre-sented graphically by erecting a price axis perpendicular to the two-dimensional indifference plane at the origin, and then defin-ing indifference surfaces with price as a variable.[3] He concludes that the analysis is too complicated in this form and substitutes the concept of preferred asset ratios, which can be handled algebrai-cally, for the demand schedule concept. There are several objec-tions to Boulding's treatment. First, preferred asset ratios (generali-zations of the Cambridge, or cash-balance approach to the demand for money to cover all assets) are not explanations of anything. They must be derived by using some treatment of investors' tastes similar to indifference analysis. Second, preferred asset ratios are probably functions of the prices of the assets under consideration, which robs them of much of their simplicity when compared to demand schedules.[4] And third, when it comes to the treatment of

---

[3] Kenneth E. Boulding, *A Reconstruction of Economics* (New York: John Wiley and Sons, Inc., 1950), Ch. V.

[4] Boulding recognizes that preferred asset ratios are generally functions of price, and that to find the relationship of the ratios to price one must revert back to indifference analysis. But he does very little in the way of analyzing the nature of the relationship.

supply, where both stocks and flows are involved, demand and supply schedules are easier devices to use.[5]

For these reasons the demand for an asset is treated here in the ordinary schedule sense. The schedules are derived from the three-dimensional indifference systems describing investors' tastes. The awkwardness of three-dimensional graphs can be avoided by comparing two-dimensional cross-sections, each defined for a given value on the third (price) axis. The cross-sections are like ordinary indifference maps, but there is a separate one for each different price of the asset so long as the investor's estimate of the contribution of the asset is not independent of its present price.

The extent of the difference between two indifference maps, each defined for a different price of the same asset, depends importantly upon the expected life of the asset. As a general rule, the longer-lived the asset is, the more its expected contribution will vary as its present price varies. We begin by studying two limiting cases, an asset that has a one-day existence and one that lasts forever.

Limiting case I: one-day asset

Suppose the market for wine were to distinguish between wines of various ages very finely, there being an established price for wine of any age. The value one day hence of a cask of wine presently 100 days old will be determined, not in the market for 100-day wine, but in the market for wine 101 days old. The investor who looks to present prices as the best indication of future prices would base his estimate of the contribution of 100-day wine, not on its present price, but on the present price of 101-day wine; the latter market is the relevant one because it is the market in which the 100-day wine, which assumes a new identity with the passage of a day, will be priced tomorrow. In this case, the prospective value of a cask of wine is independent of its present price, being determined, rather, by the present price of wine one day older.

To take a somewhat different case, if there is a market for rights to the rental income from land over the next day only, the prospective contribution of a right depends exclusively on the market for the services of land, and this market depends on the value-

---

[5] Boulding does not consider the role of flows in the pricing of stocks, which greatly differentiates his theory from the one to be developed here.

productivity of the land and is not affected by changes in the prices of rights to the income. The prospective contribution of a right to the next day's income is therefore independent of the present price of the right.

The common feature of the examples of maturing wine and of the rights to the next day's rental income from land is the determination of the prospective contributions exclusively in markets for something economically different from the asset in question. All assets with this characteristic are called *one-day assets* because they do not retain their market identities over the ensuing day. For these assets, Hicks's problem is not relevant, and the indifference maps defined for them are the same for all prices. The relationship between the price of a one-day asset and the combinations of it with other assets selected by an investor can be discussed without reference to expectational effects stemming from changes in the price.

Since the indifference system for a one-day asset is essentially the same as that for a consumption item, it would be possible to derive the demand curve from the indifference map in the usual manner. However, it will be helpful later, when shifting indifference maps are encountered, if we accustom ourselves to a translation of the relevant information from the indifference map into other forms. The first step is to see how the wealth-investment curve varies as the price is changed.

A wealth-investment curve traces all bundles for which the marginal rate of substitution of a particular asset A for all other assets measured in dollars is equal to the price of the asset, and any change in the price will therefore change its position. For a one-day asset the marginal rate of substitution at any point is invariant with changes in price and the wealth-investment curve moves rightward as price declines; for any given y value, the x value must increase sufficiently to bring the marginal rate of substitution down to equality with the new, lower price. (Only in the unlikely case that all other assets lumped together are inferior could this rule be violated.) The extent of the necessary increase in x is governed by the rapidity of the decline in the marginal rate of substitution as additional units of A are added to a given dollar value of all other assets held.

In Figure VI-2, OW, defined for a particular price P, is shown

along with OW', defined for a lower price P'. The intersection of
OW with M_1N_1 at D_1 shows the bundle chosen at the original
price P when the investor's wealth is OM_1. Similarly, the intersection, at D'_1, of OW' (tracing all bundles for which the marginal
rate of substitution equals P') with $M_1N'_1$, the constraint defined
for P', denotes the bundle chosen at the lower price, if wealth is
held constant at OM_1. Measured from point D_1, the rightward

Fig. VI-2

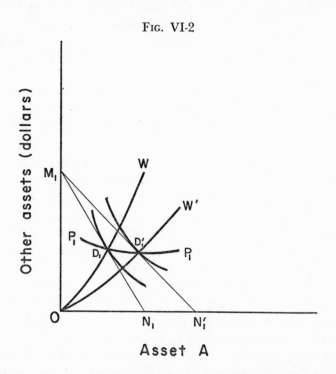

Asset A

movement of the constraint is inversely proportional to the price
decline; the investor can increase his holdings of A by the recipro-
cal of the percentage fall in its price without altering his holdings
of other assets. If the rightward movement of the wealth-investment curve from D_1 is greater than the inverse proportion of the
decline in price, the point D'_1, indicating the intersection of
$M_1N'_1$ and OW', will lie below D_1, as shown. In this case the price
elasticity of demand, defined as

$$\frac{\partial x}{x} \bigg/ \frac{\partial P_A}{P_A},$$

holding wealth constant, is greater than one. However, should the wealth-investment curve move rightward from D_1 by less than the inverse proportion of the price decline, point D'_1 will lie above D_1, indicating that demand is inelastic.

The movement of D_1 in response to declining price itself generates a curve P_1P_1, which is called the *price-investment curve*. P_1P_1 traces the intersections of all the constraints, each defined for a particular price and constant wealth OM_1, with the wealth-investment curves defined for the same prices. By definition, P_1P_1 traces

FIG. VI-3

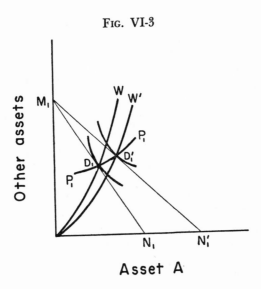

Asset A

the points at which all constraints whose y value is OM_1 are tangent to indifference curves. But when we get into the cases where indifference curves shift as price changes it is simpler to think of the price-investment curve as being generated by the movement of the intersection of M_1N_1 with OW as price changes.

If the demand for A is price elastic, P_1P_1 has a negative slope; (Figure VI-2); if the demand is price inelastic, P_1P_1 slopes upward from left to right (Figure VI-3). Since a price-investment curve is defined only for a given wealth, a change in wealth causes it to shift. The shift represents the outward movement of all the D's, each defined for a particular price, along the wealth-investment curves as the MN curve moves outward. In Figure VI-4, P_2P_2 is the price-investment curve defined for the investment wealth OM_2.

D_2 and D'_2 are the bundles the investor holds at prices P and P′, respectively.

All of the relevant information from the indifference map for any one-day asset can be translated into price-investment curves (one for each wealth) and wealth-investment curves (one for each price). Given any price of A and the investor's wealth, the bundle of A and other assets he chooses to hold through the next day is

FIG. VI-4

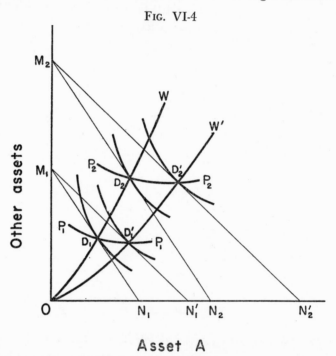

Asset A

shown by the intersection of the appropriate constraint with the wealth-investment curve defined for the given price and the price-investment curve defined for the given wealth.

The next task is to find the wealth- and price-investment curves for other types of assets, whose prospective contributions vary with their present prices. When this has been done, the problem posed by Hicks will have been surmounted and a general theory of demand can be developed.

Limiting case II: a perpetuity

Suppose we are dealing with an investor's rankings of bundles of land whose productive capacity is thought to be inexhaustible and

all other assets lumped together. In Figure VI-5, indifference curves
I, II, and III are defined for a particular price P of an acre of land,
and OW is the wealth-investment curve defined for that price.
Because the land is a perpetuity, its market identity is not changed
from one day to the next. In accordance with the neutral-expectations assumption, the investor takes the present price of an
acre of land to indicate its actuarial value one day hence. If the

FIG. VI-5

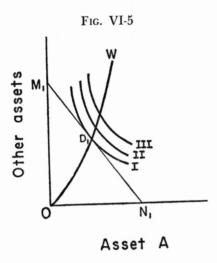

Asset   A

price is halved (from P to P′), all values in the investor's subjective frequency distribution of the possible market values of land
tomorrow are also halved, so that both the actuarial value and
the standard deviation are cut in half.

As the price of land falls, the actuarial contribution of any
bundle containing land is lowered, since it is a weighted sum of
the actuarial values of the components. The dispersion for the
bundle also falls, for the dispersion of the land component is
lowered. A new indifference map must be drawn because the
relevant cross-section of the three-dimensional indifference space
that takes into account the influence of present price on expectations is changed. To define the new wealth-investment curve
OW′, we must know various characteristics of the new indifference
map.

The marginal rate of substitution for any bundle D included
on OW, the old wealth-investment curve, tends to fall as the
price drops because the discounted marginal contribution of

land declines. If the marginal rate of substitution were to fall as fast as the price, D would also lie on OW′, which traces bundles for which the marginal rate of substitution equals P′. This will not, however, be the case. The expected contribution of land depends only in part upon the expected price of land. The other part of the contribution is rental income, and the investor's estimate of rental income is independent of land values. Therefore, although the actuarial contribution falls as the price falls, it rises relative to the price. At the same time, the importance of land relative to other assets in any given bundle falls, tending to lower

FIG. VI-6

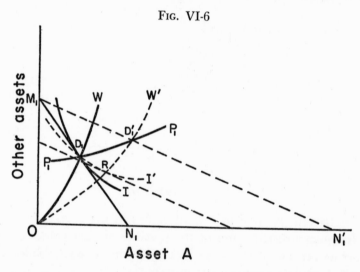

Asset A

marginal dispersion relative to price. Both the rise of the actuarial contribution and the decline in the marginal dispersion relative to the price of land work to raise its discounted marginal contribution relative to price. The marginal rate of substitution rises relative to price, although it falls in absolute terms.[6]

The wealth-investment curve moves rightward from D to an x-value high enough to reduce the marginal rate of substitution for any y-value to equality with P′. Figure VI-6, where indifference curve I is defined for starting price P, shows that the marginal rate of substitution at D_1 is equal to P, and OW passes through

---

[6] Also, the discounted marginal contribution of a dollar's worth of other assets falls since their "weight" in the total prospective contribution of any bundle increases as the prospective contribution of land declines.

D_1. Indifference curve I', shown as a dotted line, is defined for the lower price P'. It also passes through point D_1, but the marginal rate of substitution at D_1 is lowered because of the fall in price. However, because the marginal rate of substitution rises relative to price, OW', the new wealth-investment curve, passes through I' at a point R lying to the right of D_1. $M_1N'_1$ is the constraint defined for price P'. Its intersection with OW' indicates the bundle D'_1 held by the investor at the lower price, assuming his wealth is unchanged. P_1P_1 is the price-investment curve defined for wealth OM_1.

One-day assets and perpetuities share a common feature: the wealth-investment curve moves rightward as price falls. However, whereas the one-day asset loses none of its attractiveness as its price falls, the perpetuity does, for its prospective contribution depends partly on its present price. The consequence of this difference is that the rightward shift of OW is generally less pronounced in the case of perpetuities. The price elasticity of demand, which is governed by the relation between the rightward movement of OW and the rightward movement of the constraint in response to a lowering of price, therefore tends to be lower for a perpetuity than for a one-day asset.

The intermediate case

Rather than being of either the one-day or the perpetuity variety, most assets fall between the limiting cases. There may be no present market from which the estimate of tomorrow's price can be taken. For example, to return to the case of maturing wine, there may be no established price for wine one day older, perhaps because it is the first wine of a given season. The investor has no observable price on which to base his prediction of tomorrow's price. But suppose that there is an established market for wine one year older, this being the nearest reference available. The neutrality assumption would demand that the investor's estimate of the wine's value one year hence be given by the present price of the older wine. But it is his estimate of its price tomorrow that determines its prospective contribution over the next short moment. A similar problem would arise in the case of a half-ripened stand of wheat if there is no present market for wheat one day closer to maturity. Given the present price of wheat in

the bin, which serves as the basis of the investor's forecast of
the harvest-time value of the wheat in the field, what is a neutral
expectation of its value tomorrow? If its present price is anything
other than the net value projected for maturity, the investor
must expect the value of the stand of wheat to change by the time
it has matured. The question is, how much of the change will
he expect to come over the next day.

It might be presumed that the investor figures the value will
change at a constant percentage rate between now and maturity.
If this is so, a decline in the present price leads him to reduce

FIG. VI-7

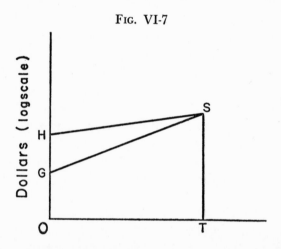

his expectation of its value tomorrow, and hence its contribution
over the next day. However, the actuarial value projected for
tomorrow rises relative to the price because the expected absolute
increase in value over the next day will become greater as the
difference between maturity value and present price increases.

This is shown by Figure VI-7. Time is measured on the horizontal axis, OT being the time it will take before the wheat is
harvested. Its actuarial value at time T is taken from the present
price for harvested wheat, measured by TS on the logarithmic
scale of the vertical axis. Measuring off any present price along
the y axis, a straight line to point S traces the time path of the
actuarial values. As the present price falls from OH to OG, all
of the expected prices for days short of day T also fall, but less
than proportionately. The finite maturity date acts as an "anchor"

on the investor's expectations. As the distance OT, the time to maturity, decreases, expected values change less in response to changes in price. In the limiting case of a one-day asset, there is no change in the expected price as present price changes.

For an asset falling into the intermediate category between the one-day and perpetuity classifications, then, the effect of a change in price on the position of the wealth-investment curve will generally be less pronounced than for a perpetuity, but more pronounced than for a one-day asset, since the marginal rates of substitution will fall as price falls, but less rapidly than for a perpetuity. Many assets may fall into the intermediate range, including any that depreciate but for which there are no observable markets for depreciated assets one day older.

The investor need not expect the price to approach maturity value at a constant percentage rate; he could expect the rate of change to increase or decrease as time passed. In this respect, his estimates would probably be based on past or present observations of similar cases. The requirement of neutrality is satisfied if the rate of approach to maturity value is unaffected by changes in the present price. As long as the maturity date is a finite number of days away, tomorrow's expected price varies directly, though less than proportionately, with the present price. Wealth-investment curves defined for assets falling into the intermediate classification move rightward as price declines.

The general rule is therefore the same for all assets from one-day assets to perpetual income assets: the wealth-investment curve moves rightward as price falls. The price effect, shown by the rightward movement of the intersections of the wealth-investment curves and the constraints (defined for a given wealth) as price declines, works in favor of the asset in question regardless of its life span.

The only possible exception to the rule that the price effect is favorable to the asset whose price is lowered arises in the case of inferior assets. In this case, the intersection of constraint and the relevant wealth-investment curve could move leftward as price declines; Figure VI-8 illustrates the possibility. OW and MN are defined for price P, OW′ and MN′ for the lower price P′. D′ lies to the left of D, and the price effect is given by the leftward movement along PP from D to D′. That the price effect does not

Fig. VI-8

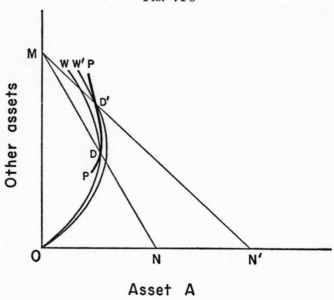

Asset A

Fig. VI-9

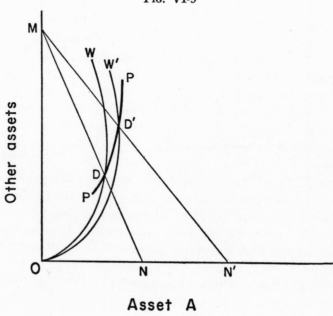

Asset A

necessarily work against A when the wealth-investment curve has a negative slope is shown by Figure VI-9, where D' lies to the right of D although both OW and OW' slope downward from left to right over the relevant ranges.

The individual's demand curve

If an investor comes into the market for a particular asset holding none of it, his wealth is independent of its price. The amounts he chooses to hold at various prices are given by the intersections of the constraints with the price-investment curve defined for his given wealth. This information can be translated into an ordinary demand curve, and the movements along it as price changes are equal to the movements along the underlying price-investment curve.

However, if the investor already holds some of the asset, his money wealth varies with its price, and he moves, not only along a given price-investment curve, but from one such curve to another as his wealth varies with the price. Suppose, to take the

F<small>IG</small>. VI-10

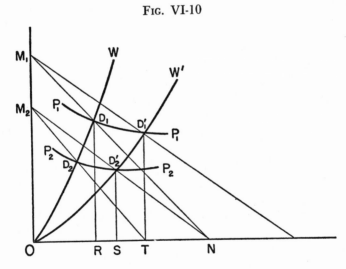

most extreme case, that the investor comes into the market holding only ON units of asset A, as measured along the horizontal axis of Figure VI-10, and no other assets. Every change in P_A, the price of A, will be accompanied by a proportional change in his dollar wealth. The equation for the constraint is $xP_A + y = ON(P_A)$, where y is the value (in dollars) of assets other than A. As P_A falls, as from P to P', the constraint falls along the y axis from M_1 to M_2, while its x intercept remains unchanged.

If P_1P_1 is the price-investment curve defined for wealth OM_1, and P_2P_2 for wealth OM_2, the investor will choose bundle D_1 at price P and bundle D'_2 at price P'. The movement from D_1 to D'_2 can be thought of as involving two stages: a wealth effect and a price effect.

The wealth effect is represented by the movement from D_1 to D_2 along the wealth-investment curve OW defined for price P. This shows what the investor would do if his wealth were lowered from M_1 to M_2 while the prices of all assets including A remained unchanged. The wealth effect will generally work against both A and all other assets; only for inferior assets, where the wealth-investment curve has a negative slope, is this not the case. The wealth effect is peculiar to situations where existing stocks of assets are already held by an investor.

The price effect is shown by the movement from D_2 to D'_2 along P_2P_2, the price-investment curve defined for wealth OM_2. This effect will almost certainly be in favor of asset A. It may or may not work against all other assets, depending on whether the price elasticity of demand for A is greater than or less than one.

Unless A is an inferior asset, the wealth effect tends to reduce the overall elasticity of demand. This can be seen by comparing the total movement from D_1 to D'_2 with that from D_1 to D'_1 along P_1P_1 that would take place if the investor's money wealth were unaffected by the change in price. In Figure VI-11, dd' is defined as the actual demand curve for the asset, while cc' is the demand curve that would obtain if the investor's money wealth were held equal to OM_1 while the price fell from P to P'.

The possibility that the demand curve will slope positively is greater when the investor already holds some of the asset. If the investor holds only A and no other assets, and if the wealth effect of a decline in P_A works relatively more against A than against other assets while the price effect works in favor of other assets as well as in favor of A (price elasticity less than one), the investor may hold less A as its price falls. This is shown in Figure VI-12, where these conditions are met.

Fig. VI-11

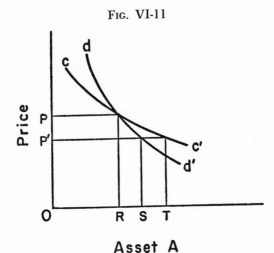

Asset A

The likelihood that an investor will enter the market holding only one asset is small. In the more general case, where he holds both A and other assets, the wealth effect is less pronounced, tending to increase the overall elasticity of demand. Nevertheless, the wealth effect adds to the possibility of encountering a positively sloped demand curve.

Fig. VI-12

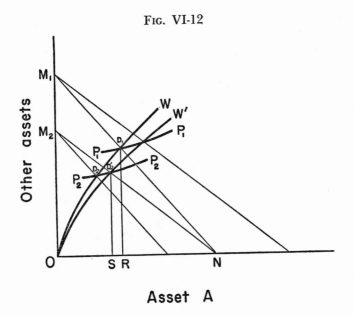

Asset A

The market demand curve

As Wicksteed has pointed out, the market demand for an asset to hold is found by summing the demand curves of all individuals, including those who may already hold some of the existing stock. The relevant facts on the demand side are the amounts people will hold at various prices, rather than whether they are buyers or sellers. The existing stocks are a part of supply, whether or not their original owners end up holding them.

However, although Wicksteed's viewpoint is preferable to the buyer-seller distinction made by Marshall and others, he fails to recognize the relationship between asset prices and wealth. In a discussion of the demand for horses he states: "If the fundamental method of [adding together the demand curves of all people in the market, whether they be buyers or sellers] is adopted, it is obvious at once that no hypothesis as to which of the persons brings the horses into the market will in any way affect the result." [7] Not only is the distribution of the given stock among those in the market thought to be irrelevant for the determination of prices, but "You may deprive [everyone with a demand for horses to own] of horses altogether, and throw [the same amount] from some other source upon the market, without reserve price . . . but you will always bring out the identical result." [8]

In other words, the demand for the stock is determined independently of its size and its distribution among those who have a demand to hold it. According to this view, a person who owns a horse will not find his demand for horses affected if his horse dies. He will wish to hold the same number of horses at any particular price, regardless of his wealth. If the government were to expropriate all horses and then throw them on the market, their prices would not be affected because neither the demand for horses nor the available supply would be changed.

This view overlooks the fact that owning an asset automatically provides the owner with sufficient wealth to hold it. If a person's $200 horse is expropriated, he is made $200 poorer. He can regain his position as a horseowner only by cutting down on his holdings

---

[7] *The Common Sense of Political Economy*, II (New York: Augustus M. Kelley, 1950), 511.

[8] *Ibid.*, pp. 510–511.

of other things, providing these are sufficiently valuable to cover the price of a horse. But he is not likely to cut down just on other things; he will probably also cut his demand for horses. A person's demand curve for horses or any other asset cannot be defined independently of his holdings of the asset. The approach offered here takes this fact into account.

The argument must now be revised to take consumption into consideration. By assuming that the investor devotes all of his wealth to holding assets over the next day, we have automatically set his consumption at zero. But people are both investors and consumers. Since consumption involves the dissipation of wealth, and is done at the expense of holding assets, consumption spending must be subtracted from wealth to determine the actual investment budget.

Chapter III presented a theory of consumption spending in which the objective determinant of consumption is a person's real consumption potential, or his command over consumption services. His consumption spending varies directly, but less than proportionately, with his real consumption potential. Consumption prices are taken as given in the discussion of the demand for an asset, so that a person's real consumption potential varies in direct proportion with his money wealth, and is therefore not independent of the prices of assets he owns.

To account adequately for consumption, two corrections must be made in the treatment of the demand curve for a particular asset as it has been outlined above. The first involves allowing for the lowering of the total demand for assets, or the investment budget, because people dissipate part of their wealth on consumption, and the second involves amending the proposition that the total dollar demand for assets varies by the full amount of changes in an investor's wealth.

Suppose a person's consumption-asset demand relationship is given by line OZ in Figure VI-13, which shows that as his wealth increases he increases both his investment budget and his consumption spending. When his wealth is equal to OM_1, he devotes OF_1 to holding assets through the next day and OG_1 to consumption spending, as indicated by the intersection of the constraint M_1M_1 with OZ.

The previous discussion of the investor's demand for asset A, based on the assumption that he did not consume, overestimates his demand for assets. If his wealth is OM_1, the relevant constraint on his asset indifference map has a y intercept, not of OM_1, but

FIG. VI-13

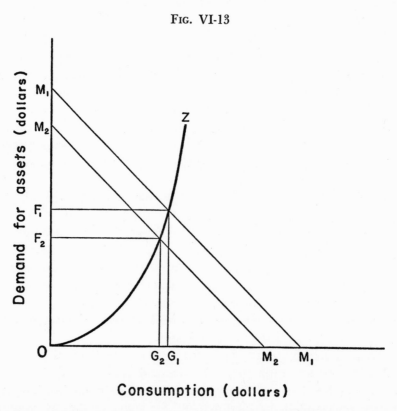

Consumption (dollars)

of OF_1, the part of his total wealth that is budgeted for investment. As is shown in Figure VI-14, he holds, not bundle D_1, but bundle D_{11}, indicated by the intersection of OW, the wealth-investment curve, and F_1H_1, the constraint he imposes upon himself by using OG_1 of his wealth for consumption spending. Alternatively, the adjustment for consumption may be thought of as a movement from price-investment curve P_1P_1, defined for a total investment budget of OM_1, to $P_{11}P_{11}$, defined for the actual investment budget OF_1. Because he consumes, the person holds less of asset A at any given price, unless it is an inferior asset. He will also hold less dollars' worth of other assets.

Moreover, if he holds only asset A, a fall in its price to P' lowers the investor's wealth proportionately from OM_1 to OM_2. As is shown in Figure VI-13, his consumption spending falls from OG_1 to OG_2, while his investment budget falls from OF_1 to OF_2. Because part of the adjustment to his reduced wealth takes the form

FIG. VI-14

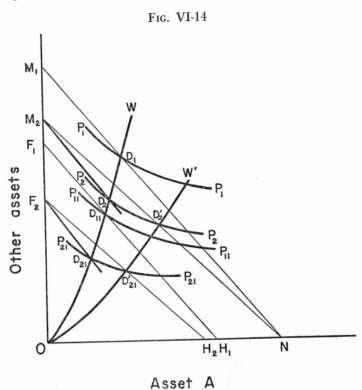

Asset A

of reduced consumption spending, the investment budget falls by less than the full amount of the decline in wealth; the wealth effect on the investor's demand for A is tempered by the partial absorption of the reduction in his wealth through lowered consumption spending. The relevant constraint for asset holdings falls from F_1H_1 to F_2H_2 in Figure VI-14. F_2H_2 shows, by its intersection at D'_{21} with OW' (defined for price P'), the amounts of A and all other assets lumped together that he holds at the lower price for A. This compares with the bundle D'_2 that he would choose if he devoted none of his wealth to consuming. The movement, allowing for consumption, is from D_{11} to D_{21} to D'_{21}, taking first the wealth effect and then the price effect, rather than from D_1 to D_2 to D'_2 as is indicated if consumption is not considered.

FIG. VI-15

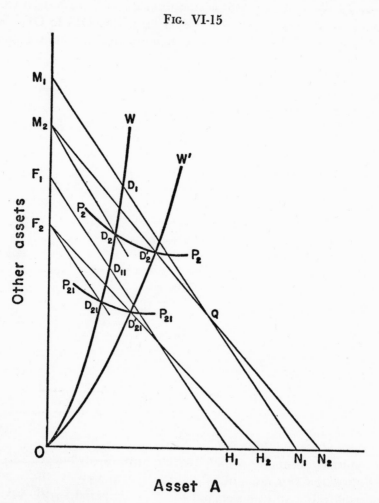

Asset A

The upshot of these corrections is to lower the demand curve for asset A and also, probably, to make it less elastic. The elasticity tends to fall because an investor will probably reduce his consumption less than proportionately to the decline in his wealth that accompanies a reduction in the price of A, taking instead a larger proportional cut in his holdings of assets over the next day.

The wealth effect becomes relatively more powerful, for the percentage reduction in the investment budget is greater than the percentage reduction in wealth, whereas when consumption is neglected the two fall equally. Since the wealth effect normally works against both A and other assets, and since its importance, relative to the price effect, is increased by accounting for consumption, the demand curve for A will be less elastic than was indicated by the first approximation, where consumption was neglected.

At the other extreme, when the investor holds none of asset A, his investment budget will also be lower if we account for his dissipation of part of his wealth on consumption. But his response to changing prices is still indicated by a movement along one price-investment curve, albeit a lower one, since his wealth, and hence his consumption, is independent of the price of A.

In the general case, where an investor holds both A and other assets, there will be a wealth effect and therefore an induced change in consumption associated with changes in P_A; they will be more important the more his inherited holdings are concentrated in A, as opposed to other assets. Figure VI-15 shows a case where the investor inherits bundle Q, worth OM_1 at price P for asset A and OM_2 at a lower price P′. If OF_1 is his investment budget when his wealth is OM_1 and OF_2 when his wealth is OM_2, he will select bundle D_{11} at price P and bundle D'_{21} at price P′, where OW and OW′ are the respective wealth-investment curves and $P_{21}P_{21}$ is the price-investment curve for an investment budget of OF_2. The wealth effect shown by the movement from D_{11} to D_{21} is less than it would be if the investor held only asset A, since in that case his total wealth would fall by the full proportion of the decline in the price of A. If consumption were neglected, the relevant points would be D_1, D_2, and D'_2. Again, allowing for consumption reduces the amount of A held at any price as long as A is not an inferior asset.

VII

Trading Costs and Liquidity

MONEY AS AN INVESTMENT

In arranging his affairs, an investor provides himself with enough cash to meet his current obligations, including his consumption spending, leaving his remaining wealth available for investment over the next day.

As an investment, given the assumptions of perfect markets and costless trading, cash is on an equal footing with all other assets. Because its future value is known with certainty, there is no discount for dispersion, and the marginal contribution of one dollar of cash is always one dollar. Indifference curves tracing bundles of cash and noncash assets lumped together reflect this constancy of the marginal contribution of cash.[1]

People will hold money balances only if the discounted marginal contribution of every available real asset is less than one dollar per dollar of its price. The special quality of cash is its perfectly certain prospective contribution, which is always equal to its "price."

The simplicity of this cash-balance theory traces to the assumptions of perfect markets, costless asset trading, and neutral expectations. In keeping with the intention to examine the demand for assets only under conditions of neutral expectations and per-

---

[1] They need not be straight lines, however, unless the rate of discount for dispersion is unaffected by changes in the actuarial contribution and dispersion of the bundle held.

fect competition, attention is concentrated on the effects of introducing trading costs into the investor's expectations.

"Spread" due to trading costs

An investor's prospective cash wealth is the expected net sales value of the bundle of assets he will own at the start of the next short moment, including those assets he holds through the period and any that have accrued as income. If trading is costless, the net sales value is the same as the market cost of the bundle. An investor will maximize his discounted prospective cash wealth because as his cash wealth is greater he can consume more and hold more of any asset in the future.

If trading real assets involves a cost to the investor, the net sales value of an asset is less than its market price, the difference being the "spread" due to the trading cost. In this case, an investor's cash wealth is an accurate reflection of the value of his holdings to him only if he should sell all of them. But if he is in the market buying additional amounts of some asset he already owns, the value of any unit of the inherited stock is, to him, equal to its market price, since that is what he is willing to pay for additional units. In general, an investor's holding of any real asset may be worth, to him, any amount between its net sales value and its market cost. Similarly, the prospective actuarial contribution of any bundle of assets (including accrued earnings) may lie anywhere between its prospective net sales value and its prospective market cost.

The presence of selling costs makes the expected contribution of a bundle of real assets depend upon the chances the investor will be selling real assets to raise cash. Money balances take on added significance, because by holding them an investor can reduce the chances of having to sell real assets to raise cash. Adding cash balances to any bundle of real assets raises the prospective contribution of the entire holdings by the nominal value of the added cash plus any increase in the prospective value of the real assets, to the investor, resulting from the lessened expectation of having to sell them. The entire increase in the prospective contribution is due to the added cash, so that the marginal contribution of a dollar of cash exceeds one dollar as long as adding the cash reduces the chance of having to sell real assets.

Successive increases in cash holdings will have successively smaller marginal contributions because the prospect of having to raise additional dollars by selling noncash assets diminishes as more cash is held. At some point, the cash balance may be large enough to make the investor certain he will not have to raise more cash by selling real assets. Beyond this point the marginal contribution of cash is no more than one dollar, its nominal value. The diminishing marginal contribution of cash balances tends to make the marginal rate of substitution of cash for other assets diminish as more cash is held.

VARYING DEGREES OF LIQUIDITY; TWO DIMENSIONS OF "MONEYNESS"

Cash is a special asset in three respects: its certain value, its role as the medium of payment, and its divisibility. Divisibility aside, a real asset whose trading costs were nil would differ from cash only in that its prospective value would be uncertain, and a real asset whose future value were certain would differ from cash only in that its trading costs were greater. An asset that had both of these characteristics, along with perfect divisibility, would be a perfect substitute for cash.

To the extent that some assets have more uncertain cash values or greater trading costs than do others, they are less perfect as substitutes for cash. Given two assets whose trading costs, as a percentage of their market values, are the same, the one whose prospective net sales value is more certain will be a better substitute for cash. The probability of having to raise at least some given amount of cash varies inversely with the amount in question. Hence, the greater the probability of an asset's having some minimum net sales value, the more protection it will provide against having to sell other assets. The asset with the more certain net sales value is therefore a better substitute for cash, or is more liquid. This feature tends to raise its marginal contribution relative to the asset whose net sales value is less certain. Similarly, if two assets have prospects identical in all respects except that the trading spread is less for one than for the other, the one with the smaller spread is more liquid and has the higher marginal contribution.

In the absence of any trading costs, cash balances do not protect the value of an investor's holdings of real assets from falling because he has to sell them, and the only unique feature of cash balances is their certain contribution. Although this study is concerned primarily with asset pricing in competitive markets, a short digression will bring out the similarity between trading costs and market imperfections as sources of illiquidity. If an investor envisages depressing the price of an asset he owns by selling it in an imperfect market, the marginal contribution of cash balances is further increased, since the net sales value of the asset will be smaller the more of it he has to sell. Similarly, if markets are imperfect in the sense that they are poorly organized, sales made in a hurry, without sufficient time to scare up potential buyers, may entail "sacrifices." Additional cash balances will reduce the prospect of being forced to sell such assets under adverse conditions, thereby raising the expected contribution of the bundle of real assets with which they are held by more than their nominal value. Imperfect markets of either type raise the marginal contribution of cash balances in much the same way as do trading costs. In a society where the markets for many assets are thin, this may be an important source of demand for cash and other highly liquid assets.

Liquidity and Asset Selection

The presence of trading costs increases the marginal contribution of cash, working against the demand for all real assets taken together. At any given set of prices for real assets, the investor will hold more cash and less real assets the greater is the general level of the spread between buying and selling prices for real assets.

To the extent that some assets are more liquid than others, in the sense outlined above, their marginal contributions will be raised, relative to those of less liquid assets. It is possible that they will rise so much that, even though the investor holds more cash and less of all other assets lumped together because of trading costs, he also holds more of these liquid assets at given prices than he would if there were no trading costs attaching to any assets.

VIII

The Workings of the Asset Markets

We are now prepared to examine the equilibrium system of asset prices when investors are uncertain and do not regard assets as being perfectly substitutable. Taking consumption prices as given, thoroughgoing equilibrium in the assets markets requires a set of prices for all real assets such that every market clears—there is neither excess demand nor excess supply in any market. Let us at first sidestep complexities arising on the supply side by assuming that inherited stocks of real assets constitute the sole source of supply, there being no way in which new assets can be produced or old ones used up, a condition similar to the one set up in Chapter III.

There, because of the perfect-substitutability assumption, the demand for and the supply of real assets, taking consumption prices as given, could be shown by a single pair of curves, with the demand curve sloping down to the right over the relevant range, as is shown in Figure VIII-1. At sufficiently low prices for real assets, people are poor enough so that they wish, as a group, to add to their real asset holdings. This being impossible because supply is limited to the inherited stock, there is excess demand for real assets. Measured in dollars, the excess demand is equal to the difference between aggregate demand, or the dollar value of assets people wish to hold and aggregate supply, the dollar value of assets available to hold.

The real assets market can be in equilibrium only when the

excess demand is eliminated. As P_A rises in response to the excess demand, people's wealth rises by the increase in the market value of the inherited stock of real assets. Aggregate demand for real assets to hold rises by less than the increase in wealth because people devote a part of their increased wealth to higher consumption spending and to higher cash balances, which are assumed in this simplified setting to be a constant fraction of the total

FIG. VIII-1

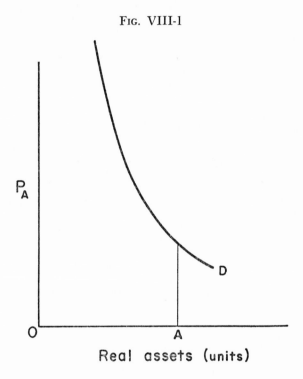

Real assets (units)

demand for assets to hold. The aggregate supply of assets to hold rises equally with their market value. Thus the increased consumption spending and cash holdings accompanying the rise in P_A reduce the excess demand for real assets by holding the increase in aggregate demand for real assets below the increase in aggregate supply. A sufficient rise in P_A brings the market for real assets into equilibrium by channeling all of the original excess demand into consumption expenditures and cash holdings. The equilibrium price is indicated by the intersection of the demand curve and the (vertical) supply curve shown in Figure VIII-1.

The graphical statement of the argument may be revised to pinpoint the essentials. In Figure VIII-2, the aggregate supply, or the market value of the inherited stock of real assets, is plotted against P_A, giving line AP_A. The aggregate money wealth of the group is shown by adding the inherited stock of money (OL) to AP_A at every price, giving $AP_A + OL$, the total wealth line.

People divide their wealth among consumption, holding cash, and holding real assets, and in equilibrium aggregate demand for

Fig. VIII-2

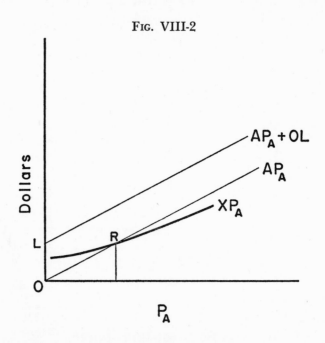

all three must equal aggregate money wealth. As P_A rises, people divide their increased money wealth among increases in the three uses. Because all rise as P_A increases, XP_A, the aggregate money demand for real assets, rises by less than the increase in AP_A, the market value or aggregate supply of real assets.

The equilibrium price of assets is shown by the intersection of the XP_A curve with line AP_A at point R. Only at this price is the group willing to hold just the inherited stock of real assets. Starting from any lower P_A, the excess of aggregate demand over aggregate supply forces P_A to rise until all excess demand is diverted to consumption spending and cash holdings. At any P_A higher than the equilibrium level, there is negative excess demand, or excess supply, causing P_A to fall until people are induced to divert sufficient consumption spending and cash holdings into the demand for real assets to eliminate the excess supply. By assumption there can be no new investment spending, so all of the stock of money must be used to finance spending on consumption or held as idle balances.

When the simplifications of Chapter III are dropped, so that assets are not perfect substitutes for one another and people do not necessarily hold cash balances equal to some constant fraction of their total wealth, the analysis becomes more complex. The requirement for equilibrium throughout the markets for real assets is now that there be neither excess demand nor excess supply in *any* of the markets for particular assets; they must all clear simultaneously. When they do, it follows that the aggregate demand for all real assets taken together equals aggregate supply.

As a preliminary to generalizing about the case of many real assets, the reasonably manageable case of two real assets is useful. Until problems on the demand side have been cleared up, the assumption of no new production and no capital consumption is retained. Given the inherited stocks of two real assets A and B, their initial distribution, the supply of money and its distribution, and the prices of consumption services, the demand for asset B can be derived, given the price of asset A, in the manner shown in Chapter V. Suppose the price of A, denoted by P_A, is shown by OH in Figure VIII-3, and that D_B in Figure VIII-4 is the demand curve for asset B, given $P_A = OH$. The intersection of D_B with the vertical stock supply curve for B, erected at O′, determines the equilibrium $P_B = OJ$.

The demand curve for A, given price OJ for B, can now be derived. If it intersects the vertical stock-supply curve erected at O′ in Figure VIII-3 at $P_A = OH$, we have the pair of prices that equilibrates both markets at once. Such a simultaneous clearing of both markets would indicate that, since the aggregate money demand for real assets is equal to their aggregate market value, people wished to spend on consumption or to hold idle an amount of cash precisely equal to the money supply, or the excess of their dollar wealth over the value of inherited stocks of A and B.

But suppose that when $P_B = OJ$, clearing the market for B

at the assumed price OH for A, there is excess demand for A at $P_A = OH$, as is shown in Figure VIII-3 where D_A, the demand curve for asset A, given $P_B = OJ$, lies to the right of the stock supply curve at $P_A = OH$. The excess demand for A will tend to raise its price until the market clears. Taking the market for A

FIG. VIII-3

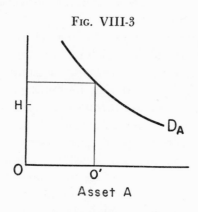

Asset A

FIG. VIII-4

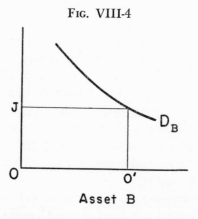

Asset B

by itself, the increase in P_A can eliminate the excess demand for A as long as the demand curve has a negative slope and crosses the supply curve. But will the increase in P_A eliminate any of the excess demand for A and B taken together? The problem is basically the same as it was in the case of only one real asset. If, as P_A rises, none of the increase in the dollar wealth of the holders of asset A is drained off into an increase in the sum of their cash holdings and consumption spending, the increase in P_A has no "efficiency" in eliminating the excess demand for both assets taken together.

Consider now the wealth effect brought about by the increase in P_A. In response to an increase in their wealth, holders of asset A increase both their consumption spending and their total investment budgets. The increased consumption drains off part of the excess demand; the aggregate demand for all assets, including money, rises by less than the increase in their market value, or aggregate supply. As long as none of the three assets people can hold (money, A, and B) is inferior, the increased investment budget is spread among all three. To the extent that people increase their cash holdings as their wealth rises, the wealth effect provides a second avenue of escape, in addition to increased consumption, for the excess demand for real assets. So far, the process is much the same as it is in the one-asset case of Chapter III: the excess demand tends to bring about its own elimination by generating an increase in the market value of existing real assets in excess of the accompanying increase in the aggregate demand for them.

But since there is now more than one real asset to hold, and since we no longer assume that cash holdings are kept equal to a fixed proportion of the investment budget, it is also necessary to consider the price effects of an increase in P_A. A rise in P_A, given people's wealth, is likely, first of all, to operate in favor of cash holdings.

As was seen in Chapter V, the discounted marginal contribution of a real asset rises less proportionately than its price, so the attraction of cash balances rises relative to that of holding real assets, thereby raising the marginal rate of substitution of cash balances for all real assets lumped together. The risk of getting involved in transactions costs is the same, but the "reward for not hoarding," determined by the prospective yields from real assets, is reduced. With wealth held constant, investors therefore tend to raise their holdings of cash at the expense of real assets as P_A rises. This increase in cash holdings provides an additional escape for the excess demand for real assets.

Thus the wealth effect, by inducing additional consumption and, possibly, additional holdings of cash, and the price effect, by inducing additional cash holdings only, contribute to the reduction of excess demand as P_A rises. The aggregate demand for A and B taken together rises by the increase in the market value of A less the sum of the induced increases in people's consumption spending and the induced increases in their cash balance demands. The aggregate supply rises by the full amount of the increase in the market value of A.

It is necessary to distinguish among various possible repercussions of the increase in P_A on the demand for B before the precise values of P_A and P_B necessary to the achievement of simultaneous equilibrium in the two markets can be determined.

Case 1: positive cross-elasticity. Suppose that A and B are very good substitutes, so that the price effect of an increase in P_A operates strongly in favor of B. Assuming that the wealth effect also favors B (that is, that B is not an inferior asset), the increase in P_A needed to equilibrate the market for A taken by itself may be very small. However, the efficiency of a small rise in P_A in reducing the aggregate demand for A and B taken together is low because it provides correspondingly small inducements to consume more and to hold more cash. The excess demand for A is diverted chiefly into an increased demand for B, creating excess demand in that market. However, some progress is made toward increasing consumption and hoarding as P_A rises. Because the excess demand not diverted away from the markets for A and B taken together is now in the market for B, P_B must rise. As it does, while much of the excess demand is diverted back to the market for A, again some goes into increased consumption and cash holdings due to wealth and price effects. The process of successive increases in P_A and P_B must continue until they have risen sufficiently to divert all of the original excess demand into increased consumption spending and cash holdings.

Case 2: zero cross-elasticity. In contrast to Case 1 above, a rise in P_A leaves the demand for B unaffected if the sum of the wealth effect and the price effect of a rise in P_A is neutral on the demand for B. If the wealth effect of an increase in P_A raises the demand for B, as we would normally expect, zero cross-elasticity of demand would require that the price effect work against B just enough to offset it. Since none of the excess demand for A finds its way to the market for B as P_A rises, this increase must be 100 per cent efficient in eliminating the excess demand for real assets in general; P_A must rise until it induces sufficient increases in consumption and cash holdings to eliminate all of the excess demand for A taken by itself, P_B remaining unchanged.

Case 3: negative cross-elasticity. The third possibility is that the demand for B falls as P_A rises—the sum of the wealth and price effects of an increase in P_A works against the demand for B. Equilibrating the market for A taken by itself then requires a rise in P_A sufficient to induce additional consumption and cash holdings equal to the sum of the original excess demand at $P_A =$ OH *and* the reduction in the dollar demand for B that accompanies increases in P_A. Because the rise in P_A leaves excess supply in the market for B, it is more than 100 per cent efficient in eliminating the excess demand for both real assets taken together. The price of B must now fall in order to eliminate the excess supply in the market for B taken by itself. However, if the cross-elasticity of demand remains negative, so that the demand for A increases as P_B falls, the price of B must fall by enough not only to eliminate, through induced reductions in consumption and hoarding, the excess supply existing at the start, but also by enough to make up for the diversion of demand to the market for A as P_B falls. The change in price needed to restore equilibrium in the market for B taken by itself is more than 100 per cent efficient in eliminating the excess supply of A and B taken together. There is now excess demand in the market for A, and the whole process must be repeated.

However, if every successive rise in P_A leaves less excess supply in the market for B than did the previous one, overall equilibrium will be achieved by a sufficient rise in P_A and fall in P_B. This may not occur, at least at first. Suppose, for example, that holders of B reduce their consumption very rapidly as P_B falls, while the consumption spending of people who hold A is fairly insensitive to changes in their wealth. Then total consumption spending may decline after both P_A and P_B have been allowed to change, increasing the excess demand for A and B taken together. Similarly, the increase in P_A and reduction in P_B may lead to an overall reduction in cash balances. However, P_B cannot fall below zero, so the process must stop eventually. If P_B reaches zero, equilibrium in the market for A is sufficient to provide simultaneous equilibrium in the markets for both real assets and we have, in effect, only one real asset.

The chain of events outlined above seems highly unlikely. If people expect a positive yield from holding B (they must if there is to be any demand for B at prices greater than zero), every successive equal decrease in its price brings a greater increase in its anticipated percentage yield, since its discounted marginal contribution rises relative to its price. As P_B tends toward zero, the expected yield becomes indefinitely large, and at some point it seems reasonably certain that people will stop attempting to increase their holdings of A as P_B falls—that is, the cross-elasticity of demand rises to zero. We then have the conditions of Case 2.

Thus, although the cross-elasticity of demand determines the precise nature of the adjustments in P_A and P_B needed to achieve simultaneous equilibrium in the two markets, there is always some set of prices that satisfies the condition that aggregate demand equals aggregate supply.

THE ROLE OF FLOW SUPPLIES

In Chapter III we saw that opportunities to produce new real assets or to use up old ones make the supply of assets to hold differ from the inherited stock. We noted that net flow supply, or the difference between new production and capital consumption, differs from the inherited stock in two important respects: it is a function of price and it is not a current source of wealth to anyone.

Continuing with the case of two assets only, suppose that OR and OT shown in Figures VIII-5 and VIII-6 are the prices that equilibrate the markets for both A and B simultaneously when inherited stocks constitute the sole supplies. If we now assume that changes in the stock of A (but not B) can take place over the next day through capital consumption and production, the supply of asset A available to investors will differ in size from the inherited stock at all prices of A except the one at which capital consumption just equals the amount of A that can be profitably produced, that is, where net flow supply as defined in Chapter III is zero. Given the prices of all things other than A, the demand curve for A as a productive input to be used up slopes downward to the right because of the positive output and substitution effects of a fall in its price. On the production side, in the limiting case of perfect substitutability of resources between the production of A and other uses, flow supply from new production is perfectly

Fig. VIII-5

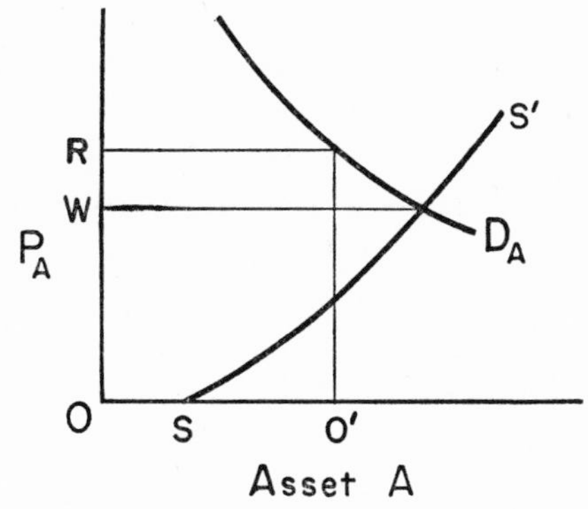

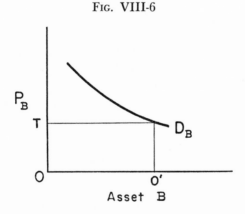

Asset A

Fig. VIII-6

Asset B

elastic at a price equal to its constant marginal cost. In the opposite limiting case of absolutely no substitutability of resources, flow supply from production is perfectly inelastic. In the general case of imperfect substitutability of resources, it pays to produce more A as its price rises.

The net flow supply curve is found by subtracting capital consumption, at each price, from the amount of profitable production, the result being the excess of the amount it pays to produce over the amount used up. In general, as price falls, net flow supply falls too, since capital consumption is increased and production is reduced. In Figure VIII-5, SS', drawn with reference to O' as origin, is the net flow supply curve for asset A. The total stock-flow supply of A, found by adding net flow supply to the inherited stock OO' at each P_A, is shown by SS' when O is taken as the origin. Unless SS' cuts the vertical stock supply curve erected at O' at the price OR, the introduction of net flow supply upsets the equilibrium of the market for A at that price. Here SS' is drawn so that it lies to the right of O' at $P_A = $ OR, indicating that the introduction of flows creates excess supply in the market for A at that price. People have an incentive to substitute investment in new units of A for holdings of inherited units. As P_A falls in response to the excess supply, people are made willing to hold or invest in the production of more of asset A, while the excess of the amount it pays to produce over the amount of capital consumed is lowered. Equilibrium is restored at $P_A = $ OW, where people are willing to hold or invest in producing just the sum of the inherited stock and the amount that can be profitably produced in excess of capital consumption.

If the reduction in P_A to OW leaves the demand for B unaffected, both markets considered together will be in equilibrium when equilibrium is restored to the market for A taken by itself. The aggregate demand for both real assets taken together exceeds the value of the inherited stocks by an amount precisely equal to the value of net investment in A. Since, before net flow supply is introduced into the market for A, equilibrium requires that aggregate demand be equal to the aggregate value of inherited stocks, the introduction of flow supply leads to a reduction in the sum of consumption spending and cash balances equal to net investment spending, the value of current additions to the group's inherited holdings of real assets. New investment spending generates its own financing by holding down the prices of real assets, diverting money from consumption spending and cash balances.

The general principle that new investment must come at the expense of holdings of cash or consumption remains unchanged by the recognition of more complicated cases where the demand for B depends on P_A. If the demand for B falls as P_A declines, equilibrating both real asset markets taken together when flow supplies of A are introduced requires a fall in both prices sufficient to reduce consumption spending and cash holdings by an amount equal to the profitable amount of net investment in A. If the cross-elasticity is negative, P_B rises as P_A falls, and the establishment of equilibrium requires that the changes in their prices be such that the total profitable investment in A be offset by an equal reduction of consumption and holdings of cash balances below what they would be with no flow supply of asset A.

The effect of introducing opportunities to produce and use up asset B is similar, reducing the equilibrium price of B for any given P_A when net flow supply is positive at the price that makes

Fig. VIII-7

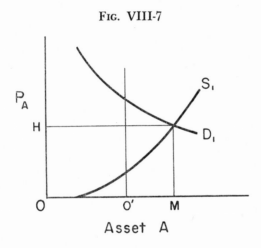

Asset A

people willing to hold just the inherited stock. For every P_B, an equilibrium price for B is so defined that it equals the marginal cost of producing B. Equilibrium in the two markets taken together is achieved when P_A and P_B are both equal to their marginal costs of production. Complications encountered when the cost of producing B is not independent of the price of A and vice versa can be handled in the manner shown in Chapter III to treat the interrelations between the cost of producing consumption goods and the price of real assets.

It is important to keep in mind the fundamental difference between stock supply and flow supply. Suppose that the demand curve and the stock-flow supply curve for asset A, given $P_B = OT$, are shown by D_1 and S_1 in Figure VIII-7, while D_1 and S_1 in

Figure VIII-8 show the demand and stock-flow supply of asset
B defined for $P_A = OH$. OO' on each graph measures the inherited stock. OH and OT are equilibrium prices at which both
markets clear. Investors add $O'M$ units of A and $O'N$ units of B
to their inherited holdings of the assets over the day.

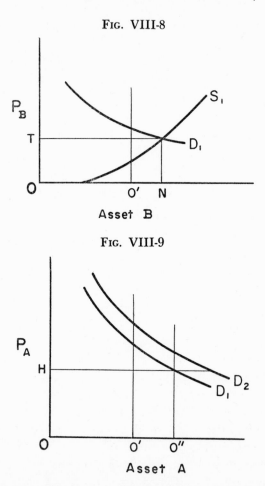

FIG. VIII-8

Asset B

FIG. VIII-9

Asset A

Now suppose alternatively that net flow supply is zero for both
assets at all prices, and that, in the place of new investment opportunities, we add $O'M$ units of A and $O'N$ units of B to the
inherited stocks, increasing the OO''s of Figures VIII-7 and
VIII-8 to the OO'''s of Figures VIII-9 and VIII-10. At $P_A = OH$
and $PB = OT$, the aggregate supply of A and B taken together

is unchanged by this substitution of stock supply for flow supply. But in changing the form of supply, we have changed the conditions determining demand. Holders of the increased stocks of A and B are made wealthier, and they devote a part of the increase in their wealth to increased demand for real assets to hold. Provided neither A nor B is an inferior asset, the demand curves for both shift upward. In Figures VIII-9 and VIII-10, the demand curves labeled D_2 are higher than the D_1 curves taken from Figures VIII-7 and VIII-8. At prices OH and OT, there is excess demand in each market, and asset prices must rise. *The demand for assets to hold cannot be defined independently of the size of the in-*

FIG. VIII-10

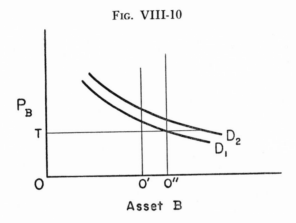

Asset B

herited stocks; the roles of stock supply and flow supply in the determination of prices are not coordinate.

This matter is of special importance in the analysis of accumulation over extended periods of time. *Ceteris paribus,* as the inherited stock of assets increases due to net investment, the demand curves for assets shift upward, although the increase in aggregate demand at any set of prices is less than the increase in aggregate supply due to accumulation since people dissipate a part of their increased wealth on consumption. Analyses positing stable demand curves for assets in the face of accumulation are deficient because they fail to recognize the effect of accumulation on demand.[1]

---

[1] For example, R. W. Clower's analysis of "The Dynamics of Investment," *American Economic Review,* XLIV (March, 1954), 64–81. Clower's analysis of stocks and flows is taken up later in another connection.

THE CASE OF MANY REAL ASSETS

Although the equilibrating mechanism becomes more complex when more than two real assets are considered, the general outlines remain the same. The presence of excess demand or supply in the market for any asset when the markets for all other assets are equilibrated has the same implications as it does in the case of two assets. The excess demand or supply is eliminated from the markets for all real assets taken together by changes in their prices sufficient to generate equal changes in consumption spending plus cash holdings plus net new investment. In equilibrium, the price of any asset that can be produced currently cannot exceed its marginal cost of production.

With many real assets to be considered, the possibility of encountering negative cross-elasticity of demand is greater than it is in the case of two assets. It is still unlikely, however, that the price of any asset will fall to zero as other asset prices rise.

SECURITIES ISSUED AGAINST REAL ASSETS

A minimal frame of reference for treating securities is needed to round out the description of equilibrium in the assets markets. Suppose that all real assets are owned by corporations that in turn are owned by individual shareholders; individuals do not own real assets directly. The demands for corporation shares, which depend upon the expectations and tastes of potential buyers, can be handled as were the demands for real assets in Chapter V. If no new real assets can be produced and no existing ones used up, the determination of the equilibrium prices of shares can be treated just as it was in the earlier portion of this chapter, where it was assumed that all real assets were owned directly. The essential fact is that, since all assets are covered by securities, security issues do not constitute an addition to the net supply of assets available to hold, but simply a different form of ownership.[2]

---

[2] However, if the trading costs should be less for securities than for real assets, the desire for idle balances will be reduced, raising the overall demand for and value of ownership claims above what it would be if people could own only the real assets. This is one of the reasons why organized securities markets are thought to promote capital formation.

When the possibility of producing new real assets is considered, the flow supply of new shares is governed by the marginal cost of producing real assets. Whenever the prices of securities exceed the cost of producing the real assets underlying them, it pays corporations to float new issues to finance investment in new real assets; the earning power of the corporation expands more than commensurately with the increase in claims against it, enlarging the prospective income of present share owners. Similarly, when the prices of securities are lower than the costs of producing the real assets underlying them, corporations have an incentive to buy up existing securities while selling off real assets. Therefore, in equilibrium the prices of shares equal the marginal costs of the real assets underlying them. If real assets are produced under conditions of increasing marginal cost, it pays to issue more securities, or retire fewer, as their prices mount. Net flow supply curves for securities slope upward to the right, reflecting the rising supply prices of real assets.[3]

The equilibrium value of any particular type of security, given the prices of all other securities and of consumption services, is given by the intersection of its demand curve with its stock-flow supply curve. The process by which all securities markets are equilibrated simultaneously is similar to that discussed above for the case where real assets are owned directly. In equilibrium, the value of any security cannot exceed the marginal cost of producing the real assets underlying it. Just as cost of production partly governs the equilibrium prices of real assets, so it partly governs the prices of securities issued against real assets.

---

[3] The equilibrium total value of shares in a corporation may exceed the market value of underlying real assets by an amount equal to the value of any intangible assets owned by the corporation ("goodwill"). Under perfect competition, many intangible assets, such as patents, franchises, and brand names would not exist. However, the mere fact of being organized for production may constitute an intangible asset. To the extent that there is a marginal investment in organization entailed in the use of additional real assets, the flow supply of new shares is reduced at any given prices for real assets. The equilibrium price per share cannot exceed the sum of the marginal cost of the underlying real assets plus the marginal investment cost of organization. But if existing organization capital cannot be traded, then the minimum value of a firm's shares may be as low as the marginal cost of producing the underlying real assets alone. Thus there may be a discontinuity in the net flow supply of new shares at the point where net flow supply equals zero.

CLOWER'S CONTRARY VIEWS

The view of the role of costs in the determination of asset prices presented here is not shared by R. W. Clower, who contends that the current prices of real assets and securities are independent of their current flow supplies.[4] According to Clower, the demand curve for any real asset or security to hold slopes downward to the right, given all other prices, for reasons he does not state. The current price of any asset is determined by the intersection of its demand curve with its stock supply curve. This intersection sets the price of the asset over the ensuing short moment, independent of conditions of flow supply. In the case of real assets, production is then carried up to the point where marginal cost is equal to the current price set by the intersection of the demand curve with the stock supply curve. Similarly, issues of new securities are carried up to the point where the marginal cost of the real assets under-lying existing issues is equal to the predetermined value of securities outstanding against them. In Clower's view, although changes in the cost of producing real assets change the flow supply curves, they cannot affect the current prices of real assets and securities, since current prices are determined independently of flow supplies.

Clower justifies this view by asserting that the demand curve for new assets "is infinitely elastic at the level of current market prices since, by hypothesis, the market period is so short that current new supply is negligible with relation to current stocks; i.e., all durable goods which are newly produced during the period can be added to previous holdings without any noticeable reduction in price." [5] People do not require an inducement to increase their holdings of assets because the increase is small in relation to inherited holdings. However, since any increase in spending on new real assets or securities issued to finance new real investment must be accompanied by an equal reduction in the sum of consumption spending and cash balances, Clower's view implies that the latter are passively determined. Clower's implicit theories of consumption and the demand for cash balances do not square with the

---

[4] In *op. cit.*, and "Productivity, Thrift, and the Rate of Interest," *Economic Journal*, LXIV (March, 1954), 107–115.

[5] "The Dynamics of Investment" *op. cit.*, pp. 67–68.

ones proposed here, according to which an increase in the flow supply of assets induces additional spending on new assets by lowering asset prices, leading in turn to lowered holdings of cash and lowered spending on consumption. It is the view that increased spending on new real assets must be induced by changes in asset prices that makes this theory differ from Clower's, and that gives to current costs a role in the determination of current prices. While it is true that the magnitudes involved in flow supply may be small in relation to the value of the inherited stock because the day is very short, it may be similarly true that people's consumption spending is also small in relation to that value. A small increase in investment spending accompanied by a small reduction in consumption spending may imply a very large percentage reduction in consumption, measured in terms of, say, annual rates. Clower's view that changes at the margin are small and can therefore be neglected is a very dangerous one. Marginal analysis loses meaning when marginal changes are held to be insignificant.

Clower's notion that current costs and current prices are independent is not an unusual one. It is, for example, similar to Marshall's view of the determination of the market prices of assets, discussed in Chapter III. Boulding too uses the notion.[6] Keynesian theory, on the other hand, recognizes the influence of current costs on current asset prices, although as a rule the relationship is not stressed. Viewed in the framework of Keynesian equilibrium, any change in the cost of producing real assets changes the marginal efficiency of capital. If costs fall, the marginal efficiency of capital rises, encouraging additional investment spending. This, however, converts hoards into active balances, and the drawing down of hoards involves an increase in interest rates, or a fall in bond prices. In equilibrium, the rate of interest on bonds must be equal to the expected rate of return at the margin of new investment and therefore it depends on the costs of new real assets. Keynes criticizes Marshall for failing to recognize this relationship between the prices of old assets and their current costs of production.[7] Fisher, too, recognizes the influence of costs on prices

---

[6] Kenneth E. Boulding, "A Liquidity Preference Theory of Market Prices," *Economica*, N.S. IX (1944), 55–63. Reprinted in *Readings in Price Theory* (Chicago: Richard D. Irwin, Inc., 1952), pp. 311–328.

[7] John Maynard Keynes, *The General Theory of Employment, Interest, and Money* (New York: Harcourt Brace and Co., 1936), p. 187, esp. n. 2.

through his rate of return over cost function. It appears that the role of costs in determining prices is likely to be lost only when discussions of the prices of particular assets are undertaken; indeed, it is hard to imagine devising a theory of the level of asset prices (the interest rate) that completely neglects the relationship.

Clower also contends that current thrift has no influence on current asset prices: "Even a large current change in thrift, since its effects will be spread among a myriad of assets, will ordinarily have little effect upon the demand for any one asset. Moreover, in the short run any increase in the demand for assets to hold will necessarily be small in relation to total (historically accumulated) demands, so that thrift can play no *direct* part in determining the current rate of interest." [8]

But the notion that an increase in demand, coupled with less than perfectly elastic supply, does not affect prices simply because it is small in relation to total demand is not admissible. The increase creates excess demand that can be worked out only through an increase in prices. Clower's notion, which implies that price is independent of demand, is inconsistent with his contention that price is set by the intersection of the supply and demand schedules.

According to the approach adopted here, Clower's two rules, that current asset prices are independent of current costs of production and current thrift, must be replaced with the rules that current asset prices are higher the higher are their costs of production and the thriftier people are.

Personal Debt Instruments

Just as real assets can provide the underlying basis for security issues, so can the earning power of human beings. Claims against human earning power have value in the market for assets because they serve as substitutes, for investment purposes, for other assets. Given any set of prices for all other assets, the demand for claims on a particular person's earning capacity will be finite in the sense that there will be some maximum amount a person can raise by selling them. Even if there are no institutional restrictions on mortgaging oneself, a person's possible earnings over his lifetime are limited. In practice, claims against persons are generally fixed-

---

[8] "Productivity, Thrift and the Rate of Interest," *op. cit.*, p. 111.

value claims, rather than common stock type shares in income. The demand curve for any person's I.O.U.'s, given other asset prices, slopes downward from left to right because, as he sells more debt, the possibility of his not being able to pay it off increases, reducing its discounted marginal contribution to potential buyers.

The existence of a market for claims to his earning power raises a person's dollar wealth, given the prices of other assets he owns.[9] His total money demand for assets to hold (including his "reservation" demand for his own unissued I.O.U.'s) is higher by the same amount only if this increased wealth does not induce him to consume more. As long as it does, the effect of introducing personal borrowing is to raise consumption and depress the markets for assets in general, since the aggregate market value of the I.O.U.'s exceeds the addition to the aggregate demand for assets on the part of their owners. It is not necessary that people sell any I.O.U.'s. They may simply try to hold less of other assets, feeling more secure because of the reserve provided by the untapped borrowing power. Many people profess to object to borrowing against future income, but this need not mean that they would not change their consumption habits if a law were passed forbidding personal indebtedness. This result is in line with the common-sense conclusion that a law forbidding people to borrow against their earning power would lower consumption spending and raise the demand for real assets and securities. Forbidding such borrowing would have the same general effect on consumption demand as would the destruction or appropriation by the state of existing real assets or claims to them. People would be made poorer at any set of prices for these assets, and, since their consumption would fall as they attempted to restore a part of the lost wealth, asset prices would rise.

---

[9] But not his "net worth" as this term is commonly used, because a person's earning power is not included among his assets. This accounting practice, though quite understandable, seems to distort the facts; one type of valuable (salable) stock being singled out for omission from the balance sheet. Consistency requires that total borrowing power based on human earning power be carried as an asset, outstanding securities issued against it be listed as liabilities, and the difference be added into net worth, or the owner's residual claims to the assets he possesses. The net worth figure is then more useful as an indication of the quality of any additional claims he might issue.

IX

The Economics of Government Debt

The effects of an existing government debt and of changes in its magnitude coming about through current debt operations (government purchases and sales of its own debt) constitute an outside influence on asset prices. This chapter will help to clarify the treatment of asset values set forth so far by showing how it can be used to treat the effects of such an outside influence.

The economics of government debt is a subject of considerable importance because debt management is a widely used instrument of government financial policy. Sovereign governments with the power of issue need never sell debt to private investors because they need money; debt policies may be formulated quite independently of budgetary policies for governments that are not subject to financial constraints. As Lerner has correctly pointed out, debt policies of such governments should be judged solely by their own effects and should not be analyzed as if there were some functional relationship between debt to the private sector and government expenditures.[1]

GOVERNMENT DEBT: THE SIMPLIFIED CASE

Under the simplifying assumptions employed in Chapter III, only two prices had to be determined—P_O, the price of a fixed-composi-

---

[1] Abba P. Lerner, "The Burden of the National Debt," in *Income, Employment, and Public Policy* (New York: Macmillan Co., 1945), pp. 255–275.

tion bundle of consumption services, and P_A, the price of a unit
of real assets. All real assets were perpetuities and all investors
were assumed to be perfectly certain and to agree. Rates of substitution among assets were therefore fixed and were the same for
all people. Choosing any particular real asset to serve as *numeraire*,
quantities of all other real assets could be expressed in terms of
units of the *numeraire*. Given the inherited stocks of real assets
and money together with people's tastes as between consuming and
thrifting and given the production possibilities of the economy,
the supply and demand, and hence the equilibrium price for con-

FIG. IX-1

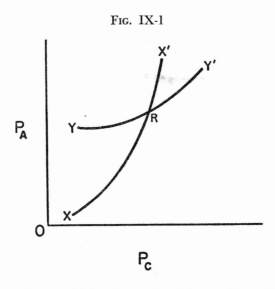

sumption services could be determined for each possible level of
P_A, the price of a unit of real assets; conversely, the equilibrium
P_A could be determined for each possible level of P_C, the price of a
unit of consumption services. Plotting the equilibrium P_C's for
each possible P_A yielded the XX′ curve, and plotting the equilibrium P_A for each possible level of P_C yielded the YY′ curve,
shown in Figure IX-1.

The XX′ curve was shown to be inelastic $(\frac{\Delta P_C}{P_C} / \frac{\Delta P_A}{P_A} < 1)$.
Starting with the equilibrium P_C defined for any P_A we choose, a
doubling of both P_C and P_A (or any other equi-proportionate rise
in the two prices) leaves the supply of consumption services forthcoming unchanged, for supply depends solely on P_C/P_A. But it

reduces the amount the group is willing to consume because people who hold inherited stocks of money experience a decline in their real consumption potentials. Thus the equilibrium P_C falls relative to P_A as P_A is raised.

The YY' curve is elastic $(\dfrac{\Delta P_C}{P_C} \Big/ \dfrac{\Delta P_A}{P_A} > 1)$. Starting with the equilibrium P_A defined for any given P_C, an equi-proportionate rise in both prices generates excess supply in the real assets markets. The stock-flow supply of real assets, which depends on P_A/P_C, is unchanged when both prices rise by the same proportion. But people who hold cash experience a decline in their real consumption potentials and they respond, not only by consuming less, but by thrifting less (lowering the value of the assets they hold relative to the price of consumption services), so that equal percentage increases in P_A and P_C leave excess supply in the assets markets. Therefore the equilibrium P_A falls relative to P_C as the assumed level of P_C is increased.

The intersection of the XX' and YY' curves, shown at point R in Figure IX-1, indicates the pair of prices that equilibrates both markets simultaneously. Because the XX' curve is inelastic and the YY' curve is elastic, the two can intersect only once. The ratio of P_A to P_C (measured by the slope of a ray drawn from the origin to point R) indicates the equilibrium marginal rate of transformation of real assets for consumption services. The higher this equilibrium ratio is, the greater is the equilibrium demand for, and rate of production of, consumption services relative to the equilibrium demand for, and rate of production of, real assets.

The influences of existing government debt and of current debt operations can be analyzed in terms of their effects on the positions of the XX' and YY' curves, and hence on the pair of prices required to equilibrate both markets taken together. For simplicity we shall assume that government debt is in the form of perpetual income bonds which have an earning power just sufficient to make them perfect substitutes, for holding purposes, for one unit of the *numeraire* real asset.

Inherited holdings of government debt

Suppose that $X_1X'_1$ and $Y_1Y'_1$ in Figure IX-2 apply for a situation in which no inherited government bonds are held. R_1 shows the

equilibrium pair of prices for real assets and consumption services.
If we now add to the group's holdings of real assets and money a
given number of government bonds, each the equivalent for investment purposes of one unit of real assets, the XX' and YY'
curves must shift. At any P_A, people who hold the newly added
bonds are wealthier than they were before, making their consumption demand higher. The supply of consumption services, given
any P_A, is not affected, so that the equilibrium price of consumption services is raised. The XX' curve shifts rightward as bonds

FIG. IX-2

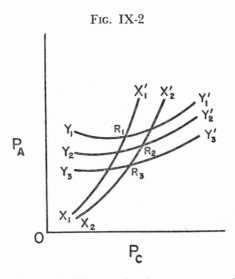

are added to people's holdings of other assets, as from $X_1X'_1$ to
$X_2X'_2$ in Figure IX-2.

On the other hand, given any P_C, the demand curve for earning
assets—real assets and bonds—is raised as holders of the added
bonds devote a part of their additional wealth at any given P_A to
holding earning assets. But since these people also consume more,
their dollar demands for earning assets rise by less than the market
value of the added bonds. By adding more to stock supply than to
the demand for earning assets, adding bonds to people's inherited
asset holdings reduces the equilibrium P_A defined for any given P_C.
The YY' curve shifts downward, as from $Y_1Y'_1$ to $Y_2Y'_2$ in Figure
IX-2.

As XX' moves rightward and YY' moves downward, their intersection moves downward and to the right, from R_1 to R_2. Giving

people bonds, by making them wealthier, raises their demand for consumption relative to their demands for new earning assets. As the equilibrium ratio of P_A to P_C is lowered, the production of consumption services increases at the expense of the production of new real assets.

The conclusion that adding government bonds to holdings of other assets raises consumption agrees with Lerner's contention that the demand for consumption grows as government debt increases.[2] Lerner, however, employs a setting where the increase in the debt comes from past sales by the government to the private sector; the above analysis simply posits an increase in holdings of debt *ceteris paribus*. It is necessary to see whether sales of government debt actually speed up the rate at which people accumulate earning assets before Lerner's proposition can be adequately judged. If every sale of a bond were accompanied by a reduction of one unit in the production of new real assets, people's holdings of earning assets would not rise as the government debt grew and there would be no reason to suppose that they would increase their consumption over time. Current debt operations must be considered.

The effects of current government debt operations

Current government debt operations, whether they involve net sales to the public or net purchases from them, are flow supplies. Like capital consumption and the current production of new real assets, they involve changes in the quantity of assets available to hold without simultaneous changes in investors' ability to hold them, that is, without simultaneously raising or lowering inherited stocks.

Starting from point R_2 in Figure IX-2, denoting the equilibrium P_A and P_C when the supply of bonds available to hold is limited to bonds inherited from the past, suppose instead that the government is offering a specified number of new bonds for sale, without any current debt retirement. The new issues are perfect substitutes for old bonds, old real assets, and new real assets. Given any P_C, the net flow supply of earning assets is increased by the amount of bonds (each the equivalent of one unit

---

[2] Abba P. Lerner, *The Economics of Control* (New York: Macmillan Co., 1944), Ch. XXIV.

of real assets) offered for sale by the government. Since the current debt offering does not alter the stock supply of government bonds, it raises only the supply of assets to hold, given any P_C, without altering the demand for them. In this respect current offerings of government debt are similar to reductions in the cost of producing new real assets. The greater supply lowers the equilibrium P_A for any assumed level of P_C, moving the YY' curve downward, as from $Y_2Y'_2$ to $Y_3Y'_3$ in Figure IX-2.

Given any P_A, the demand for consumption services is independent of the flow supply of bonds because people's wealth depends only on the value of their inherited stocks of assets. The supply of consumption services depends only on the relation between P_A and P_C and is therefore the same, at any given P_A, regardless of current government debt operations. Since neither the supply nor the demand for consumption services defined for any given P_A is influenced by current debt operations, the XX' curve is not affected.

The equilibrium pair of prices for real assets and consumption services is indicated by the intersection of $Y_3Y'_3$ and $X_2X'_2$ at point R_3. The effect of the current debt operation is to lower both P_A and P_C, but P_A falls relatively more than does P_C, since the current debt operations cause a movement of the equilibrium point downward along the XX' curve, which is inelastic (P_C/P_A rises as P_C falls). The current debt offering raises the supply of earning assets relative to the demand for them. This reduces asset prices, and hence the cost of producing consumption services, by more, relatively, than it reduces the wealth of anyone who holds cash, and the demand for consumption rises relative to supply. As P_C rises relative to P_A, it pays resource owners to shift them from the production of new real assets to the production of consumption services. This change in the pattern of demand for new output has a differential incidence on resource owners. Resources specialized to the production of new real assets find their incomes lowered relative to those of resources used more intensively in the production of consumption services.[3]

Since current debt operations reduce the rate of production of real assets, the accumulation of government debt over time is

---

[3] Cf. Earl R. Rolph, "The Incidence of Public Debt Operations," *National Tax Journal,* IX (December, 1956), 339–353.

accompanied by a reduced rate of accumulation of real assets. The more government debt people are presently absorbing, the less real assets they will hold at any future date. However, the rate at which they accumulate both earning assets taken together is raised by current sales of government debt. The government sales cause the equilibrium rate of consumption to rise because they lead to increases in people's real consumption potentials. But as real consumption potentials rise, people also increase their thrifting (the value of the assets they hold relative to the price of consumption services). Therefore, in equilibrium, the total dollar demand for assets to hold is higher, relative to P_C, than it is when there are no current debt offerings. The decline in P_A relative to P_C as a result of the offering induces people to increase their total holdings of earning assets and the production of new real assets does not fall by the full amount of the increase in the private sector's holdings of bonds. Therefore, Lerner's contention that sales of government debt tend, through time, to raise the demand for consumption spending by raising the value of accumulated assets is valid, even though the sales of debt do reduce the rate of production of new real assets.

GOVERNMENT DEBT UNDER MORE COMPLEX DEMAND CONDITIONS

The analytical framework outlined in Chapters V to VIII can now be used to treat the more complex aspects of the influence of government debt that arise out of imperfect substitutability among assets and between assets and cash balances. No attempt is made to exhaust the analytical problems raised by government debt; instead, the emphasis is on the kinds of problems raised and the extent to which the general implications of government debt can be specified.

For these limited purposes, it will suffice to confine the analysis to a setting where there are but three assets that can be held— government debt, identical real assets, and cash balances. Alternatively, it could be assumed that all real assets are owned by corporations which issue common stock; as was shown in Chapter VII, the treatment is essentially the same in both cases.

Again the implications of existing stocks of government debt are found by comparing two situations identical in all respects save that in one people inherit government debt from the past and in the other they do not. The effects of current government debt operations are found by comparing cases where the only difference is with respect to the debt operations.

Starting with a situation in which there are no current government debt operations, and no inherited supplies of government debt, the equilibrium pair of prices for real assets and consumption services is determined as before. Given the inherited supplies of identical real assets and money and their distribution, along with people's tastes and the production possibilities of the economy, the equilibrium pair of prices is denoted by the intersection, as at R_1 in Figure IX-2, of $X_1X'_1$ and $Y_1Y'_1$.

Inherited holdings of government bonds

The effects of adding government bonds to inherited holdings of real assets and money can be divided into two categories, the price effect of making an additional asset available to hold, given people's wealth, and the wealth effect of adding bonds to people's inherited holdings of other assets. To isolate the price effect, it is necessary to see how people react to the opportunity to hold bonds when bonds are not currently a source of wealth to anyone. Given any pair of prices for real assets and consumption services, a demand curve for bonds can be constructed. Since no one's wealth is affected by bond prices, no one's investment budget changes as the price of bonds varies. The amount of bonds any person holds depends on P_B, the price of bonds. For any given P_B, this amount is indicated by the intersection of the investment budget line or constraint defined for the given price with the price-investment curve defined for the person's given investment budget. At sufficiently high prices no one will wish to hold bonds, but as price is lowered the discounted marginal contribution of bonds rises relative to their price, so that at sufficiently low prices people are induced to hold them. The price effect of making bonds available at prices that induce people to hold them must work against the demand for other assets (real assets and cash balances), since investors with given investment budgets must hold less of other assets if they are to hold bonds.

In Figure IX-3, d is the market demand curve for bonds found by summing the individual demand curves, each representing movements along the price-investment curve defined for a given investment budget and the given P_A and P_C. If OO′ bonds are made available at a price of OJ while no one's wealth is allowed

FIG. IX-3

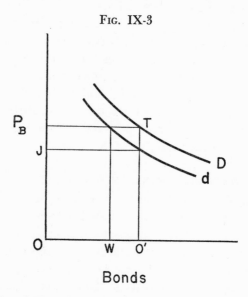

Bonds

to change, the dollar demand for real assets and cash balances must be lower by OO′(OJ) than it is when no bonds are available at any price.

The precise workings of the price effect of making bonds available without changing anyone's wealth depend on the substitutability of bonds for cash relative to their substitutability for real assets. It might be supposed that investors would normally reduce their holdings of both real assets and cash to acquire bonds, and this might well be the case. However, two alternatives are also feasible. People might consider bonds good substitutes for cash at bond prices too high (yields too low) to make it worthwhile to substitute real assets for bonds. This is more likely to be the case if the bonds are of very short maturity; in the limiting case of bonds that mature "tomorrow," the price of a bond is certain, making it a perfect substitute for cash balances if the yield is high enough to cover whatever transactions costs are involved in turning in the bond at maturity. But even perpetuities might be considered good substitutes for cash at prices too high to induce substitution of bonds for real assets if people feel considerably more certain about the future prices of the bonds than they feel about the future prices of real assets. Beyond this, the price effect may not work against the demand for real assets if investors expect future bond prices to vary inversely with the prices of real assets. The liquidity problems arising out of holding noncash assets are then diminished by the prospective canceling out of market price fluctuations when bonds are held along with real assets, and the liquidity advantages of cash balances are reduced.

For either or for both of these reasons, it cannot be categorically asserted that the price effect of making bonds available at a price that induces investors to substitute them for cash must work against the demand for real assets. It is possible for bonds and real assets to be complementary, so that as people substitute cash for bonds the demand for real assets rises.

But price effect is only part of the story concerning the effects of adding bonds to people's inherited holdings of other assets. The holders of the added bonds are made wealthier at any positive price for bonds, and the increase in their wealth must be accompanied by an equal increase in their total dollar demands for all things. The typical response to increased wealth, given P_A and P_C, is to increase both consumption spending and the investment budget. The wealth effect of adding bonds to a person's inherited holdings of other assets can be measured, for any given price of bonds, by the movement along the wealth-investment curve as the investment budget increases. So long as bonds are not inferior assets, the wealth effect works in favor of bonds.

If OO' bonds are inherited, bondholders are made wealthier by $OO'(P_B)$ where P_B is the price of bonds (Figure IX-3). Since they will typically devote a part of their added wealth to consuming and to holding other assets, the wealth effect raises the demand for bonds by some amount less than OO' at each P_B. By adding the wealth effect to d, the demand for bonds when only a price effect is allowed, the total demand for bonds (D) is obtained. D lies to the right of d, but by less than the distance OO' at any given price. Assuming that there is no flow supply of bonds coming from current government debt operations, the equilibrium price of bonds, taking P_A and P_C as given, is indicated

by the intersection at point T of DD' with the vertical stock supply curve erected at O'. The sources of the demand for bonds
fall into two classes. At $P_B = OT$, people are willing to hold OW
of bonds without any changes in their wealth, so that O'T(OW)
of their demand comes at the expense of holdings of cash and real
assets combined. The rest of the dollar demand for bonds,
O'T(WO'), traces to the added wealth of bondholders.

The effect of adding bonds to inherited stocks of real assets
on the over-all equilibrium of the system may now be described,
using the XX' and YY' curve analysis introduced earlier. Given

Fig. IX-4

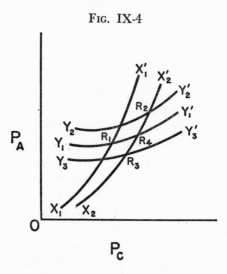

any P_A, adding bonds to inherited holdings of other assets increases wealth, and thereby leads to a rise of the consumption
demand curve. Hence addition of the bonds leads to an increase
in the equilibrium P_C defined for any P_A, just as it did under the
simpler assumptions taken from Chapter III. The XX' curve
shifts rightward, as from $X_1X'_1$ to $X_2X'_2$ in Figure IX-4.

The effect on the YY' curve is less easily determined. As was
indicated previously, it is not certain that the price effect of making bonds available to hold works against the demand for real assets. The wealth effect of adding bonds to people's holdings of
other assets works in favor of real assets unless real assets are
inferior. Given any P_C, it is possible for the demand for real assets either to rise or to fall when bonds are added to people's

holdings of other assets. Other things equal, the demand for real
assets is more likely to rise the more willing people are to substitute bonds for cash and the more eager they are to hold more
real assets as their wealth rises.

If adding bonds should raise the demand for real assets, given
P_C, the YY′ curve moves upward, as from $Y_1Y'_1$ to $Y_2Y'_2$. This is
the opposite of what was found under the assumptions of Chapter II. If, on the other hand, the demand for real assets is lowered,
the YY′ curve falls, as from $Y_1Y'_1$ to $Y_3Y'_3$. This is more likely to

Fig. IX-5

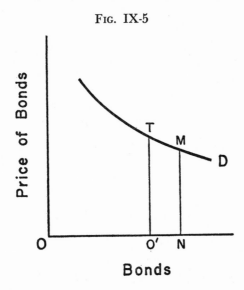

Bonds

be the case the more willing people are to substitute bonds for
real assets.

Since the new curves, $X_2X'_2$ and either $Y_2Y'_2$ or $Y_3Y'_3$, are drawn
on the assumption that the bond market clears when OO′ bonds
are inherited from the past, their intersection at either R_2 or R_3
indicates the combination of P_C and P_A that allows all three markets to clear simultaneously. The equilibrium price of bonds is
shown by O′T in Figure IX-5, where D is the demand curve defined for the equilibrium pair of P_C and P_A (R_2 or R_3 in Figure
IX-4) and the inherited supply of bonds OO′. Any change in the
amount of bonds inherited from the past would upset this three-
way equilibrium by changing both the supply of bonds available
to hold and the wealth of bondholders at any given price for bonds.

The effects of current government debt operations

Current debt operations upset the three-way equilibrium discussed above by making the supply of bonds available to hold differ from OO', the inherited stock shown in Figure IX-5.

Suppose, for example, that the government offers O'N new bonds for sale. At price O'T, investors are willing to hold only OO' bonds. Every investor has adjusted his asset holdings so that the discounted marginal contributions of a dollar's worth of all three assets are equal. Since the discounted marginal contribution

FIG. IX-6

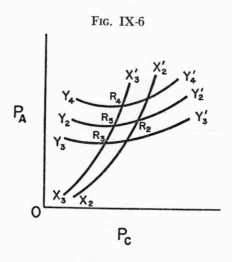

of bonds, given their price, declines as more bonds are held, no investor will be willing to hold more bonds at price O'T, and the current debt offering creates excess supply at this price. As bond prices fall to NM, the price that equilibrates the bond market taken by itself, bondholders experience a reduction in their wealth that leads them to economize on their consumption. The equilibrium P_C defined for the given price of real assets is reduced. Thus the XX' curve is moved leftward as from $X_2X'_2$ to $X_3X'_3$ in Figure IX-6. This result differs from that found when bonds and real assets were treated as perfect substitutes; in that case the *ceteris paribus* demand for bonds was perfectly elastic, and the current debt operation left bond prices, and hence the demand for consumption services, unaffected given any P_A, the price of a unit of real assets.

The effect of the current sales of government debt on the demand for real assets, given P_C, depends on the cross-elasticity of demand between the two earning assets. If the cross-elasticity is zero, equilibrating the bond market, taken by itself, is sufficient to restore equilibrium to the markets for both types of earning assets taken together, and the YY′ curve is unaffected. If the cross-elasticity is positive, the YY′ curve shifts downward, and if it is negative the YY′ curve shifts upward. The cross-elasticity depends on the sum of the price and wealth effects of a fall in bond prices on the demand for real assets.

So long as real assets are not an inferior asset, the wealth effect of a reduction in bond prices works against the demand for real assets. As was noted earlier, the price effect of a reduction in bond prices may work either in favor of or against the demand for real assets, depending on the degree to which investors consider the two assets to be substitutable for one another. The cross-elasticity must be positive if both the wealth and price effects of a decline in P_B work against the demand for real assets. In this case the current debt sales act to hold down real asset prices, given any P_C, since equilibrium in the bond market is achieved partly at the expense of the demand for real assets, and the YY′ curve is moved downward, as from $Y_2Y'_2$ to $Y_3Y'_3$ in Figure IX-6.

If, on the other hand, the cross-elasticity of demand for real assets with respect to bond prices should be negative, the YY′ curve moves upward, as from $Y_2Y'_2$ to $Y_4Y'_4$. This might happen if real assets are an inferior asset or if people regard bonds as very good substitutes for cash balances and at the same time expect that future variations in bond values will be opposite in direction to variations in real assets prices. The third possibility is that the reduction of bond prices does not affect the YY′ curve at all because the cross-elasticity of demand is zero.

Because of the lack of any necessary relation between bond prices and the demand for real assets, the effect of the current sale of new debt on P_A and P_C is less easily determined than it was when the assumptions of Chapter III were employed. Depending on the effect of the debt sale on the YY′ curve, the equilibrium pair of prices might be shown by R_3, R_4, or R_5 in Figure IX-6. It is no longer possible to speak in terms of the change in *the* level of asset prices or *the* interest rate, since the relative prices of real assets and bonds are changed by the current sale of new government debt. For example, if the cross-elasticity of demand for real assets is zero, the effect of the debt sale on the price of real assets comes about only through its effect on the consumption market; the movement of R is from R_2 to R_5 along $Y_2Y'_2$, and in equilibrium P_C/P_A is lowered, so that the current debt operation raises the rate of production of real assets even though the rate of interest on bonds is raised. In the earlier analysis, where real assets and bonds were treated as perfect substitutes, precisely the opposite was true. Current sales of debt lowered YY' without affecting XX', raising the equilibrium ratio P_C/P_A, so that the rate of production of new real assets was reduced by current sales of debt.

Even though it seems reasonable to suppose that the cross-elasticity of demand for real assets will be positive so that YY' falls as new bonds are sold, the current sale of new debt may still lower P_C/P_A since the XX' curve shifts leftward. The relevant issue here is one of fact: only if the leftward movement of XX' is relatively smaller than the downward shift of YY' will P_C/P_A rise as new government bonds are sold.

It is possible that the proceeds of government debt operations may come chiefly at the expense of the demand for cash balances. If the cross-elasticity of demand for real assets with respect to bond prices is zero, bond sales have no direct impact on investment spending. If, in addition, people regard cash and bonds as good substitutes, so that a small reduction in bond prices leads them to substitute bonds for cash on a large scale, bond prices may fall very little in response to a current debt offering, and the demand for consumption services and hence the XX' curve are only slightly affected.

Alternatively, if the current debt operation leaves YY' unaffected and at the same time bonds are held chiefly by people of great wealth, whose consumption is affected very little by changes in current bond prices, the XX' curve may be affected only slightly even though bond prices may fall significantly. As long as the demand for cash balances is considerably more sensitive to changes in bond prices than is either the demand for real assets or the demand for consumption services, the effect of current debt operations on P_A and P_C may be slight.

The findings with respect to the effects of current sales of new government debt may be reversed to cover the case of current debt retirement. If the government undertakes to buy up a given amount of its debt, the supply of bonds available to hold is reduced, but without any direct effect on the demand for bonds, for the inherited supply is unaffected. Consequently, the price of bonds tends to rise. Holders of bonds experience an increase in their wealth, and are thereby led to consume more, moving the XX' curve rightward. So long as the cross-elasticity of demand for real assets with respect to bond prices is positive, the YY' curve moves upward. However, should the cross-elasticity be negative, the YY' curve moves downward.

Current debt retirement encourages production of new real assets only if the YY' curve shifts upward relatively more than the XX' curve shifts rightward; again the imperfect substitutability of bonds and real assets makes possible a reversal of the earlier findings under the condition of perfect foresight.

Debt retirement by raising bond prices probably results partly in increased holdings of cash balances, and this cushions the impact on the demands for real assets and consumption services. Although under the theory of asset choice used here cash balances cannot be perfect substitutes for bonds, it is possible that the increasing price of bonds that results from current debt retirement works mainly to induce people to hold more cash, while having little impact on the XX' and YY' curves.

X

Government Finance
and Aggregate Demand

This final chapter attempts to draw out, in a very general way, the implications of the kind of analysis so far proposed for problems of governmental financial policies affecting aggregate demands for new output. Monetary and fiscal policies are most often thought of, not in terms of their effects on interest rates or on particular demands as such, but in terms of their effects on aggregate demands for flows of new output. Although the analysis of particular markets is an essential ingredient of our viewpoint of overall equilibrium, it is possible to discuss the way particular governmental financial policies affect the aggregate of demands for new products without building up the analysis in detail. Such a discussion may be helpful in showing the relationship between the analysis of assets markets used here and theories of aggregate demand.

Accordingly, the main purpose here is not to trace out the ultimate impact of such policies on the total equilibrium of the system; the object is, instead, to point out the routes by which variations in governmental financial policies are transmitted to the markets for new products. To do this, we need to think only in terms of the influence of government financial policies on demands for consumption services and new real assets at given prices, without having to inquire into the details of their effects on the final equilibrium of the entire system. Since a great deal of the literature on monetary and fiscal policies concerns economies where prices (including money wages) are not completely flexible, the kinds of full-employment solutions obtained in previous chapters are not directly comparable with other views. By limiting our present inquiry to the effects of various financial policies on demands for new output at given product prices, we deliberately avoid some of the complicated problems that arise when supply prices of resources are not flexible.

Two Types of Monetary Variations

The discussion involves two types of governmental policies that affect private money holdings: debt operations and tax policies. The important distinction between the two is that debt operations change the privately held supply of government debt at the same time they change private cash balances, while tax policies involve "pure" changes in private cash balances without any offsetting change in other private asset holdings.

Debt operations of government are often thought of as "monetary policies," at least when they are conducted by central banks. There is, however, no relevant analytical distinction between the case of central bank operations in government debt and those of a treasury, just as there is no economic necessity for having a central bank that is separate from the national treasury.[1]

Government Debt Retirement
and Demand for New Products

We may conveniently pick up where we left off in Chapter IX. Since government debt operations change private cash balances

---

[1] Commercial banks, operating with fractional reserves, have not been discussed here. However, the activities of commercial banks are analytically the equivalent of the debt operations of a governmental authority. Commercial banks influence the nonbank sector of an economy through their purchases and sales of assets to and from nonbank investors. These assets may be government debt, in which case the analysis is simply an extension of our earlier findings, or they may be the IOU's of private parties, including businesses and individuals. In either event, an increase (decrease) in commercial banks' demand for noncash assets leads to an increase (decrease) in private cash holdings that is matched by sales (purchases) of noncash assets to the banks. Commercial banks are, in this sense, an arm of governmental debt-monetary policies, though their behavior is conditioned by the profit motive.

as well as private holdings of government securities, we shall refer to them here as debt-monetary policies.

So long as the demand curve for government bonds is negatively sloped, and the cross-elasticity of demand for real assets with respect to bond prices is positive, current retirement of government debt through market purchases operates in favor of demands for both new real assets and consumption services. In the literature on debt-monetary policies, there is, so far as I know, no suggestion of the possibility of negative cross-elasticity of demand between bonds and other assets. Quite the opposite, it is often held, through use of a certainty-equivalent assumption, that bonds and real assets are perfect substitutes. On the basis of the analysis presented here, the certainty-equivalent formulation of investors' tastes must be rejected, and the possibility of negative cross-elasticity can probably also be safely ignored. When these two cases are ruled out, we are left with the proposition that a change in bond prices operates to change demands for real assets in the same direction. It also induces a sympathetic variation in consumption demands because of wealth effects of changing asset values.

If these propositions are accepted, doubts concerning the efficacy of monetary-debt policies as methods of controlling the volume of demand for new products can be narrowed considerably. There exist first the possibility that within the relevant range investors treat bonds and cash as perfect substitutes, so that current debt operations leave bond prices intact, and, second, the possibility that, although current debt operations do affect them, the range over which they can move bond prices is so proscribed that it may not be possible to attain a given level of aggregate demand through the use of debt-monetary operations.

The first case is analytically the equivalent of Keynes's "liquidity trap." Keynes held that expected future bond prices were independent of present prices. This view is considerably different from the neutral-expectations assumption used here, except in the case of a "one-day" bond. Whereas the neutral-expectations assumption implies that in general a change in current bond prices leads to a change in the same direction of the discounted marginal contribution of a bond, Keynes's assumption means that a bond's discounted marginal contribution is independent of its price. On the investor's indifference map, the marginal rate of substitution at any point does not shift in favor of bonds when bond prices rise, for the change in present price has no influence on expectations as to future price.

Because Keynes's assumption concerning expectations does not make the attractiveness of a bond depend on its present price, it implies a more elastic demand curve for bonds than does the neutral-expectations assumption. However, this is not a sufficient condition for a perfectly elastic demand for bonds. The Keynesian liquidity trap depends also on the assumption that investors consider bonds and money to be perfect substitutes for one another. At a sufficiently high price for bonds, there are no "bulls" in the bond market, and government debt retirement does not affect bond prices; all bondholders are willing to substitute cash for bonds at no change in price. In this case the excess demand for bonds resulting from current debt retirement is dissipated in greater private cash holdings.

In Keynesian analysis, if debt operations do not change interest rates, they cannot affect aggregate demand. Since, according to the analysis of Chapter IX, "communication" between the market for government debt and other markets depends on the price and wealth effects accompanying a change in bond prices, we would agree that aggregate demands can be influenced by debt operations only insofar as bond prices are responsive to variations in the net flow supply of bonds. However, the analysis used here leads to the presumption that in general variations in the net flow supply of government debt do in fact imply variations in the equilibrium price of bonds.

In equilibrium, every investor holds bonds up to the point where his marginal rate of substitution of bonds for all other assets (including cash) is equal to the price of bonds. So long as asset indifference curves are convex, investors may hold mixed portfolios of assets, including bonds and money. Any investor who holds a mixed portfolio will not reduce his holding of bonds unless bond prices change; a reduced holding of bonds implies a decrease in the marginal rate of substitution of bonds for money. Similarly, an investor who chooses to hold only bonds and no other assets has a marginal rate of substitution of bonds for money equal to or above the market price, and will not reduce his bond holding without a change in price. Even if the neutral-expectations assumption is dropped in favor of Keynes's assumption that expected future prices are independent of present bond prices, so that the marginal rate of substitution of bonds for other assets does not vary directly with price, the conclusion holds when indifference curves are convex.

Therefore, so long as cautious investors dominate the market, variations of the net flow supply of bonds cannot be absorbed without the inducements provided by changed bond prices. This is true up to the point where all government debt is retired and its amount and price cease to have economic meaning.

It is nonetheless possible that small changes in price do induce considerable changes in the amount of debt people hold. If the cross-elasticity of demand for money-balances with respect to the price of bonds is high, debt operations may lead to a result that approaches Keynes's liquidity trap situation. Large retirements through market purchases may result primarily in increased demand for cash balances to hold, with little effect on bond values. It may not be possible, even if all outstanding government debt is retired, to achieve the kinds of price and wealth effects that would bring the desired stimulation of aggregate demand for new output at given prices.

"Pure" Variations in Private Claims on Government

Debt-monetary operations are only one of the several types of financial relations of government to the private sector of an economy. Whereas buying or selling debt to the public involves an exchange of assets, another important class of transactions, government transfers (taxes or subsidies), involves net additions to or subtractions from private money balances, and hence brings about "pure" changes in public holdings of cash.

These pure monetary changes as discussed here involve variations in government tax collections in the face of constant government outlays and unchanged debt operations. The reader may find it useful to think of this as involving either a variation in the level of government cash balances or in the amount of government debt held by the central bank. The example to be used here is that of a temporary tax moratorium, a fiscal device often recommended to raise aggregate private demands for new output.

Given the level of government outlays to the private sector, and with no variation in government debt operations, a reduction in taxes leaves private holdings of money balances higher than they would otherwise be. Raising people's money balances increases their wealth at any given set of prices for real assets. According to the analysis set forth here, an increase in private wealth that takes the form of added money balances will raise demands in the markets for both nonmoney assets and for consumption at given prices. Consumption demands are higher because adding money balances to asset holdings raises real consumption potential. However, only part of the increase in real consumption potential is devoted to higher consumption demand, so that demand for assets to hold also increases. As people's investment budgets rise, given any set of prices for nonmoney assets, they can be expected to hold both more cash and more nonmoney assets. The increased demand for nonmoney assets implies a higher demand for new real assets because at any price for a particular real asset people typically will wish to hold more of it.

Since the monetary effect of reducing taxes is to raise demands for both consumption services and real assets, it follows that, in a full-employment economy of the kind discussed in the previous chapter, tax reductions cause an outward movement of both the XX′ and YY′ curves. The intersection of these curves, which denotes the prices at which equilibrium is achieved simultaneously in all markets, is also moved outward; prices rise in both markets. The specific impact of the XX′ and YY′ curves depends importantly on the tastes, as among consumption, holding real assets, holding securities, and holding money, of those who find themselves with more cash.

The point to be stressed in the present connection, where we are concerned with the impact of a tax reduction on aggregate demand at given prices, is that reduced taxes raise demands because they leave more cash in private hands. Unlike debt retirement, the increased private cash holdings do not involve compensating reductions in private holdings of government debt. If taxes are later reimposed, the moratorium has nonetheless left private balances higher than they would have been in the absence of a tax cut. Aggregate demand is therefore raised permanently above what it would have been in the absence of the moratorium. The longer the moratorium, the greater will be its effectiveness in stimulating aggregate demand.

In most of the literature on fiscal policy, the effects of manipulating tax collections are viewed in a Keynesian framework, which differs fundamentally from the one used here. These discussions commonly neglect the money market implications of variations in tax collections. Such a treatment is justified in Keynesian theory only if the liquidity preference function is perfectly elastic, so that changes in the amount of money available to hold do not affect interest rates, or, alternatively, if it is assumed that debt policies are followed to hold interest rates constant. Once either assumption is made, then the entire influence of alterations in the amount of taxes collected shows up in an upward movement of the consumption function.

For the sake of simplicity, let us assume the first condition, that asset prices cannot rise because the liquidity preference function is perfectly elastic. Suppose that, in Figure X-1, line C represents consumption, measured along the vertical axis, as a function of disposable income (Y_d), measured horizontally. The relationship of disposable income (national income minus total taxes) to total spending is shown by tax line MT, where the horizontal distance MS measures total tax yields. (If tax yields were zero, the relationship of disposable income to total spending would be shown by line ON.) The equilibrium level of national income, given taxes of MS, is shown by the intersection of $C + \overline{I} + \overline{G}$ with line MT at point H, where net investment (I) and government outlays (G) are given.[2]

A lowering of taxes is represented by a rightward movement of the relevant tax line; in Figure X-1, if tax receipts are lowered from MS to RP, the relevant tax line becomes RV. With a given rate of government spending and no influence on investment, such a reduction of taxes engenders an increase in the equilibrium level of income because it raises disposable income at any given level of Y. The increase in the equilibrium level of national in-

---

[2] An exposition of this method of treating the effects of taxes on the equilibrium level of income is given in John G. Gurley, "Fiscal Policies for Full Employment," *Journal of Political Economy*, LX (December, 1952), 525–533.

come is equal to $\Delta T \left[\dfrac{C'(Y)}{1 - C'(Y)} \right]$ or the amount of tax relief

times the transfer multiplier. This increase is represented by the movement of the "Keynesian Cross" from H to F. The higher equilibrium rate of spending depends on the continuation of tax

Fig. X-1

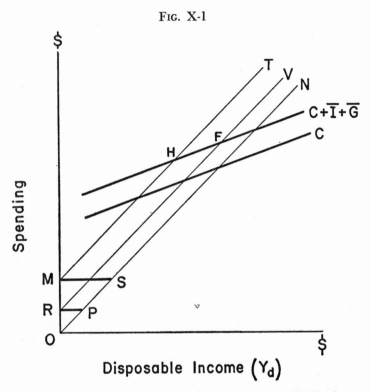

Disposable Income (Y_d)

relief. If taxes are raised again to their former level MS, the multiplier process is reversed and equilibrium is restored at H. Since, by assumption, the increased money supply that accompanies a tax reduction does not affect interest rates, there can be no permanent effect on total spending. The added money is all absorbed in increased saving, none of which is applied to the purchase of nonmonetary assets.[3]

_____
[3] If the liquidity-trap assumption is dropped, it is necessary to assume that government debt operations are employed to hold interest rates constant, since we are investigating only the effects of the deficit on consumption. In this case, the

This conclusion contrasts sharply with that found when the kind of consumption theory used in this study is employed to analyze tax policy. The latter approach, as we have shown, leads to the conclusion that a tax reduction provides a permanent stimulus to consumption, for consumption is related objectively to wealth—not to income. The additional money supply provides a permanent addition to people's money wealth, and restoration of taxes merely brings to a halt the augmentation of money holdings from what they otherwise would have been. It does not destroy the effect on consumption of the higher cash holdings resulting from earlier tax reduction. Even if asset prices were unaffected, consumption would increase.

The distinction made here between the effects of government debt operations and those of variations in tax collections clarifies the monetary theory underlying the analysis used in this study. Government debt operations produce variations in the money supply which are accompanied by compensating variations in private holdings of government debt instruments, and their effectiveness in shaping aggregate demand depends entirely on their ability to change securities prices. On the other hand, monetary changes due to variations in tax receipts directly affect private wealth and hence affect spending on consumption.

Eclectic theories, employing a modified Keynesian framework which relates consumption spending to net private asset holdings as well as to income, yield results more closely akin to those found using the analysis suggested here. Whether such eclecticism is necessary is open to question, however, since no income variable seems needed when consumption is related to wealth; wealth, by definition, includes recent income.

The monetary theory implied by the analysis used here involves considerations of the importance of money both as a particular asset to hold because of its superior liquidity and as a source of wealth or spending power to its holders. Our discussion therefore is in line with much of the current literature on monetary theory. However, the money stock is only one of the

augmented private saving that accompanies tax reduction is applied to the purchase of government debt rather than to holding cash. The effect on private wealth is the same in either case, the only difference being in the form in which people hold their augmented claims on government.

interrelated parts of a stock-flow analysis of spending and prices. Such a stock-flow analysis must, ultimately, deal with the kinds of questions that have been raised in earlier chapters concerning the processes by which all assets markets are involved in the establishment of economic equilibrium.

Index

Actuarial value, of an asset-bundle, 63
Annuity programs, 18
Accumulation of assets: effect on demand, 17; explained by time preference theory, 14–18; simple taste explanation, 16–18
Asset demand curve: for all real assets, 33–42; for particular asset, 91–93
Asset prices, relative, 22
Assets, demand for, as mirror image of consumption demand, 4

Boulding, K. E., 2–3; on demand for particular assets, 79–80, 121
Break, George F., 24 n. 10

Capital consumption, 44–45, 112–114
Cash balances, demand for: and government debt, 131–133, 138; simplified view of, 33–34; under uncertainty, 100–103, 109–112
Central bank, not distinguished from Treasury, 141
Certainty-equivalents, 63–64
Clower, R. W., 117 n. 1; on flow-supply of assets, 120–122; on thrift and asset prices, 122
Commercial banks, as arm of government, 141 n. 1
Constraint, on demand: defined, 25; income as, 4–7, 24–25; wealth as, 4–7, 25
Consumption budget: as part of wealth, 5; related to particular asset prices, 95–99, 109
Consumption, constraint on. See Constraint
Consumption function, Keynesian, 2, 146
Consumption services, demand for: 27–28, 95–99; and borrowing power, 59–60,

123; and current government debt operations, 129; and government debt outstanding, 126–128; in time-preference theory. See Time-preference
Consumption services, price of, related to asset prices, 30–33, 47–49
Consumption services, supply of, 28–29
Cross-elasticity of demand: between bonds and cash, 144; between government bonds and other earning assets, 137–139, 142; between real assets, 110–112

"Day," Robertsonian concept of, 13
Debt, government: effects of retirement of, 139, 141–144; as source of wealth, 127
Debt management of government, independence from budget policies, 124
Debt, personal: demand for, 123; as source of demand, 5–6, 24–25, 123; as form of wealth, 59–60, 123
Dispersion, marginal: defined, 66; related to price, 86
Domar, E., 61 n. 1, 62 n. 2, 68

Elasticity of demand; for asset: related to consumption, 98–99; for one day asset, 82–83; for perpetuity, 87; reduced by wealth-effect, 92–93
Equilibrium, stability of, 39–40
Estates, under time-preference theory, 18–19
Expectations, neutral, 9; and asset indifference curves, 78–79, 84–85; and Keynesian liquidity trap, 142–144

Fellner, William, 61 n. 1, 62 n. 2.
Fisher, Irving, 61 n. 1, 64 n. 4; quoted,

14 n. 4, 19 n. 12; rate of return over
cost, 121–122; on time preference, 14, 17
Flow demand for assets. *See* Capital consumption
Flow supply: of real assets: net, 43–44,
112–115; distinguished from stock supply, 45, 115–118; of securities, 119. *See
also* Marginal costs
Friedman, Milton, 2; on constraint, 24 n.
4; permanent income hypothesis, 27;
on uncertainty, 68–69, 72, 74

Goodwill. *See* Intangible assets
Gurley, John G., 146 n. 2.

Hawtrey, Ralph, 15 n. 5
Hicks, J. R., 2, 8, 9, 61 n. 1, 69 n. 10, 81,
84; on constraint, 24 n. 4; on general
equilibrium prices, 49 n. 12; on indifference curves, 78

Imperfect markets, effect on liquidity,
103
Income, as source of demand. *See* Constraint, income as
Inferior assets, 77–78, 92, 99, 109
Indifference curves for assets, 8–9. *See
also* Marginal rate of substitution
Inflexibility of prices, 140
Institute of Life Insurance, 18 n. 10
Intangible assets, owned by corporation,
119 n. 3
Interest, rate of: common explanation of,
1–2, 22–23; as determinant of capital
values, 1; determined by capital values,
50
Investment budget: as part of wealth, 5;
related to particular asset prices, 95–
99, 109
Investment opportunities, effect on asset
prices, 47, 114
Investment in real assets, related to outstanding government debt, 128–130

Joint probabilities, 65

Keynes, John Maynard, 10, 15 n. 5, 64 n.
4, 121, 142–144
Keynesian analysis: of government debt
operations, 142–144; of tax reduction,
146–148
Keynesian theory of asset prices, 121
Klein, Lawrence R., 2, 27
Knight, F. H., 17, 30 n. 10; on marginal
costs and capital values, 58

Lerner, Abba P., 124 n. 1; on outstand-
ing government debt, 126–128, 130
Life insurance, 18
Liquidity of assets, 102–103
Liquidity trap, Keynesian, 142–144, 146–
147
Lutz, Friederich, 61 n. 1, 68
Lutz, Vera, 61 n. 1, 68

Makower, Helen, 3, 23, 61 n. 1
Marginal contribution of an asset, discounted: defined, 66; equalized for all
real assets, 72; and marginal rate of
substitution, 67. *See also* Marginal rate
of substitution
Marginal costs: and prices of real assets,
56–59, 115–118, 122; and prices of
securities, 119. *See also* Flow supply
Marginal efficiency of investment: influence on asset prices, 121; lowered
by tax, 51–56; relation to marginal
costs of real assets, 56, 121–122
Marginal rate of substitution: between
two assets, 66–69; related to changes in
wealth, 77–78; related to asset prices,
84–91
Markowitz, Harry, 65 n. 5, 65 n. 6
Marschak, Jacob, 3, 23, 61 n. 1
Marshall, Alfred: on constraint, 24 n. 10;
on marginal costs and asset prices, 57,
121; on saving and interest, 51–56
Mehr, Robert I., 18 n. 11
Metzler, Lloyd A., 3
Money, as constraint on demand, 13. *See
also* Cash balances, demand for
Multiplier, Keynesian transfer, 146–147
Musgrave, R. A., 61 n. 1, 62 n. 2, 68
Myrdal, Gunnar, 61 n. 1

Net worth, 123 n. 9

One-day asset, 81–84
Osler, Robert W., 18 n. 11

Packard, Vance, 20 n. 14
Patinkin, Don, 3
Perfect foresight, assumption of, 23, 105–
106
Perpetuity, indifference map for, 84–87
Pigou, A. C., on "amenity" of savings, 16;
quoted, 19 n. 12; time preference views
contrasted with Fisher's, 17; on un-
dervaluation of future consumption,
19–20
Preferred asset ratios, limitations as
analytical device, 79–80
Price effect: 9, 75, 89–90, 92–93, 98, 109–

LOS ANGELES

CULT RECIPES

LOS ANGELES
CULT RECIPES

VICTOR GARNIER ASTORINO

MURDOCH BOOKS
SYDNEY · LONDON

BETH. ELECTRIC AVE & CALIFORNIA AVE

CONTENTS

INTRODUCTION

'Dear Victor, parts 12 and 16 of your report are not relevant to the topic. You do understand that this is a reflection on your academic experience and not a travel guide. Kindly remove these sections.'

It was with these stinging words that the academic dean of my school received the report of my university exchange to Los Angeles in 2010. Too many photos of hamburgers! And yet as soon as I returned, still obsessed with this subject, I started working on opening a gourmet burger restaurant in Paris. I dreamed it, created it, called it Blend Hamburger, and it saw the day in late 2011. I was quickly joined by my partner, accomplice and friend Adrian, without whom no page of this book could have been written, and since then we make sure we each eat at least one hamburger a day. Six years later, when this Los Angeles travel diary was proposed, life gave me the opportunity to bring my two passions together: cooking and photography. An amazing fate for what was once seen as 'off topic'! Even better, it was in the city that has always pushed me to do what I love.

To carry out this project, I chose to go alone and take only my analogue cameras. Not being able to see the shots before I went back to France made each moment last much longer, and now, with the developed film I take precious care of the material trace of this total immersion. I will never, for example, forget my dinner with Richard, who invited me to join him at his table because there was a 45-minute wait at Little Dom's for its spaghetti and meatballs, and night was falling. In the end, the photo was ruined ... If I had known at the time, I'm not sure I would have had such a good time.

In Los Angeles, no door is ever closed. Wherever I was, and even when it was not a good time, I was always given a chance. I didn't receive a single negative response from anyone I approached. I feel like once you throw yourself (or lose yourself) in something that makes you happy, people don't judge you, whatever it is. This is a city that lets people live their dream.

This dream is everywhere. It is in the manners and attitudes ... It is also at the heart of its economy, as Los Angeles lives to the beat of the film, television and music industry. It works itself into the diversity of its landscapes: from the enormous freeways I spent so many hours on, to the heights of Hollywood, where a few minutes' walk takes you outside of civilisation. And it fully comes into its own on the Pacific Coast Highway, which runs alongside the massive, powerful and omnipresent ocean ...

All of these elements that inspire dreams and meditation surely explain why Los Angeles is home to some of the most creative and healthy food in the world. The menus of the restaurants seem totally freed from convention. It is also perhaps the meeting of the city's many cultures, combined with certain American eating habits, that produces these extraordinary ideas. Only in Los Angeles, for example, is it normal to eat a Thai pizza or order a Korean taco.

The quest for wellbeing fosters their creativity. Alex, the co-founder of Caffe' Delfini, told me the idea of serving julienned zucchini (courgette) with his bolognese sauce was as a replacement for high-calorie spaghetti. So some of the most delicious, non-conformist dishes in this food diary start from the imperative to do oneself good, without dogma or limits.

The shared, unbendable rule of this game, the safeguard of all these ideas, is the worship of local produce, elevated to the level of the sacred. The restaurants effectively develop a sacred bond with their local environment, in particular through the farmers' markets, their preferred source of supply. The city's nickname in fact is 'the farm of the United States', because of the diversity and volume of its agricultural production. The possibilities on restaurant menus are limitless.

This book of cult recipes pays tribute to the Angelenos and the incredible fecundity of Los Angeles, both for the body and the mind. I hope it will help persuade you to go and discover or rediscover the City of Angels, and especially to taste the original versions of these dishes, some of which seem straight out of a dream to me.

Chap. 1
WEST LOS ANGELES
SANTA MONICA
BRENTWOOD
SAWTELLE

HICKORY BURGER WITH CHEESE

SERVES 4

Grapeseed oil

Fine sea salt

500 g (1 lb 2 oz) minced (ground) beef

2 teaspoons liquid smoke (American food stores)

8 cheddar cheese slices

4 hamburger buns

4 tablespoons mayonnaise

1 large pickle (gherkin)

1 iceberg lettuce

2 teaspoons Smoky tomato sauce (page 258)

In a hot frying pan brushed with grapeseed oil, cook four seasoned minced beef patties over medium heat on one side for 3 minutes. Mix together 150 ml (5 fl oz) water and the liquid smoke. Pour a quarter of the mixture onto each burger. The frying pan must be hot enough for the water to evaporate immediately. Flip the burgers and arrange two slices of cheddar in a star shape on each burger. For a rare burger, keep cooking for another 3 minutes; for medium, 4 minutes; for well done, 5 minutes. To assemble the burger: spread the bottom half of the bun with mayonnaise, then add rounds of pickle, three to four lettuce leaves cut to the width of the hamburger, the burger with the melted cheese and the smoky tomato sauce, then top with the other half of the bun.

What a pleasure to eat at The Apple Pan! Despite the fact you often have to queue and you can't stay forever because you have to give up your seat. It is one of the oldest restaurants in Los Angeles. The sodas are still served in paper cones, just like in the 1940s. And the smoky flavour of their hickory burger remains a secret that many fans would dream of decoding. My version, which is not the restaurant's, reveals an accessible technique that brings us closer to that unique flavour.

1970 PLYMOUTH HEMI CUDA, CARS WITH CLASS, WILSHIRE BLVD SANTA MONICA

OLD-FASHIONED APPLE PIE

MAKES 1 PIE

THE PASTRY
400 g (14 oz/2⅔ cups) plain (all-purpose) flour
200 g (7 oz) butter, cut into cubes
30 ml (1 fl oz) iced water

THE APPLES
1.4 kg (3 lb 2 oz) apples
125 g (4½ oz) caster (superfine) sugar
2 pinches cinnamon, plus extra to sprinkle
1 pinch ground nutmeg
45 g (1½ oz) plain (all-purpose) flour
2 tablespoons lemon juice
1 pinch coarse salt
50 g (1¾ oz) butter
1 egg yolk
2 tablespoons soft brown sugar

For the pastry: blend the flour with 1 teaspoon salt in a food processor. Add the butter and pulse until mixed evenly but not pasty. Add the iced water, little by little, continuing to mix in short bursts. Shape the dough into two flattened rounds and place them in the refrigerator in two plastic bags for 45 minutes. Preheat the oven to 220°C (425°F). Roll each pastry round out to a circle 5 mm (¼ inch) thick, one with a diameter 5 cm (2 inches) larger than the edge of the pie dish for the base, the other 5 cm (2 inches) smaller for the top crust. For the apples: cut the apples into medium-sized slices and mix well with the sugar, 2 pinches of salt, the spices, flour and lemon juice. Let this mixture rest for 10 minutes. Sprinkle with the coarse salt. Lay the larger circle of pastry in the bottom of the pie dish, pour the apple mixture onto the pastry, cut the butter into small cubes and dot over the apples. Cover with the other circle of pastry and seal the edges by pressing them with a fork. Brush the pastry with the egg yolk. Sprinkle with the brown sugar and a little cinnamon. Cut slits in the top two thirds of the way down. Cook the pie in the lower part of the oven for 30 minutes at 220°C (425°F). Reduce the temperature to 180°C (350°F) and cook for a further 45 minutes, covered with foil.

1963 FORD RANCHERO, ABBOT KINNEY BLVD & N VENICE BLVD

CORA'S COFFEE SHOPPE

CHICKEN BREAKFAST BURRITO

MAKES 4 BURRITOS
4 large tortillas (wheat or corn)
1 avocado
8 cheddar cheese slices
80 g (2¾ oz) crème fraîche or
sour cream
Fresh fruit, to serve
SCRAMBLED EGGS
8 eggs
15 g (½ oz) butter
45 ml (1½ fl oz) thin (pouring/whipping)
cream
MEXICAN RICE
280 g (10 oz) rice
20 ml (½ fl oz) grapeseed oil
320 g (11¼ oz) tomatoes
70 g (2½ oz) onion
Coriander (cilantro), to taste
CHICKEN
400 g (14 oz) skinless chicken breast
fillets
25 ml (¾ fl oz) olive oil

Scrambled eggs: whisk the eggs and season with salt and freshly ground black pepper. Cook the eggs for at least 5 minutes in a hot frying pan greased with butter. Add the cream to stop the cooking process and mix in. For the Mexican rice: wash the rice three times and drain well. Heat the oil in a saucepan and brown the rice for 3 minutes, stirring, on a high heat. Blend the tomatoes in a food processor with 300 ml (10½ fl oz) water, the chopped onion and some salt until smooth, at least 2 minutes. Once the rice has browned, reduce the heat to medium and add the puréed tomato and coriander. Once the liquid has reduced down to the level of the rice, cover and cook for 2 minutes. Let it rest for at least 20 minutes. For the chicken: season the chicken on all sides with salt and pepper. Drizzle with olive oil and bake on a baking tray at 180°C (350°F) for 18 minutes. Heat the tortillas on a medium heat in a lightly oiled frying pan for 3 minutes. Make a layer of Mexican rice in the middle of the burrito, add some cold, shredded chicken, thin slices of avocado, scrambled eggs, two cheddar cheese slices, and spread with crème fraîche. To assemble: fold two opposing sides of the burrito inwards and then roll it up starting from an unfolded side. Brown the burrito by rolling it in the hot frying pan for about 2 minutes. Cut in half and serve with fresh fruit.

20TH & OLYMPIC BLVD

BUCKWHEAT BLUEBERRY PANCAKES

MAKES 4 PANCAKES
50 g (1¾ oz/⅓ cup) plain (all-purpose) flour
200 g (7 oz/1½ cups) buckwheat flour
½ teaspoon baking powder
½ teaspoon bicarbonate of soda (baking soda)
2 eggs
75 ml (2¼ fl oz) milk
375 ml (13 fl oz/1½ cups) buttermilk
45 g (1½ oz) melted butter, plus extra for frying
½ pinch salt
2 teaspoons sugar
1 handful blueberries
Maple syrup, to serve

Quickly mix all of the ingredients together, except the blueberries and maple syrup. Do not overmix or the batter might thicken. Pour a ladleful of batter into a frying pan brushed with a little butter. Add the blueberries and cook for 2 minutes on a medium heat until bubbles appear in the pancake. Turn over and cook for 1 more minute. Serve with the maple syrup.

It was at Cora's that I first discovered that, as well as being delicious, a burrito can also be an excellent breakfast (see previous page), especially before a big day. Even at 7 am, their garden patio is sometimes packed.

MUSCLE BEACH VENICE SMOOTHIE

MAKES 1 SMOOTHIE
240 ml (8 fl oz) fresh almond milk
1 frozen banana
1 small handful frozen raspberries
1 small handful frozen blueberries
1 small handful frozen blackberries
1 scoop vanilla flavour plant protein
powder (organic food stores)
1 scoop green superfood powder
(organic food stores)
1 scoop BCAA (essential amino acid food
supplement)*
1 scoop amino acid powder*
1 scoop creatine powder*
1 scoop glutamine powder*
*specialty fitness stores

Blend all the ingredients together in a food processor for
2 minutes. Serve well chilled.

*A few steps from Muscle Beach, the LA Urban Fitness Nutrition
Center is a temple, not only of bodybuilding, but also wellbeing,
with one of the most comprehensive juice bars in Los Angeles.*

PINKBERRY

FROZEN YOGHURT

MAKES 6 YOGHURTS

1.2 kg (2 lb 12 oz) Greek-style yoghurt (non-fat)
320 ml (11 fl oz) low-fat milk
75 g (2½ oz) caster (superfine) sugar
15 ml (½ fl oz) agave syrup
1 teaspoon natural vanilla extract
30 ml (1 fl oz) fresh lemon juice
1 big handful strawberries, to serve
1 handful blueberries, to serve
1 handful pomegranate seeds, to serve
1 handful Granola (page 196), to serve

Mix together the yoghurt, milk, sugar and agave syrup until the mixture is smooth and the sugar has dissolved. Add the vanilla and lemon juice. Mix together. Pour into the bowl of an ice cream machine and follow the instructions. Serve immediately for a very smooth and creamy texture (or take it out of the freezer 15 minutes before serving). Add the cut fruit or granola when serving.

I always find it very hard to settle sensibly for one or two fresh fruits and some cereal when I am faced with the full array of Pinkberry toppings. Each one is more tempting than the last. This is however the best way to enjoy Pinkberry's non-fat frozen yoghurt. They were the first to establish themselves in Los Angeles in 2005.

4TH & BROADWAY, SANTA MONICA

SANTA MONICA SEAFOOD

CIOPPINO (FISH & SEAFOOD STEW)

SERVES 2

2½ tablespoons chopped basil
4 tablespoons olive oil
10 clams (vongole)
10 mussels
4 garlic cloves
40 g (1½ oz) French shallots, chopped
1 teaspoon chilli flakes
185 ml (6 fl oz/¾ cup) white wine
125 ml (4 fl oz/½ cup) fish stock made with water and 1 fish stock cube
120 g (4¼ oz) firm white fish
10 prawns (shrimp)
50 g (1¾ oz) crabmeat
2 tablespoons chopped parsley
4 slices artisan-style bread, toasted

TOMATO SAUCE

½ celery stalk
1 onion
Olive oil
½ teaspoon sugar
½ teaspoon onion powder
½ teaspoon chilli flakes
½ teaspoon oregano
300 g (10½ oz) fresh tomatoes
100 g (3½ oz) tomato paste (concentrated tomato purée)

Make the tomato sauce in a saucepan: sauté the chopped celery and chopped onion in 2 tablespoons olive oil on a medium heat for 5 minutes. Add the sugar, onion powder, chilli flakes, oregano, 2½ teaspoons salt and ½ teaspoon freshly ground black pepper. Cook for another 5 minutes, stirring all the time. Add the diced fresh tomatoes with the tomato paste. Cook for 5 minutes, stirring. Reduce the heat and cook, covered, for 15 minutes. Put ½ tablespoon of the basil and 2 tablespoons of the olive oil in a frying pan on a high heat. Add the clams and mussels. Crush two of the garlic cloves and add those, along with the chopped shallots, 2½ teaspoons salt and the chilli flakes. Sauté for 3–4 minutes, stirring constantly. Add the wine and reduce for 3 minutes. Add the fish stock, stir well and cook for 4 minutes. Add 230 g (8 oz) of the tomato sauce, along with the fish, prawns and crabmeat. When the fish is cooked, serve with the parsley, remaining basil and two slices of toasted bread rubbed with the remaining halved garlic cloves and drizzled with the remaining olive oil.

It was a ritual: my friend Aymeric, who lived in LA, and I would go once a week to Santa Monica Seafood for its lobster roll and swordfish sliders. Spending an afternoon with Stefani, I realised the full extent of their activities and understood why they are leaders in their field. They play a pioneering role with their policy of controlled and responsible fishing.

SANTA MONICA SEAFOOD
LOBSTER ROLL

SERVES 2
1 fresh lobster or 300 g (10½ oz) frozen
or tinned lobster meat
40 g (1½ oz) butter
2 tablespoons light crème fraîche (or
light sour cream)
20 ml (½ fl oz) lemon juice
1 teaspoon grated lemon zest
2 garlic cloves
200 g (7 oz) mayonnaise
½ bunch chives
2 hot dog buns
French fries, to serve

Cook the lobster in a large pot of boiling salted water for
6 minutes, adding the claws half way through the cooking
time. Remove all of the meat and drain. Sauté the cooked
meat for 3–5 minutes in a frying pan on a medium heat with
half the butter; the lobster flesh should be golden. Whip the
light crème fraîche with the lemon juice and zest, then add
the crushed garlic and beat for 2 minutes. Gradually incorporate
this mixture into the mayonnaise. Season with ½ teaspoon
salt and ½ teaspoon freshly ground black pepper and add the
chopped chives. Set aside in the refrigerator for at least 1 hour.
Add the lobster to the sauce and mix together well. Split open
the hot dog buns and heat them in a 180°C (350°F) oven for
3 minutes, then fill the buns with the lobster mixture. Serve
with French fries.

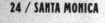

SWORDFISH SLIDERS

MAKES 3 SLIDERS

1 carrot

1 onion

A few white cabbage leaves

1 teaspoon mustard

2 tablespoons mayonnaise

½ teaspoon sugar

2 tablespoons olive oil

3 small swordfish fillets

White pepper

3 mini hamburger (slider) buns

Chipotle aïoli (page 258)

1 tomato, sliced

3 cornichons (baby gherkins)

French fries, to serve

Julienne the carrot, finely chop the onion and finely shred the cabbage leaves. Mix together the mustard, mayonnaise and sugar. Add the mayonnaise sauce to the vegetables and mix together well. Heat the olive oil in a hot frying pan on a medium heat and cook the swordfish fillets for 3–4 minutes on each side; the surface should be golden brown. Season with the white pepper just before the end of the cooking time. Toast the halved hamburger buns for 3 minutes in a 180°C (350°F) oven. To assemble: spread the bottom halves of the buns with chipotle aïoli, then top with pan-fried swordfish fillets, a slice of tomato and some of the coleslaw. Top with the other half of the bun. Skewer a small cornichon on a toothpick and insert in the slider. Serve with French fries.

THAI DISHES

CHICKEN PAD SEE EW

SERVES 1

100 g (3½ oz) wide flat rice noodles
1 tablespoon vegetable oil
1 garlic clove
125 g (4½ oz) skinless chicken breast
fillets, cut into pieces
1 egg
½ teaspoon rice vinegar
½ teaspoon soy sauce
1½ tablespoons sugar
1 handful Chinese broccoli (gai larn)
½ teaspoon dark soy sauce
½ teaspoon oyster sauce
½ teaspoon fish sauce
1 pinch white pepper

Cook the noodles as directed on the packet. Pour the oil into a very hot frying pan. Add the chopped garlic and stir for about 30 seconds. Add the chicken and stir-fry for about 3 minutes, until browned. Add the cooked rice noodles and mix well. Add the egg and stir vigorously for about 2 minutes to coat all of the mixture. Add the rice vinegar, regular soy sauce and sugar, continuing to stir vigorously for about 2 minutes. Add the Chinese broccoli, dark soy sauce, oyster sauce and fish sauce and stir-fry for 1 minute. Finish with white pepper, and mix.

What an honour it was that Henry opened the doors of his kitchen to me and I could finally find out how to achieve this complex flavour. At the bottom of my apartment in Santa Monica, I crossed the threshold of this Thai restaurant, family-run since 1986, countless times. This is the dish I miss most when I am in France, it is the taste of Los Angeles for me.

PRAWN PAD THAI

SERVES 1

100 g (3½ oz) wide flat rice noodles
1 tablespoon vegetable oil
1 garlic clove
5–7 large raw prawns (shrimp)
1 egg
1 teaspoon rice vinegar
1 tablespoon fish sauce
1½ tablespoons sugar
1 tablespoon peanuts
2 spring onions (scallions)
½ teaspoon paprika
1 handful bean sprouts
1 pinch white pepper
1 tablespoon lime juice

Cook the noodles as directed on the packet. Pour the vegetable oil into a hot wok and sauté the crushed garlic for 30 seconds, then add the peeled and deveined prawns. Cook for at least 3 minutes, until browned. Add the noodles. Mix together well. Add the egg and stir vigorously for about 2 minutes; the whole mixture needs to be coated. Add the rice vinegar, fish sauce and sugar and cook, stirring constantly, for about 2 minutes. Add the roughly crushed peanuts, sliced spring onions, paprika and bean sprouts. Stir-fry for 1 minute. Add the white pepper, stir-fry for a few seconds, take off the heat and sprinkle with lime juice.

VEGGIE GARDEN WRAP

MAKES 1 WRAP
1 carrot
1 zucchini (courgette)
Soy-ginger sauce (page 258)
40 g (1½ oz) brown rice
1 large corn tortilla
Butter, for greasing
60 g (2¼ oz) hummus
1 handful baby English spinach
½ avocado
¼ cos (romaine) lettuce
2 tomatoes
Tahini sauce (page 258)
Hot sauce, to serve

Cut the carrot and zucchini into sticks and cook them in boiling water. Drain. Add 60 ml (2 fl oz/¼ cup) of the soy-ginger sauce to the vegetables and keep them warm. Cook the rice according to the instructions on the packet. Heat the tortilla for 3 minutes in a frying pan greased with butter on a medium heat. Turn the tortilla over. To assemble the wrap: in the frying pan, off the heat, spread the tortilla with hummus and add the spinach, hot rice, pickled carrot and zucchini, sliced avocado, cos lettuce, and rounds of sliced tomato. Top with tahini sauce. Fold two edges of the tortilla inwards and roll up the wrap starting from one of the non-folded sides. Cut in half. Serve with hot sauce or what's left of the other sauces.

À VOTRE SANTÉ
KALE PIZZA

MAKES 1 PIZZA
200 g (7 oz) kale
Olive oil
1 tablespoon lemon juice
½ onion
1 ball mozzarella cheese (125 g/4½ oz)
60 g (2¼ oz) fresh goat's cheese
1 pinch chilli powder
170 g (6 oz) Pizza dough (page 262)
½ handful pine nuts

Slice the kale and marinate it in 2 tablespoons olive oil and the lemon juice for at least 1 hour in the refrigerator. Preheat the oven to its hottest setting. Slice the half onion and caramelise it on a high heat in a frying pan brushed with olive oil for about 5 minutes, stirring. Season with salt and freshly ground black pepper. Dry the mozzarella with paper towel and cut it into six or eight pieces. Mix together the kale, goat's cheese, chilli powder and onion. Season. Spread the seasoned pizza dough with the kale mixture and arrange the mozzarella on top. Bake for 15–20 minutes until the edges are brown and the mozzarella is melted. Sprinkle with the pine nuts that have been toasted in a frying pan with a drizzle of olive oil on a high heat for 4 minutes, stirring well.

I met Bashar, one of the two happy owners of this restaurant, when I sat next to his daughter there, by chance. A real institution for Angelenos, this Brentwood neighbourhood restaurant manages the delicate balance of combining pleasure and wellbeing, with generous, luscious dishes that are also fresh and balanced.

BUTTERMILK BISCUIT WITH SUNNY-SIDE UP EGGS

SERVES 6

500 g (1 lb 2 oz) blueberries
115 g (4 oz) caster (superfine) sugar
25 ml (¾ fl oz) lemon juice
450 g (1 lb/3 cups) plain (all-purpose) flour
20 g (¾ oz) bicarbonate of soda (baking soda)
100 g (3½ oz) butter
14 eggs
265 ml (9½ fl oz) buttermilk
1 tablespoon milk
6 thick slices ham
Olive oil for frying

Preheat the oven to 175°C (345°F). Bring half the blueberries, 75 g (2½ oz) of the sugar and the lemon juice to the boil, stirring. Turn off the heat, add the remaining blueberries, stir well and cool. Mix the flour, 40 g (1½ oz) of the sugar, the bicarbonate of soda and 10 g (¼ oz) salt with the cubed butter. Whisk two eggs with the buttermilk. Combine the two mixtures and knead for 5 minutes. Flatten the dough on a floured work surface to a thickness of 1.5 cm (⅝ inch). Cut out 8 cm (3¼ inch) rounds using a cookie cutter. Mix two eggs with the milk and lightly brush the top of the rounds. Bake in the oven for 15 minutes. In a frying pan on a medium heat brushed with olive oil, brown the ham on each side for 2 minutes. Fry the remaining eggs, sunny side up, in the same frying pan. For the sandwich: open up the biscuit, spread each side with blueberry jam, and insert one slice of fried ham, folded in half. Serve with the two eggs.

I still have in my memory the handshake of Brian, the chef at Farmshop, and the smile of Sarah, the manager, as well as the spectacular energy that Farmshop devotes to innovation and making sure everything is good. There are always new things in their food store, and the same applies to their menu, which changes with the seasons and the rhythm of what's available at the local farmers' markets, their only source of supply.

FARMSHOP
STEAK & EGGS

SERVES 2

125 g (4½ oz) honey
2 bunches flat-leaf parsley
20 g (¾ oz) mint
20 g (¾ oz) fresh oregano
185 ml (6 fl oz/¾ cup) freshly squeezed
orange juice
250 g (9 oz) carrots
3 or 4 long-stem artichokes
1 garlic clove, crushed
Olive oil
1 pinch thyme
A few black olives
Pulp of 1 lemon
2 underblade steaks
Peppercorn mix (page 260)
4 fried eggs (page 262)
1 pinch ras el hanout

Bring the honey to the boil with one bunch of the parsley, the mint and oregano tied up in a piece of muslin (cheesecloth). Add 185 ml (6 fl oz/¾ cup) water, the orange juice and carrots, sliced thinly lengthways. Mix and bring to the boil. Wait for the carrots to soften, about 5 minutes. Remove the carrots and keep reducing the liquid, stirring (about 15 minutes). Remove the outer fibres of the artichoke stems, and the leaves from the top until you reach the heart. Cut into four lengthways. Cook the crushed garlic for 3 minutes in a frying pan on a medium heat with 1 tablespoon olive oil. Add the thyme and artichoke quarters, and cook for 5 minutes. Coat the carrots in the reduced glaze and add them to the artichokes with some black olives and the pulp of the lemon, mixed with the remaining chopped bunch of parsley and drizzled with a little olive oil. Cook, stirring, for 3 minutes. Season. Season the steaks with some peppercorn mix and a pinch of salt and cook on a very high heat for 30 seconds on each side, then for about 1½ minutes on each side and another 30 seconds again on each side for a rare steak. For medium, add 1 minute on each side; for well done, 2 minutes on each side. Cut the steaks in half and serve with the sautéed vegetables and two fried eggs. Finish with a pinch of ras el hanout.

19TH ST SANTA MONICA & COLORADO

HARA SUSHI INC

TANGO MAKI ROLL
ARNOLD PALMER

DRY CLEAN EXPRESS. SANTA MONICA BLVD & BROCKTON AVE

SERVES 2

TANGO MAKI ROLL

100 g (3½ oz) Vinegared sushi rice (page 261)
2 sheets nori seaweed
1 avocado, sliced very thinly
1 mango, sliced very thinly
4 Tempura prawns (page 261)

UNAGI SAUCE

125 ml (4 fl oz/½ cup) mirin
125 ml (4 fl oz/½ cup) soy sauce
100 g (3½ oz) sugar
1 tablespoon soft brown sugar
1 carrot, sliced into rounds
1 onion, sliced into rounds
1 daikon (white radish), sliced into rounds
10 g (¼ oz) fresh ginger

ARNOLD PALMER

A legendary drink named after the golfer
whose nickname in the 1950s was The King.

TANGO MAKI ROLL

For the unagi sauce: place all of the sauce ingredients in a
saucepan and bring to the boil. Keep stirring on a low heat until
the texture is thick. Filter through a fine strainer. To assemble the
roll: spread the vinegared rice on one of the nori sheets, placed
on a sushi mat covered with plastic wrap on both sides. Place
the other sheet on top, a little above the rice. Make a line of
avocado and mango slices across the full width of the nori sheet
(reserving four slices of avocado and four slices of mango), 3 cm
(1¼ inches) high and 8 mm (⅜ inch) thick. Arrange the prawns two
by two, with the tails poking a little outside the sheet of nori on
both sides. Roll up with the help of the mat. Cut into four maki and
place a thin sliver of avocado and mango on top of each. Serve with
the unagi sauce.

ARNOLD PALMER

Pour 150 ml (5 fl oz) Home-made lemonade (see page 262) over
ice cubes, then 150 ml (5 fl oz) iced tea.

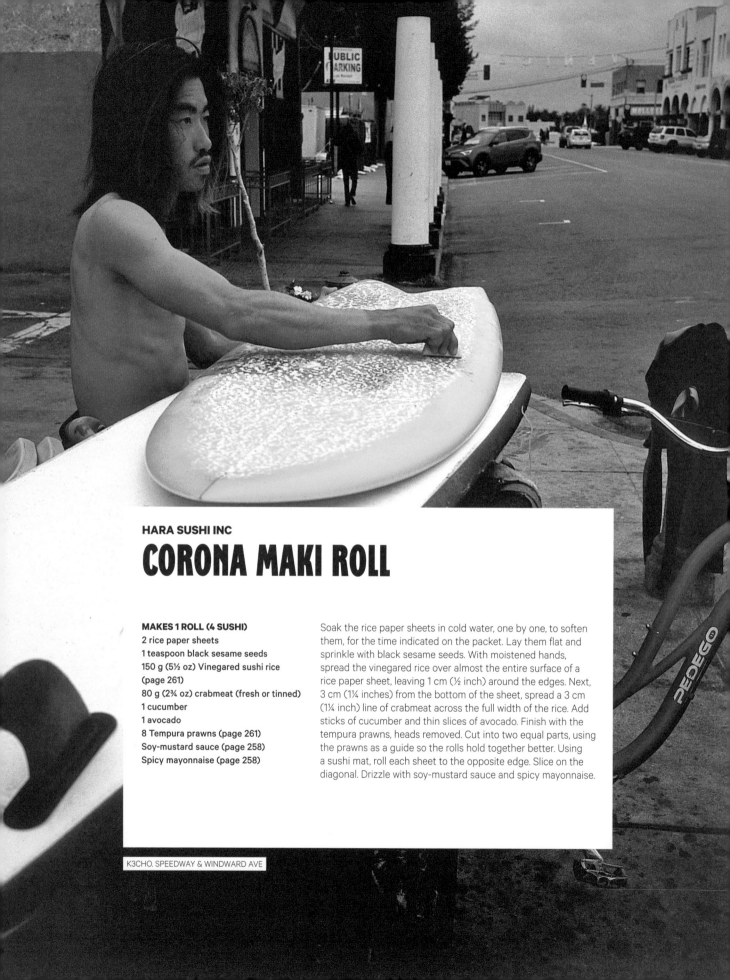

HARA SUSHI INC

CORONA MAKI ROLL

MAKES 1 ROLL (4 SUSHI)
2 rice paper sheets
1 teaspoon black sesame seeds
150 g (5½ oz) Vinegared sushi rice
(page 261)
80 g (2¾ oz) crabmeat (fresh or tinned)
1 cucumber
1 avocado
8 Tempura prawns (page 261)
Soy-mustard sauce (page 258)
Spicy mayonnaise (page 258)

Soak the rice paper sheets in cold water, one by one, to soften them, for the time indicated on the packet. Lay them flat and sprinkle with black sesame seeds. With moistened hands, spread the vinegared rice over almost the entire surface of a rice paper sheet, leaving 1 cm (½ inch) around the edges. Next, 3 cm (1¼ inches) from the bottom of the sheet, spread a 3 cm (1¼ inch) line of crabmeat across the full width of the rice. Add sticks of cucumber and thin slices of avocado. Finish with the tempura prawns, heads removed. Cut into two equal parts, using the prawns as a guide so the rolls hold together better. Using a sushi mat, roll each sheet to the opposite edge. Slice on the diagonal. Drizzle with soy-mustard sauce and spicy mayonnaise.

K3CHO. SPEEDWAY & WINDWARD AVE

SAKE BOMB

MAKES 1 GLASS
1 small glass heated sake
2 chopsticks
1 cold beer

Sit the glass of sake on the two chopsticks, resting parallel to each other on top of the glass of beer. Bang your fist on the table to make the sake drop down and drink in one go, shouting: 'Kanpai!'.

Located at the foot the Santa Monica apartment where I lived in 2010, every birthday, end of semester, etc. was celebrated at Hara Sushi Inc. It was always a feast. It is where I discovered the madness of Californian sushi, made from all kinds of unexpected fruit, vegetables and sauces.

S MUIRFIELD ROAD & WILSHIRE BLVD

MELROSE AVE & VINE ST

DOWNTOWN LA
CHINATOWN
UNIVERSITY PARK
ART DISTRICT

SPRINKLES CUPCAKES
VANILLA CUPCAKES

MAKES 25 CUPCAKES

VANILLA CAKE BASE
300 g (10½ oz/2 cups) soft (cake) flour or plain (all-purpose) flour
320 g (11¼ oz) caster (superfine) sugar
12 g (¼ oz) bicarbonate of soda (baking soda)
135 ml (4½ fl oz) milk
2 eggs
4 egg yolks
3 drops natural vanilla extract
180 g (6½ oz) butter

FROSTING
1½ egg whites
85 g (3 oz) caster (superfine) sugar
170 g (6 oz) butter
2 drops natural vanilla extract

For the cake base: mix together the flour, sugar, bicarbonate of soda and ¼ teaspoon salt. Separately, mix together the milk, eggs, yolks and vanilla. Put the dry mixture, cubed butter and half the wet mixture into the bowl of an electric standmixer. Beat on high speed for 4 minutes. Add the rest of the wet mixture in three stages, beating for 2 minutes at medium speed after each addition. Bake in muffin tins at 170°C (325°F) for 16 minutes. For the frosting: heat the egg whites and sugar in the top of a double boiler until the sugar dissolves. The mixture should be hot to the touch. Whisk with a beater to make a meringue. Add the cubed butter, ½ pinch salt and the vanilla and continue beating until light and creamy. Use a piping (icing) bag to ice the cakes.

It was in front of Sprinkles in February 2010 that I witnessed a stampede outside a restaurant for the first time. Candace, the founder, can claim to have opened the world's first cupcake bakery in Beverly Hills. Her fresh cupcakes are inimitable. This is the cupcake recipe from Blend, developed with Camilla Malmquist, a talented American pastry chef based in Paris.

NZ SINNERS. N LARCHMONT BLVD & ROSEWOOD AVE

CALIFORNIA PIZZA KITCHEN
THAI CHICKEN PIZZA

MAKES 1 PIZZA
1 large skinless chicken breast fillet
Olive oil
Thai sauce (page 257)
Pizza dough for 1 base (recipe page 262)
225 g (8 oz) grated mozzarella cheese
4 spring onions (scallions)
75 g (2½ oz) carrots
50 g (1¾ oz) bean sprouts
2 tablespoons peanuts
2 coriander (cilantro) sprigs

Flatten the chicken breast with a rolling pin, drizzle with olive oil, and season with a pinch of salt and freshly ground black pepper. In a hot frying pan brushed with olive oil, cook the chicken on a medium heat for about 2 minutes on one side. Lower the heat, turn over the breast and cook for 7–8 minutes on the other side. Dice the chicken and add to a bowl containing half the Thai sauce. Mix well. Cool, then place in the refrigerator. Spread out the dough on a floured baking tray to about 30 cm (12 inches) in diameter. Spread the rest of the Thai sauce over the base using the underside of a ladle, starting from the middle and tracing a spiral outwards. Scatter with the mozzarella cheese. In an oven heated to its maximum temperature (ideally on a pizza stone), bake for 12–15 minutes, or until the edges are golden brown. Top the cooled pizza with the diced marinated chicken and drizzle with the Thai sauce marinade left in the bowl. Bake for 5 minutes Add the thinly sliced spring onions, julienned carrots, bean sprouts, crushed peanuts and coriander.

For me, this pizza is an emblem of the Los Angeles food scene and of California, generally. All the cultures combine their inspirations and techniques in this dish, using local ingredients. This is a reinterpretation of a Thai dish as a pizza, where a peanut sauce replaces the famous tomato sauce base.

DTLA CHEESE

AVOCADO TOAST

MAKES 4 TOASTS
1 bunch chives
120 g (4¼ oz) ricotta cheese
1 teaspoon lemon juice
2 avocados
4 slices artisan-style bread
½ pinch paprika
½ pinch cumin
1 bulb spring onion (scallion)

Mix the chopped chives with the ricotta. Add a pinch of salt and 5 pinches freshly ground black pepper, mix, then add the lemon juice and mix again. Roughly mash the avocados. Spread the toasted bread with the ricotta-chive mix and cover the whole surface with avocado. Sprinkle with the paprika, cumin, chopped bulb spring onion and a little salt and pepper.

Bringing together generosity and finesse, DTLA CHEESE, the Grand Central Market cheese shop with a thousand different products elevates what, everywhere else would be a side-dish, to the level of a main meal. Their secret is perhaps that each item on their menu is taken very seriously. If you are not a fan of avocado, you must go there for their grilled cheese.

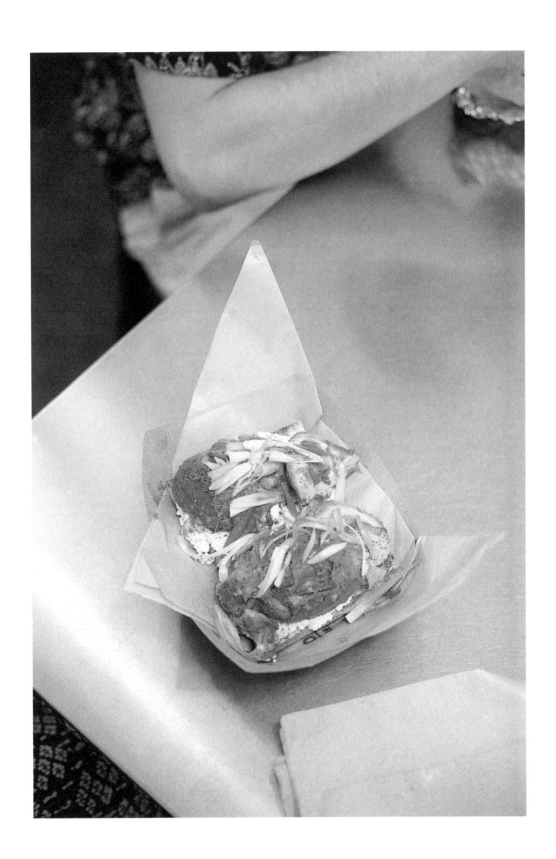

VITALITY SMOOTHIE

MAKES 1 JUICE
1 apple
200 g (7 oz) pineapple flesh
2 kale leaves
1 handful English spinach
½ avocado
½ cucumber
1 piece fresh ginger

Seed and quarter the apple and place with the rest of the ingredients in a blender. Blend for 3 minutes. The texture should be smooth and homogenous.

A customer who bought his vitality smoothie at Press Brothers Juicery very kindly made sure I did not fall from the stool I stood on to take the picture of the queue at Eggslut. Kindness and taking care of others are in the DNA of this business, created by two brothers raised on juiced fruits and vegetables, describing their mother as 'an avid juicer of 20 years'.

EGGSLUT
BACON & EGG SANDWICH

MAKES 4 MUFFINS
6 eggs
30 g (1 oz) butter
1 bunch chives
4 English muffins or brioche buns
60 g (2¼ oz) Chipotle aïoli (page 258)
4 rashers bacon
4 cheddar cheese slices

Break the eggs into a frying pan on a medium heat and add the diced butter. Stir to break the yolks. Season after 2 minutes with salt and freshly ground black pepper. Stop cooking after 5 minutes. Add the chopped chives and stir. To assemble: spread the inside of the muffin with chipotle aïoli, add the scrambled eggs topped with a rasher of bacon – fried for 5 minutes each side in a frying pan on a medium heat – a slice of cheddar, and close the muffins.

After more than an hour of waiting and almost falling off a stool, I found that Eggslut deserves this obsession. I didn't have the patience to take a photo of my sandwich. Muriel, Whitney and their friend agreed to let me hold them back a few minutes so I could immortalise theirs. Starting with unbeatable raw materials (including fresh buns), Eggslut sets itself apart with its egg-cooking know-how. It is with great humility therefore that I have created this interpretation of their dish. Obviously, the waiting time at Eggslut makes their sandwiches taste even better.

HAWTHORN AVE & HIGHLAND AVE

DUKE'S, LOS FLORES CANYON RD, MALIBU

AVOCADO-PESTO-RICOTTA TOAST
CHIA SEED PUDDING

SERVES 4
AVOCADO-PESTO-RICOTTA TOAST
4 slices wholemeal (whole-wheat) bread
100 g (3½ oz) ricotta cheese
Lemon zest
2 avocados
WALNUT PESTO
1 garlic clove
50 g (1¾ oz/½ cup) walnuts
45 g (1½ oz) basil leaves
75 ml (2¼ fl oz) olive oil
2 pinches salt
50 g (1¾ oz) finely grated parmesan cheese
CHIA SEED PUDDING
450 ml (16 fl oz) coconut milk
60 ml (2 fl oz/¼ cup) agave syrup
2 pinches cinnamon
2 ripe bananas
45 g (1½ oz) chia seeds (organic food stores)
25 g (1 oz/¼ cup) desiccated coconut

AVOCADO-PESTO-RICOTTA TOAST

For the walnut pesto: crush the garlic and process with the rest of the pesto ingredients, except the parmesan, in a food processor for about 20 seconds until the texture is smooth. Add the parmesan and process for 10 seconds. For the avocado-pesto-ricotta toast: spread the toasted bread with the walnut pesto, add the ricotta, sprinkle with lemon zest and season with salt and freshly ground black pepper. Place half an avocado, sliced into rounds, on top.

CHIA SEED PUDDING

Blend together the coconut milk, agave syrup, cinnamon, a pinch of salt and one mashed banana in a food processor for about 20 seconds. The texture should be smooth. Add the chia seeds and mix. Chill for about 2 hours. Before serving, add some rounds of fresh banana and a little desiccated coconut.

Impresso Cafe felt like an oasis in the middle of downtown Los Angeles. You need to drink something slightly sour with these sweet, mild dishes, such as a kombucha tea. The coffee range is impressive here – this place is a local institution.

FRUTA CON CHILE Y LIMÓN

MAKES 1 CUP
Your choice of fruit or vegetable
Lime juice
Chilli powder

Cut up the fruit or vegetable and place it in a bowl. Pour over the lime juice and sprinkle with salt and chilli powder.

Whatever fruits or vegetables you choose, the important thing is the three secret ingredients that the holders of these stands add to give the fruits their kick. They go up and down the sidewalks at Los Angeles' major intersections as soon as the sun comes up. This recipe works with all fruits and vegetables, but the best sellers are cucumber, melon, pineapple, mango and coconut.

S HILL ST & W 3RD ST

PHILIPPE THE ORIGINAL

FRENCH DIP SANDWICH

MAKES 4 SANDWICHES

1 beef stock cube
1 onion
1 carrot
1 celery stalk
1 leek
2 garlic cloves
A few thyme sprigs
900 g (2 lb) piece roasting beef
¼ teaspoon oregano
¼ teaspoon nutmeg
¼ teaspoon sage
½ teaspoon cloves
½ teaspoon allspice
4 halved baguettes or 4 buns
90 g (3¼ oz) mustard
A few large pickles (gherkins)

Preheat the oven to 150°C (300°F). Make up the beef stock with the stock cube, according to the amount of water indicated on the packet. Chop the onion and slice the carrot, celery and white part of the leek into rounds, then mix with the chopped garlic and thyme in a large baking dish. Cover the beef with all the dried herbs and spices, season well with salt and freshly ground black pepper and roast in the oven for 45 minutes, fat side up. Take the beef out of the oven, wrap it in foil and let it rest for 30 minutes. Pour the contents of the baking dish into a frying pan and cook on a high heat, stirring, until all the liquid has evaporated. Transfer to a saucepan with 480 ml (16½ fl oz) beef stock, bring to the boil on a medium heat, then reduce the heat to low. Cook for about 30 more minutes, stirring, or until half the liquid has evaporated. Strain the sauce and add a pinch of salt and pepper. Keep warm. Heat the halved baguettes in a 180°C (350°F) oven for about 3 minutes. Just before filling the sandwich, wet the cut side of the bread with the sauce, a little or a lot, and lay thin slices of roast beef on top. Serve with the mustard and the pickles, cut into quarters lengthways, on the side.

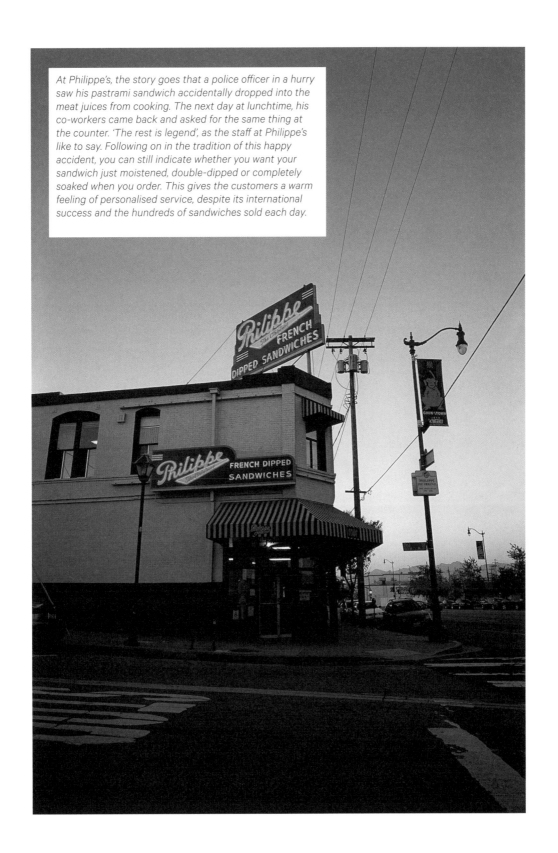

At Philippe's, the story goes that a police officer in a hurry saw his pastrami sandwich accidentally dropped into the meat juices from cooking. The next day at lunchtime, his co-workers came back and asked for the same thing at the counter. 'The rest is legend', as the staff at Philippe's like to say. Following on in the tradition of this happy accident, you can still indicate whether you want your sandwich just moistened, double-dipped or completely soaked when you order. This gives the customers a warm feeling of personalised service, despite its international success and the hundreds of sandwiches sold each day.

BANANA CREAM PIE

MAKES 1 PIE

PASTRY

150 g (5½ oz/1 cup) plain (all-purpose) flour

½ teaspoon caster (superfine) sugar

80 g (2¾ oz) butter

60 ml (2 fl oz/¼ cup) iced water

FILLING

200 g (7 oz) caster (superfine) sugar

40 g (1½ oz/⅓ cup) cornflour (cornstarch)

735 ml (25 fl oz) milk

4 egg yolks

½ teaspoon natural vanilla extract

40 g (1½ oz) butter

2½ ripe bananas

CHANTILLY CREAM

230 g (8½ oz) thin (pouring/whipping) cream, cold

2 teaspoons icing (confectioners') sugar

1 teaspoon natural vanilla extract

For the pastry: mix together the flour, ½ teaspoon salt, the sugar and cubed butter. Add the iced water, little by little, and mix; the texture should be smooth and not sticky. Shape into a ball. Roll the dough out between two sheets of baking paper. Set aside in the refrigerator for at least 1 hour (ideally 24 hours), with the baking paper. Place the pastry in a cake tin, fold the overhang inwards and press the pastry against the inside of the tin with a fork. Cover with foil, place a weight on the foil to stop it puffing up and bake at 200°C (400°F) for 20 minutes. Remove the foil and cook for 5–10 minutes more to lightly brown. For the filling: mix together the sugar, cornflour, ½ teaspoon salt and the milk. Cook on a medium heat for about 7 minutes or until bubbles appear. Reduce the heat to low and cook for a further 2 minutes. Off the heat, gradually mix in the whisked yolks. Return to a medium heat and, when it comes to the boil, cook for another 2 minutes, making sure not to scramble the eggs. Remove from the heat, stir in the vanilla and the butter in cubes, mix and let it stand. Spread half of the filling on the cooled pastry, top with some slices of banana, then make another layer of filling. Chill for 2 hours, ideally overnight. For the chantilly cream: beat the cream for 2 minutes, add the sugar and vanilla. Beat for another 2 minutes. Spread on top of the filling.

JACKS N JOE

SOUTHERN CALIFORNIA PANCAKES

MAKES 10 PANCAKES
2 eggs
200 ml (7 fl oz) milk
250 g (9 oz/1⅔ cups) plain (all-purpose)
flour
175 g (6 oz) caster (superfine) sugar
1 sachet (11 g/¼ oz) baking powder
1 tablespoon icing (confectioners') sugar
120 g (4¼ oz) crème fraîche
Melted butter
A few strawberries
1 small handful blueberries
Whipped cream, to serve

Mix together the eggs and milk and, separately, mix together the flour, sugar, baking powder and a pinch of salt. Combine the two mixtures and mix until smooth. Put this batter in the refrigerator for 1 hour. Whisk the icing sugar and crème fraîche in a chilled mixing bowl until peaks form. For one pancake, pour a ladleful of batter into a non-stick frying pan brushed with melted butter. Cook for 2 minutes, or until bubbles appear. Turn and cook for two-thirds of the time the first side was cooked. Serve with sliced rounds of strawberry, blueberries and whipped cream.

Whatever the hour of day, when you go to Jacks N Joe all the staff give off the same positive energy and lightness that's essential to a successful breakfast. It's as if Jacks N Joe is protecting customers from bad news, emails and phone calls, one pancake at a time.

INTELLIGENTSIA COFFEE

ICED COFFEE

SERVES 2
350 g (12 oz) ice cubes
100 ml (3½ fl oz) full-cream (whole) milk
15 ml (½ fl oz) agave syrup
4 espresso coffees

Place a handful of ice cubes, the milk, agave syrup and the espressos in a cocktail shaker. Shake vigorously for 2–3 minutes. Strain into two glasses filled with the remaining ice cubes. Drink through a straw.

Intelligentsia Coffee is the pioneer of the 'third wave of coffee', which strives to improve every process of coffee production. Whenever I go into one of their coffee bars, I experience a religious feeling at the sight of the architecture and the staff concentrating on operating the complex machinery. Here, everything is organised around celebrating and refining the 'black gold'.

LOS ANGELES TRADE TECHNICAL COLLEGE. RALPH T. GUTHRIE SIGN PAINTING CLASS

SIGN PAINTING, RICH LESSONS FROM THE MASTER

Having always been fascinated by the art of writing in all its forms, I was familiar with the legendary Ralph 'Doc' Guthrie from his books on sign painting, as well as through videos. His talent has made him famous around the world and, when Roxanne, his assistant, confirmed that Doc would let me attend one of his classes, I was ecstatic. Doc teaches at the Los Angeles Trade Technical College, which offers the oldest sign graphics program in the United States (since 1923). I had heard about his teaching abilities, but I didn't expect to meet someone who invested as much energy on a daily basis in helping young people (or not-so-young, and some in rehabilitation) face working life in the best possible conditions, with the odds on

their side. It doesn't matter how much time or energy they need, they don't leave the college without being equipped to live their passion. This despite a tough, heavy curriculum, and students of all stripes at very different levels. I took away a very strong message of hope from Doc Guthrie. We barely had time to talk about him, he was always showing me some wonder that one of his students had already produced, relative to their level. Doc has a gift for giving students self-confidence, which is even rarer than all the other qualities for which he is known.

AVOCADO & RADISH TOAST

MAKES 3 PIECES OF TOAST
3 slices artisan-style bread
Unsalted butter
SMASHED AVOCADO
2 avocados
2 teaspoons lemon juice
1 tablespoon finely chopped onion
Salt and freshly ground black pepper
RADISH SALAD
1 handful radishes
1 tablespoon lemon juice
2 teaspoons olive oil
½ teaspoon salt
½ teaspoon freshly ground black pepper
GARNISH
Fresh dill
Fresh chives
Freshly ground black pepper
Fine sea salt
Cherry tomatoes (optional)
Slices of lemon (optional)

Roughly mash the avocados and add the rest of the smashed avocado ingredients. Mix well. Cut the radishes into matchsticks, then mix together all of the salad ingredients. Toast the bread. Cool the toast and assemble, in this order: a layer of butter, the radish salad (spread it out with your fingers right to the edge of the toast), then the smashed avocado. Sprinkle with dill, chives, pepper and fine sea salt. Garnish with cherry tomatoes and lemon slices, if desired.

Welcoming me at the entrance to the Zinc Cafe, John was the first to tell me about Alice Waters, the mother of the Californian cuisine movement and one of its strongest inspirations. Not only is it Zinc Cafe's ambition to offer dishes all day (and every day restart from scratch, since everything is home-made, from the pastries to the juices, all the dishes, pizzas, desserts and cocktails), but also to offer a constantly changing range of decorative objects and books. It was the humility of owner, John, however, that made the biggest impression on me. He follows the seasons for his menu, just as he did on the first day, greets customers with a smile, just as he did on the first day, and the dishes are still like home cooking, as they were created by either himself or his mother.

ZINC CAFE & MARKET & BAR

ASPARAGUS SANDWICH

MAKES 4 PIECES OF TOAST
400 g (14 oz) green asparagus
Olive oil
Coarse salt
60 g (2¼ oz) Japanese (panko)
breadcrumbs
30 g (1 oz) butter
300 g (10½ oz) cauliflower
50 g (1¾ oz) onion
2 garlic cloves
125 ml (4 fl oz/½ cup) thin (pouring/
whipping) cream
1 pinch ground nutmeg
4 slices artisan-style bread
100 g (3½ oz/1 cup) grated cheddar cheese
4 eggs
Vinegar

Brush the asparagus with olive oil and add 2 pinches of coarse salt. Place the asparagus on a baking tray and bake in a 220°C (425°F) oven for 12 minutes. After 6 minutes, spread out the Japanese breadcrumbs on another tray and season with coarse salt and add a few tiny pieces of the butter. Remove the leaves and stem from the cauliflower and slice the florets. Mix with the finely chopped onion and garlic, cream, nutmeg, salt, the remaining butter and 1 large pinch freshly ground black pepper. Cook this mixture with some coarse salt on a medium heat until soft. Purée the cooled mixture. Toast the slices of bread and spread them with a generous layer of cauliflower purée, add a few asparagus spears and sprinkle with cheddar. Poach the eggs in unsalted boiling water with some vinegar added for about 3 minutes. Place them on the pieces of toast. Sprinkle with breadcrumbs. Reheat in the oven for 3–5 minutes.

PALMETTO ST & MOLINO ST

MAC & CHEESE PIZZA

MAKES 4 PIZZAS
Pizza dough for 1 base (recipe page 262 or buy from your local pizzeria)
100 g (3½ oz) grated mozzarella cheese
MAC & CHEESE
115 g (4 oz) small elbow macaroni
15 g (½ oz) butter
225 ml (7¾ fl oz) full-cream (whole) milk
60 g (2 oz/¼ cup) ricotta cheese
90 g (3¼ oz) vintage cheddar cheese, grated
125 g (4½ oz) aged parmesan cheese, grated

Preheat the oven to 180°C (350°F). For the mac and cheese: cook the pasta following the packet directions. Drain. Add the butter, milk, ricotta, 70 g (2½ oz) of the cheddar, 90 g (3 oz) of the parmesan, a pinch of salt and some freshly ground black pepper to the hot pasta. Mix together quickly. Bake the pasta sprinkled with the rest of the cheddar and parmesan for 25–30 minutes, until the top is golden brown. Flatten the pizza dough on a floured surface: starting from the middle and leaving a thick edge around the outside, stretch the dough to 30 cm (12 inches) in diameter. Add the mozzarella cheese and bake in the oven at the maximum temperature setting (ideally on a pizza stone) for 15–20 minutes until the edges are brown and the mozzarella is melted. When the pizza comes out of the oven, wait 5 minutes, then spread over some mac and cheese. Return to the oven for no more than 2 minutes before serving.

The founders of Pizzannista! have shown the self-discipline required of professional skateboarders to leave a mark on their generation with their gourmet pizzeria concept. Every Sunday night, they offer what is undeniably one of the most decadent and addictive pizzas I've ever eaten: the mac & cheese pizza. Great names in skating from all over the world can be found here.

STEF. VENICE BEACH RECREATION CENTER

Chap. 3

HERMOSA BEACH
INGLEWOOD
HUNTINGTON PARK

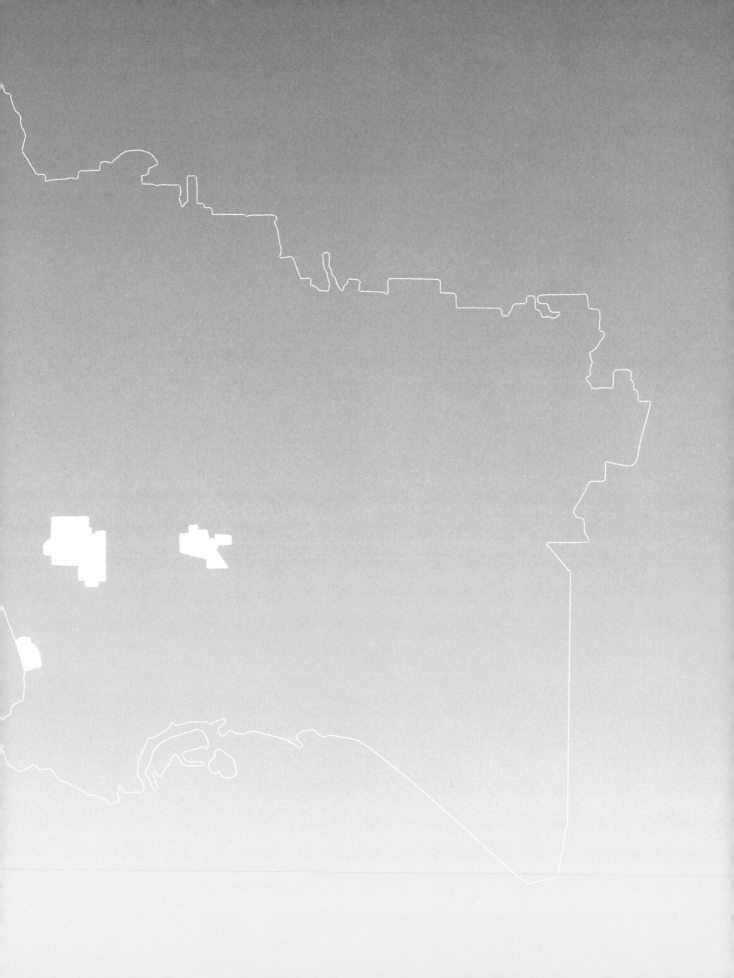

PARADISE BOWLS

STRAWBERRY SMOOTHIE

MAKES 1 SMOOTHIE
200 ml (7 fl oz) almond milk
1 frozen banana
1 tablespoon peanut butter
A big handful of strawberries

Blend all the ingredients together in a food processor for 2 minutes, until the mixture is smooth and creamy.

Bowl by bowl, based on the fresh produce of the day, Paradise Bowls helps make Hermosa Beach even more idyllic than it already is. It's a landmark for the locals. That day, the staff invited me to the other side of the counter with the same smile and energy they welcomed me with when I walked into their store.

CHRISTIAN. BELVEDERE SKATEPARK

PARADISE BOWLS

ACAI BREAKFAST BOWL

SERVES 1

1 small handful goji berries

125 ml (4 fl oz/½ cup) apple juice

2 tablespoons acai powder (organic food stores)

1 frozen banana

60 g (2¼ oz) frozen blueberries

60 g (2¼ oz) frozen strawberries

1 mango

1 kiwi fruit

A few fresh blueberries

Soak the goji berries in the apple juice for 5 minutes, then take them out and set aside. Blend the apple juice with the acai powder and frozen fruit in a food processor for 30 seconds, until there are no more lumps. Serve with pieces of mango and kiwi fruit, the blueberries and the goji berries.

«LOVE FOR PIE». 13TH ST & HERMOSA AVE, HERMOSA BEACH

ETHAN

93 / HERMOSA BEACH

WAFFLES WITH FRIED CHICKEN

MAKES 2 SANDWICHES

CHICKEN

25 g (1 oz) soft brown sugar

40 g (1½ oz) salt

2 chicken thighs, on the bone

500 ml (17 fl oz/2 cups) buttermilk

5 g (⅛ oz) freshly ground black pepper

1 pinch cumin

1 pinch paprika

COATING

250 g (9 oz/1⅔ cups) plain (all-purpose) flour

2 teaspoons cornflour (cornstarch)

WAFFLES

Vegetable oil

150 g (5½ oz/1 cup) plain (all-purpose) flour

1 teaspoon caster (superfine) sugar

1 teaspoon baking powder

¼ teaspoon espelette pepper (gourmet delicatessens)

50 g (1¾ oz) butter

2 large eggs, separated

240 ml (8 fl oz) buttermilk

MAPLE SYRUP BUTTER

50 g (1¾ oz) butter, softened

50 g (1¾ oz) lightly salted butter, softened

45 ml (1½ fl oz) maple syrup

1 pinch fine sea salt

Pistachio nut kernels

Apricot jam

For the chicken: dissolve the brown sugar and salt in 2 litres (70 fl oz/8 cups) water. Remove the bones and skin from the thighs and submerge them in this brining liquid overnight. Rinse them well the next day. Mix together the buttermilk, 2 teaspoons of the salt, the pepper, cumin and paprika. For the coating: mix together the flour, cornflour and season with ½ teaspoon salt and some pepper. Dip the thighs into the buttermilk mixture, then into the flour mixture. Deep-fry the chicken at 180°C (350°F) in a deep-fryer for 5–7 minutes; the crust should be golden. Alternatively, heat 4 cm (1½ inches) oil in a frying pan on a high heat and cook for 15 minutes, turning every 2 minutes. Place the fried chicken on a metal drainer or rack. For the waffles: heat a waffle maker, brushed with vegetable oil. Mix together the flour, caster (superfine) sugar, baking powder and espelette pepper. Separately, mix together the melted cubes of butter with the egg yolks and buttermilk. Gradually pour the wet mixture into the flour mixture, and mix together. Beat the egg whites to firm peaks and add them to the mixture. Mix well. Cook the waffles according to the instructions for the waffle maker. For the maple butter: whisk together the cubed, softened butters and the maple syrup, sprinkle with fine sea salt and chill. To assemble: cut the waffle in half, arrange the fried chicken on the plate and drizzle with some maple syrup and roughly crushed pistachio nut kernels. Serve with the maple syrup butter and apricot jam on the side.

Near my table at Abigaile, a large family had come together to celebrate the graduation of one of its younger members. Abigaile is that kind of place: large enough to feel comfortable and, despite a very modern menu, able to offer each generation something to their taste, because it is delicious. When you go as a group, there is another advantage, apart from being able to enjoy their novel dishes, and that is being able to share and sample them all.

OCEAN DRIVE & MANHATTAN BEACH BLVD, MANHATTAN BEACH

97 / HERMOSA BEACH

ABIGAILE
FRIED CHICKEN SANDWICH

MAKES 2 SANDWICHES
2 small potatoes
2 eggs
Harissa hollandaise (page 259)
Rocket (arugula), halved cherry
tomatoes, sliced radishes and shaved
parmesan cheese, to serve
MAPLE SYRUP-SAGE BISCUITS
5 or 6 sage leaves
500 g (1 lb 2 oz/3⅓ cups) plain
(all-purpose) flour
2 sachets (10 g/¼ oz each) baking
powder
125 g (4½ oz) salted butter, at room
temperature
115 ml (3¾ fl oz) milk
4 tablespoons maple syrup
Coarse salt
CHICKEN, MARINADE AND COATING
25 g (1 oz) soft brown sugar
2 chicken thighs
500 ml (17 fl oz/2 cups) buttermilk
1 pinch cumin
1 pinch paprika
225 g (8 oz/1½ cups) plain (all-purpose)
flour
2 teaspoons cornflour (cornstarch)

For the biscuits: finely shred, then chop the sage. Mix with the
flour, baking powder and cubed butter. Add the milk, little by little,
until it forms a slightly sticky ball. Spread the dough over a baking
tray and cut it into 12 squares. Top each biscuit with some maple
syrup and a pinch of coarse salt. Cook for 10 minutes in a 200°C
(400°F) oven. For the chicken: dissolve the sugar and 30 g (1 oz)
salt in 2 litres (70 fl oz/8 cups) water. Remove the bones and skin
of the thighs and submerge them in the brining liquid overnight.
Rinse the next day. Mix together the buttermilk, 1 teaspoon salt,
1 teaspoon freshly ground black pepper, the cumin and paprika.
Prepare the coating by mixing together the flour, cornflour,
¾ teaspoon salt and ½ teaspoon pepper. Dip the chicken into
the buttermilk mixture, then into the flour mixture. Deep-fry the
chicken at 180°C (350°F) in a deep-fryer for 5–7 minutes; until
the outside is golden. (Or heat 4 cm/1½ inches oil in a frying pan
on a high heat and cook the thighs for 15 minutes, turning every
2 minutes. Drain the excess oil.) For the potatoes: cut the
potatoes into matchsticks, rinse and drain. Heat 5 cm (2 inches)
oil to 180°C (350°F) in a frying pan on a medium heat. Gradually
add the julienned potatoes, stirring with a metal spatula. Cook
for about 4 minutes, until golden brown. Place on a baking tray
lined with paper towel. Wait for 3 minutes, then transfer them to
a mixing bowl. Season. Fry two eggs. Assemble, in this order: a
maple syrup-sage biscuit, 1 fried chicken thigh and 1 fried egg
balanced on top. Top with some harissa hollandaise and cover
with the straw potatoes. Add some rocket, halved cherry
tomatoes, sliced radish and shavings of parmesan cheese.

MANHATTAN BEACH PIER

CHICKEN WINGS HASH BROWN

SERVES 2
About 10 chicken wings
200 g (7 oz/1⅓ cups) plain (all-purpose) flour
2 litres (70 fl oz/8 cups) peanut oil
2 potatoes
50 g (1¾ oz) salted butter

Coat the chicken wings well with the flour and deep-fry them for 8–10 minutes at 180°C (350°F), or in 5 cm (2 inches) peanut oil in a deep saucepan for 9 minutes on a high heat. Cut the potatoes into matchsticks, rinse them until the water runs clear, and drain well. In a small heavy-based saucepan, melt the butter on a low heat, without stirring. Shake the saucepan and skim any white particles from the surface. Pour the butter into a deep frying pan on a high heat to a depth of about 5 mm (¼ inch). Add the potatoes, mix and cook for 4–6 minutes on each side, making sure they don't burn. Serve the chicken wings and hash brown separately with some hot sauce and fruit.

FRENCH TOAST

SERVES 5

1 vanilla bean, split and seeds scraped
250 ml (9 fl oz/1 cup) milk
10 slices brioche
100 g (3½ oz) butter
Icing (confectioners') sugar
500 ml (17 fl oz/2 cups) thin (pouring/whipping) cream, chilled
Maple syrup, to serve

Heat the vanilla seeds and milk in a saucepan over medium heat, but do not let it come to the boil or foam. Soak the brioche in the milk. Cook the slices in a buttered frying pan on a medium heat for about 2 minutes on one side, or until browned. Sprinkle with icing sugar before turning the brioche over. Cook on the second side for 3 minutes, or until crispy. Sprinkle with icing sugar before turning over and serving. Whip the chilled cream. (For a sweet whipped cream, add some icing sugar when the cream starts to thicken.) Serve the French toast with butter, maple syrup and cream.

If it was just about it being one of the oldest operating diners in Los Angeles, or being famous since a long scene from Pulp Fiction was filmed there, the parking lot at Pann's would not be as jam-packed as it is every day. Not only are all of its breakfasts mouthwatering, but the welcome from the staff means you always feel good when you eat there. I was very grateful to their chef Patrick, who is French, for letting me sit alongside him on several occasions.

EGGS BENEDICT

SERVES 4

500 g (1 lb 2 oz) beef brisket
Barbecue sauce (page 257)
1 large handful English spinach
Iced water
Lightly salted butter
4 potatoes (bintje or monalisa)
Peanut or other oil for deep-frying
4 English muffins
1 large tomato
4 Poached eggs (page 262)
Hollandaise sauce (page 257)
100 g (3½ oz) cheddar cheese
100 g (3½ oz) sour cream
1 spring onion (scallion)

Bake the brisket overnight at 100°C (200°F) in an oiled baking dish, covered with foil. The next day, slice the meat across the grain very thinly, then across the slices into matchsticks. Mix the shredded meat with half of its volume of barbecue sauce. Add the spinach, stems removed, to a saucepan of boiling water with 5 teaspoons of salt. When the water comes back to the boil, take the spinach out and plunge it immediately into iced water. Drain. Sauté the spinach for 5 minutes in a frying pan on a medium heat with a small knob of lightly salted butter. Season with salt and freshly ground black pepper. Boil the potatoes for 5 minutes, cut them in half and scoop out the middle, leaving about 5 mm (¼ inch) potato inside the skin. Deep-fry the potato shells in peanut oil for 4–7 minutes at 180°C (350°F). On a halved and toasted muffin, place a slice of tomato with a pinch of salt and 1 poached egg, drizzle with hollandaise sauce and sprinkle with grated cheddar. Serve with two potato halves, the shredded beef in barbecue sauce, the sour cream, the remaining grated cheddar cheese and the chopped spring onion.

VANILLA DONUTS

MAKES ABOUT 18 DONUTS
540 g (1 lb 3 oz) plain (all-purpose) flour
20 g (¾ oz) fresh yeast (from bakery)
150 g (5½ oz/1¼ cups) icing (confectioners')
sugar
20 g (¾ oz) salt
Peanut oil
GLAZE
150 g (5½ oz) icing (confectioners') sugar
3–4 tablespoons milk or water
2 teaspoons natural vanilla extract (optional)

For the glaze: put the sugar in a bowl and stir in the water and vanilla gradually, until the sugar has dissolved and you have a smooth, pourable glaze. For the donuts: knead the flour with 215 ml (7½ fl oz) water, the yeast, icing sugar and salt in an electric stand mixer on medium speed for 11 minutes. The temperature of the dough should stay between 25° and 29°C (77° and 84°F). Let the dough prove for 45 minutes to 1¼ hours. It should triple in size. On a floured work surface, roll out the dough to a thickness of 3–4 cm (1¼–1½ inches). Use a 10 cm (4 inch) cookie cutter to cut out rounds, then cut a hole in the middle of the rounds with a 3 cm (1¼ inch) cutter. Bring a saucepan of water to the boil. Heat the oven to 60°C (140°F). Turn off the oven and place the saucepan in the oven for 20 minutes. Place the donuts on a baking tray lined with baking paper and place in the oven for 35–40 minutes. When you touch the donut, your finger should leave an imprint. Rest the donuts for 3–5 minutes, then fry them in 4 cm (1½ inches) oil in a frying pan for about 2 minutes on each side. Glaze the donuts straight after frying.

Randy's Donuts is one of the most famous bakeries in the world. The world has seen its huge donut-shaped sign on-screen in blockbuster movies. The official recipe is a very well-guarded secret.

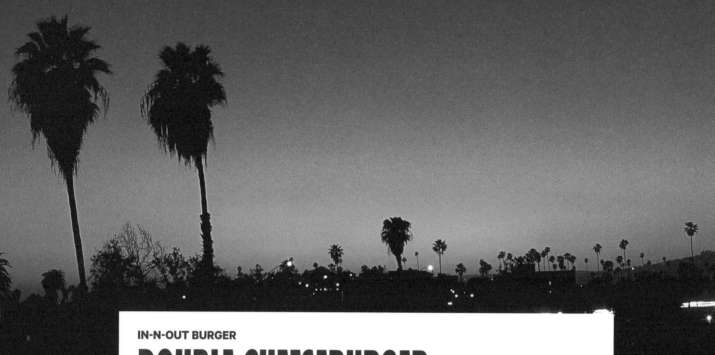

IN-N-OUT BURGER

DOUBLE CHEESEBURGER

SERVES 2

1 onion
Vegetable oil
300 g (10½ oz) minced (ground) beef
Fine sea salt
4 cheddar cheese slices
2 hamburger buns
Butter
Spreading sauce (page 257)
1 large pickle (gherkin)
1 oxheart tomato
A few leaves iceberg lettuce

Sauté the diced onion in a frying pan on a high heat with 2 tablespoons oil. Stir for 6 minutes. Shape the minced meat into four round patties and flatten them using the bottom of a plate protected with baking paper so they are thin and wide. Season with fine sea salt and some freshly ground black pepper. Cook the patties in a hot frying pan on a high heat for 2 minutes per side (for rare). After turning over the patties, lay two slices of cheddar in a star shape on each one. Halve the buns and toast them for 2 minutes in a hot frying pan with a little butter. To assemble: spread some spreading sauce on both buns and, on the bottom halves, place some rounds of pickle, a slice of tomato, two lettuce leaves (one on top of the other), some more spreading sauce, the first patty with cheese, the sautéed onion, the second patty with cheese and the top half of the bun.

This chain, which has not been franchised because it doesn't think that would be compatible with its passion for things done well, strives to offer ultra-fresh burgers, fries and milkshakes, all in an ultra-clean environment. I could spend hours watching the employees cut up their huge potatoes at the entrance of each restaurant. Considered the most popular food chain in the world, In-n-Out Burger is also known for its 'hidden menu' that lets you order sometimes decadent burgers or fries. My interpretation of their secret double cheeseburger, called a 'Double-Double, Animal Style', is still a million miles away from their own inimitable version.

N VERMONT AVE & 101 HIGHWAY

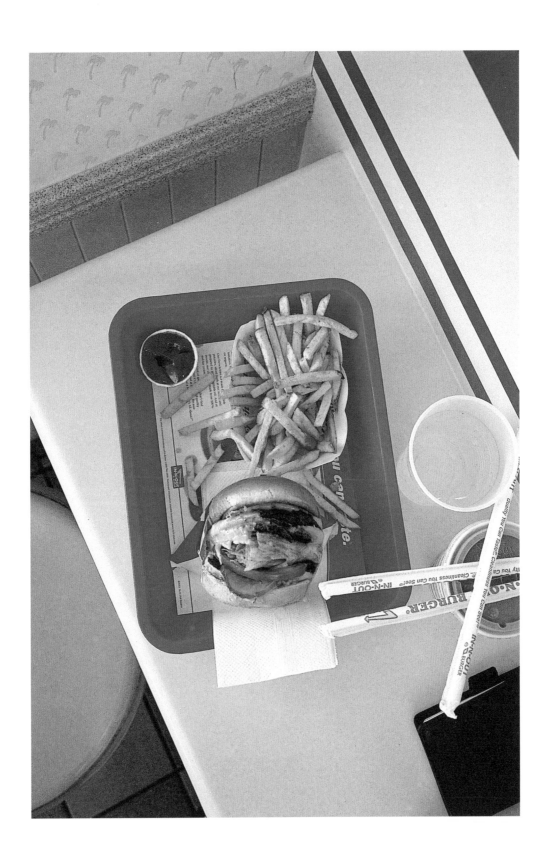

W MANCHESTER BLVD & HINDRY AVE, INGLEWOOD

Chap. 4

HOLLYWOOD
BEVERLY
FAIRFAX
STUDIO CITY
BURBANK

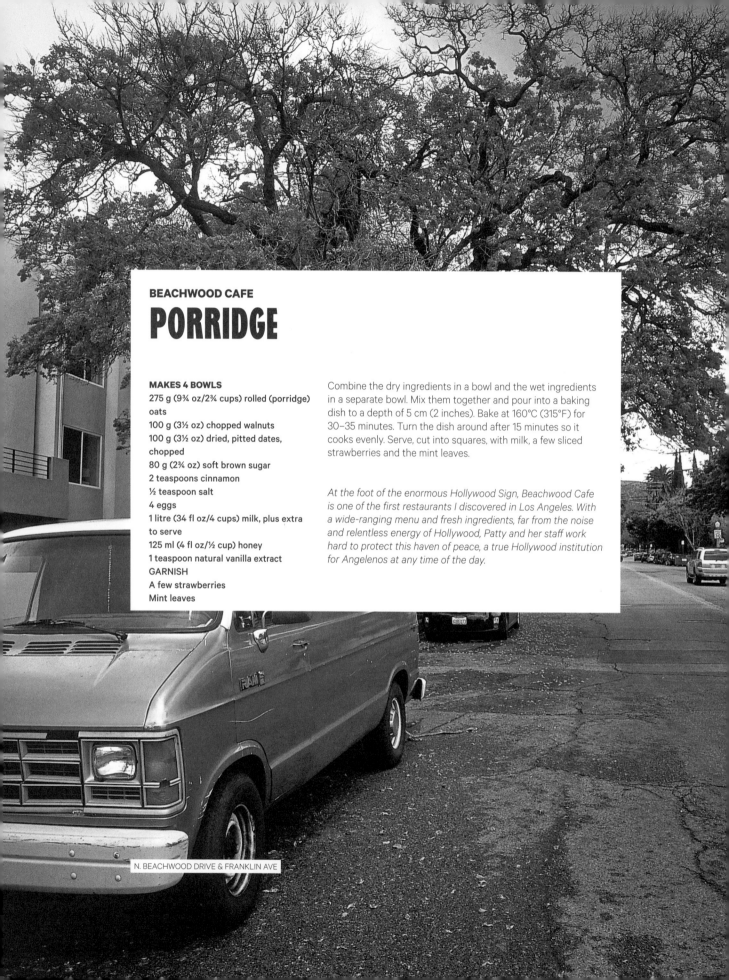

BEACHWOOD CAFE
PORRIDGE

MAKES 4 BOWLS
275 g (9¾ oz/2¾ cups) rolled (porridge) oats
100 g (3½ oz) chopped walnuts
100 g (3½ oz) dried, pitted dates, chopped
80 g (2¾ oz) soft brown sugar
2 teaspoons cinnamon
½ teaspoon salt
4 eggs
1 litre (34 fl oz/4 cups) milk, plus extra to serve
125 ml (4 fl oz/½ cup) honey
1 teaspoon natural vanilla extract
GARNISH
A few strawberries
Mint leaves

Combine the dry ingredients in a bowl and the wet ingredients in a separate bowl. Mix them together and pour into a baking dish to a depth of 5 cm (2 inches). Bake at 160°C (315°F) for 30–35 minutes. Turn the dish around after 15 minutes so it cooks evenly. Serve, cut into squares, with milk, a few sliced strawberries and the mint leaves.

At the foot of the enormous Hollywood Sign, Beachwood Cafe is one of the first restaurants I discovered in Los Angeles. With a wide-ranging menu and fresh ingredients, far from the noise and relentless energy of Hollywood, Patty and her staff work hard to protect this haven of peace, a true Hollywood institution for Angelenos at any time of the day.

N. BEACHWOOD DRIVE & FRANKLIN AVE

BEACHWOOD CAFE
SOPHIA BOWL

MAKES 2 BOWLS
120 g (4¼ oz) tofu
160 g (5½ oz) cooked brown rice
Kale side (see page 260, made without the
pomegranate)
1 small cucumber
1 tablespoon finely chopped fresh coriander
(cilantro)
100 g (3½ oz) kimchi (Asian food stores)
1 tablespoon finely sliced spring onion
(scallion)
Peanut sauce (see page 257)
MARINADE
220 g (7¾ oz/1 cup) soft brown sugar
125 ml (4 fl oz/½ cup) soy sauce
125 ml (4 fl oz/½ cup) sesame oil

For the marinade, dissolve the sugar in 150 ml (5 fl oz) water,
then add the other marinade ingredients. Cut the tofu into pieces.
Add them to the marinade and set aside in the refrigerator for
3 hours. Cook the pieces of tofu in a hot frying pan on a high
heat, 2 minutes per side. In a bowl, arrange: the heated brown rice,
kale side, marinated tofu, rounds of cucumber sliced in half, the
coriander, kimchi and finely sliced spring onion. Top with the
peanut sauce.

E HARBOR BLVD & CALIFORNIA STREET MALL, VENTURA

BEACHWOOD CAFE

COLD BREW

SERVES 6
75 g (2½ oz) ground coffee
1 litre (34 fl oz/4 cups) chilled mineral
water
Ice cubes

Pour the coffee and the chilled mineral water into a jar with a lid. Mix well and leave to infuse in the refrigerator for between 12 and 24 hours. Mix well again and filter. Serve in a glass filled with ice cubes and diluted with a little water, if you would like to soften the coffee flavour even more. It goes well with milk.

A cold brew wakes you up, but more gently than coffee because it doesn't have the bitterness. It is naturally sweet and reveals subtle aromas that you can't pick up when the coffee is hot.

N BEACHWOOD DRIVE & BEACHWOOD TERRACE

BEACHWOOD CAFE
FEZ BOWL

MAKES 4 BOWLS
1 very large kale leaf
1 large carrot
160 g (5½ oz) quinoa
1 French shallot
120 g (4¼ oz) shiitake mushrooms
2 tablespoons olive oil
1 large cooked beetroot (beet), grated
Harissa (page 259)
SHALLOT YOGHURT
1 finely chopped French shallot
2 small tubs Greek-style yoghurt
1 pinch salt
Juice of 1 lemon

Remove the stem and cut up the kale leaf. Slice the carrot into rounds and cook in boiling water for 2 minutes. Add the kale and cook for another 2 minutes. Cook the quinoa as per the instructions on the packet. Cook the finely chopped shallots and chopped shiitake mushrooms in a hot frying pan with a drizzle of the olive oil for 5 minutes. Add the carrot and cooked quinoa. Season with salt and freshly ground black pepper. Add the blanched kale and mix well. For the shallot yoghurt: mix all of the ingredients together. Serve in four bowls and add the beetroot, shallot yoghurt and harissa.

SUNSET BLVD & N EL CENTRO AVE

VEGGIE BURGER
& KALE SIDE

SERVES 6

25 g (1 oz) dried mushrooms
60 g (2¼ oz) linseeds (flax seeds)
160 g (5½ oz) brown rice
2 onions, finely chopped
125 g (4½ oz) fresh mushrooms
4 garlic cloves, finely chopped
20 g (¾ oz) flat-leaf parsley, chopped
1 teaspoon dried thyme
2 tablespoons oregano
60 ml (2 fl oz/¼ cup) olive oil
250 g (9 oz) walnuts
12 slices of bread or 6 buns
2 avocados
2 large oxheart tomatoes
Rocket (arugula)
Kale side (page 260), to serve

Soak the dried mushrooms in hot water with the linseeds for 20 minutes. Drain and reserve the water. Toast the rice in a deep frying pan and cook it with the water from the mushrooms and linseeds for the time indicated on the packet. Sauté the onions, mushrooms, garlic and herbs for 15 minutes in a hot frying pan brushed with oil. Season with salt and freshly ground black pepper. Roughly chop the nuts in a food processor. Mix together the rice, mushrooms and walnuts, then blend them in a food processor. The final texture should be thick and malleable. Shape this mixture into 10 cm (4 inch) wide patties weighing about 130 g (4½ oz). Pan-fry them on a medium heat with a little olive oil for 2 minutes on each side. Assemble, in order: bun, patty, a quarter of an avocado, a large slice of tomato, rocket, bun. Serve with the kale side.

FINLEY FARMS. HOLLYWOOD FARMERS MARKET

BEACHWOOD CAFE
CINNAMON ROLLS

MAKES 12 ROLLS

7 g (⅛ oz) fresh yeast
1 egg
520 g (1 lb 2½ oz) plain (all-purpose) flour
50 g (1¾ oz) caster (superfine) sugar
110 ml (3¾ fl oz) milk
35 ml (1 fl oz) almond milk
1 teaspoon orange blossom water
170 g (6 oz) butter
160 g (5½ oz) soft brown sugar
15 g (½ oz) cinnamon
Glaze (see page 104)

Dissolve the yeast in 90 ml (3 fl oz) water mixed with the egg. Mix together 500 g (1 lb 2 oz) of the flour, the caster sugar and 1 teaspoon salt. Heat the milks and orange blossom water on a low heat. Before bubbles form, add 60 g (2 oz) of the butter and melt, stirring. Let the mixture cool in a mixing bowl. Add the dissolved yeast to this mixture and mix together. Pour the cooled liquid into the flour and mix in. Knead the dough for 5 minutes on a floured work surface. Let it rest under a tea towel (dish towel) for 10 minutes. Blend the remaining flour into the remaining melted butter on a low heat and stir for 2 minutes. Add the brown sugar and cinnamon. Flatten the dough into a 3 cm (1¼ inch) rectangle. Spread with the cinnamon mixture, leaving a 3 cm (1¼ inch) margin around the edges. Roll the dough starting with the longer or shorter side, depending on what size roll you want. Pinch the edges and cut into 12 rolls. Place them on a baking tray lined with oiled baking paper up against each other, touching. Cover with a tea towel and let them rise until they have doubled in volume (about 1 hour). Bake in a 190°C (375°F) oven for about 25 minutes. Lightly swirl on the frosting.

WILSHIRE BLVD & S ARDEN BLVD

CHICKEN-CHEESE PITTA SPINACH & PINEAPPLE JUICE

CHICKEN-CHEESE PITTA
SERVES 4

1 chicken stock cube
Olive oil
1 red capsicum (pepper)
1 green capsicum (pepper)
2 onions
500 g (1 lb 2 oz) skinless chicken breast fillets
4 large corn or wheat tortillas
1 bunch basil
100 g (3½ oz/1 cup) grated cheddar cheese
100 g (3½ oz) grated mozzarella cheese

SPINACH AND PINEAPPLE JUICE
SERVES 1

500 g (1 lb 2 oz) pineapple
60 g (2¼ oz) baby English spinach
100 g (3½ oz) cos (romaine) lettuce

CHICKEN-CHEESE PITTA

Dissolve the stock cube in 2 tablespoons olive oil. Add some water and mix. Sauté the seeded capsicums and thinly sliced onions on a medium heat in a frying pan with olive oil. When they start to caramelise, deglaze with half the stock cube mixture. When all the liquid has evaporated, add the sliced chicken fillets and cook for about 5 minutes, until golden. Deglaze with the rest of the stock cube mixture. Heat the tortillas on one side in a medium frying pan brushed with olive oil for 3 minutes. Flip the tortillas and top with the chicken and vegetables. Add the basil, then cover with grated cheddar and mozzarella. Fold and cut the tortilla in half, cook on both sides until the sandwich is toasted and the cheese has fully melted, or another 3 minutes.

SPINACH AND PINEAPPLE JUICE

Alternate pieces of pineapple, baby English spinach leaves and shredded cos lettuce through a juicer.

What the photo doesn't show you is how quickly the cook works. What it shows well is how generous the food vendors at the farmers' market are with fresh vegetables and herbs, which gives the pitta an incomparable flavour.

STEVE

ANNA

THE OINKSTER
FRIED CHICKEN BURGER

MAKES 4 CHICKEN BURGERS
4 skinless chicken breast fillets,
4 buns, 4 lettuce leaves, 2 large pickles
(gherkins), Buffalo sauce (page 257) and
Ranch house sauce (page 257)
THE MARINADE
450 ml (16 fl oz) fermented milk or
buttermilk, 1 teaspoon salt, ½ teaspoon
freshly ground black pepper, ½ teaspoon
paprika, ½ teaspoon cayenne pepper
THE COATING
130 g (4½ oz) plain (all-purpose) flour,
½ teaspoon salt, ½ teaspoon freshly
ground black pepper, ½ teaspoon
paprika, ½ teaspoon cayenne pepper,
1 teaspoon garlic, peanut or sunflower
oil for deep-frying

For the marinade: mix together all the ingredients and pour
them into a freezer bag or mixing bowl. Add the chicken and
mix to coat with the marinade. Marinate for 4–12 hours. For
the coating: mix together all the ingredients in a bowl. Remove
the chicken from the plastic bag and cover the chicken in the
coating mixture, pressing it on firmly. Dip the chicken again in
the marinade, then again in the coating. Cook the chicken in a
deep-fryer at 180°C (350°F) for about 5 minutes, or in a frying
pan on a medium heat with 2 cm (¾ inch) oil for 4 minutes per
side. Assemble the burgers in this order: bottom half of the bun,
lettuce, rounds of pickle, the fried chicken brushed with buffalo
sauce, the top bun spread with the ranch house sauce.

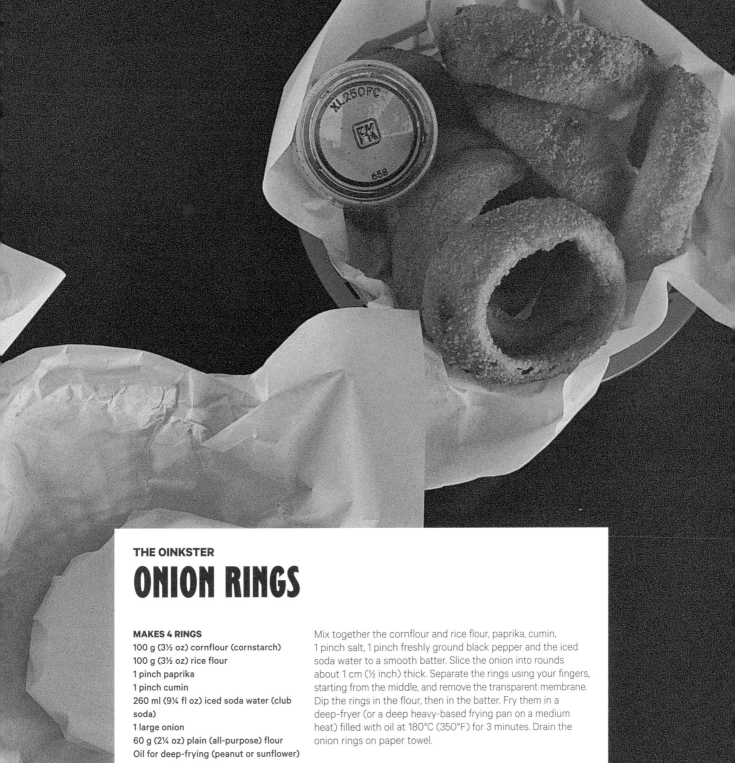

ONION RINGS

MAKES 4 RINGS
100 g (3½ oz) cornflour (cornstarch)
100 g (3½ oz) rice flour
1 pinch paprika
1 pinch cumin
260 ml (9¼ fl oz) iced soda water (club soda)
1 large onion
60 g (2¼ oz) plain (all-purpose) flour
Oil for deep-frying (peanut or sunflower)

Mix together the cornflour and rice flour, paprika, cumin, 1 pinch salt, 1 pinch freshly ground black pepper and the iced soda water to a smooth batter. Slice the onion into rounds about 1 cm (½ inch) thick. Separate the rings using your fingers, starting from the middle, and remove the transparent membrane. Dip the rings in the flour, then in the batter. Fry them in a deep-fryer (or a deep heavy-based frying pan on a medium heat) filled with oil at 180°C (350°F) for 3 minutes. Drain the onion rings on paper towel.

My hotel was right opposite; I interpreted it as a sign. The Oinkster borrows some fast food traditions, because you order at the counter and the food is served in baskets. But this establishment, beloved by Angelenos, takes so much time to do things well and with such attention to detail, it is a long way from fast food.

BBQ CHICKEN PIZZA

MAKES 1 PIZZA

1 skinless chicken breast fillet

Oil

75 g (2½ oz) Barbecue sauce (page 257)

Pizza dough for 1 base (recipe page 262 or buy from your local pizzeria)

Smoky tomato sauce (page 258)

75 g (2½ oz) grated mozzarella cheese

BLUE CHEESE CREAM

60 g (2¼ oz) light crème fraîche (or light sour cream)

150 g (5½ oz) Bleu d'Auvergne blue cheese

100 g (3½ oz) mayonnaise

½ teaspoon Worcestershire sauce

¼ teaspoon wholegrain mustard

¼ teaspoon garlic

¼ teaspoon salt

¼ teaspoon lime juice

¼ teaspoon freshly ground pepper

For the blue cheese cream: mix together all of the blue cheese cream ingredients, cover and refrigerate for 24 hours. Flatten the chicken breast, oil it lightly and season with salt and freshly ground black pepper. In a lightly oiled heated frying pan, on a medium heat, cook the chicken for about 2 minutes on one side, reduce the heat, turn it over and cook for another 7–8 minutes. Cut the cooked chicken in half and submerge it in the barbecue sauce. Cool and place in the refrigerator. Flatten the pizza dough: starting from the middle, and leaving a thick edge around the outside, stretch the base to the size you want (about 30 cm/ 12 inches in diameter). Spread with the smoky tomato sauce using the bottom of a ladle, starting from the middle and tracing a spiral outwards. Scatter over the mozzarella cheese. Cook the pizza for between 12 and 15 minutes in an oven heated to its highest temperature (ideally on a pizza stone). Take the pizza out of the oven, cool it for 5 minutes and spread with the barbecue sauce. Add pieces of marinated chicken and drizzle with the blue cheese cream. Just before serving, bake again for no more than 2 minutes.

This place is triply legendary. It is right in the middle of the Hollywood Walk of Fame. It serves some of the best pizza by the slice in Los Angeles, for Angelenos who are homesick for NYC. Finally, its menu offers this dish that symbolises Californian cuisine: pizza with chicken and barbecue sauce.

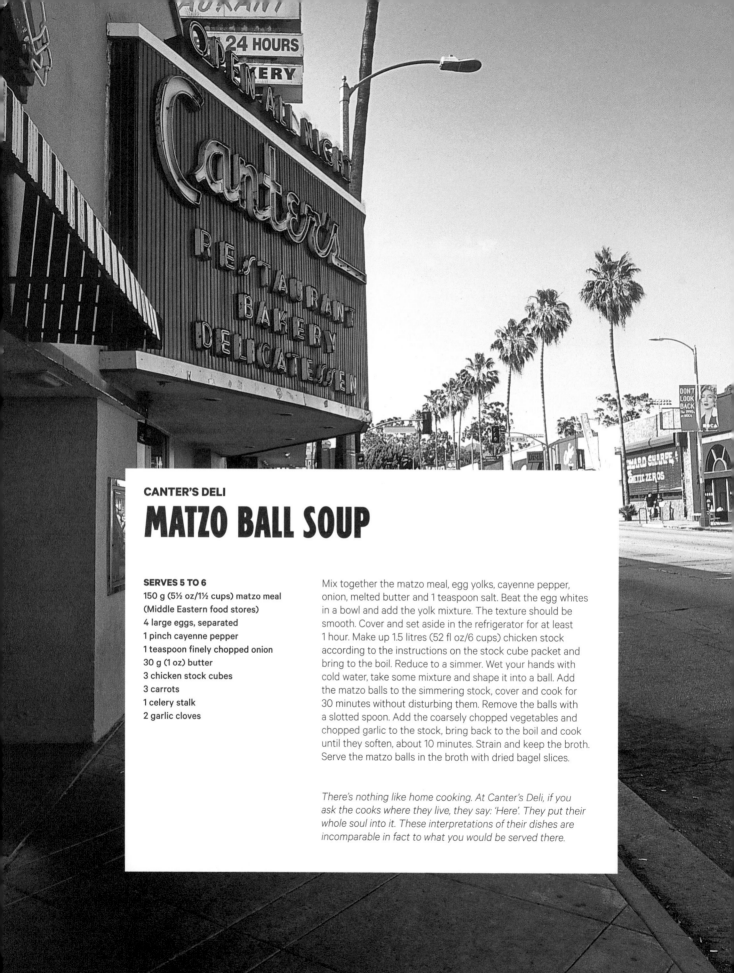

CANTER'S DELI

MATZO BALL SOUP

SERVES 5 TO 6

150 g (5½ oz/1½ cups) matzo meal
(Middle Eastern food stores)
4 large eggs, separated
1 pinch cayenne pepper
1 teaspoon finely chopped onion
30 g (1 oz) butter
3 chicken stock cubes
3 carrots
1 celery stalk
2 garlic cloves

Mix together the matzo meal, egg yolks, cayenne pepper, onion, melted butter and 1 teaspoon salt. Beat the egg whites in a bowl and add the yolk mixture. The texture should be smooth. Cover and set aside in the refrigerator for at least 1 hour. Make up 1.5 litres (52 fl oz/6 cups) chicken stock according to the instructions on the stock cube packet and bring to the boil. Reduce to a simmer. Wet your hands with cold water, take some mixture and shape it into a ball. Add the matzo balls to the simmering stock, cover and cook for 30 minutes without disturbing them. Remove the balls with a slotted spoon. Add the coarsely chopped vegetables and chopped garlic to the stock, bring back to the boil and cook until they soften, about 10 minutes. Strain and keep the broth. Serve the matzo balls in the broth with dried bagel slices.

There's nothing like home cooking. At Canter's Deli, if you ask the cooks where they live, they say: 'Here'. They put their whole soul into it. These interpretations of their dishes are incomparable in fact to what you would be served there.

CANTER'S DELI
CORNED BEEF REUBEN SANDWICH

MAKES 4 SANDWICHES
1 beef stock cube
400 g (14 oz) Corned beef (page 262)
8 slices rye bread
Russian sauce (page 257)
150 g (5½ oz) sauerkraut (fresh or tinned)
4 slices gruyère cheese
French fries, to serve
4 large pickles (gherkins), to serve

Make up the beef stock with the amount of water indicated on the stock cube packet. Cook the corned beef in the simmering broth for 3 hours. For the sandwich: spread both sides of the toasted rye bread with Russian sauce, stack with paper-thin slices of cooled corned beef, a quarter of the sauerkraut and a slice of gruyère cheese. Top with the other still-warm piece of toast. Cut the sandwiches in half and serve with fries and pickles quartered lengthways.

At Canter's, the focus is on the plate, not on the cash registers. Their corned beef, each layer of which has been scientifically tested, is a good example. Again, this is a very humble interpretation that should make you want to taste the original version, full of know-how and well-kept secrets.

FRIED CHICKEN SANDWICH & SPICY STRAWBERRY JAM

MAKES 2 SANDWICHES

Peanut or other oil for frying
2 fried eggs
2 cheddar cheese slices
SPICY STRAWBERRY JAM
130 g (4½ oz) caster (superfine) sugar
1 lemon
250 g (9 oz) strawberries
1 or 2 red chillies
BISCUIT BUNS
500 g (1 lb 2 oz/3⅓ cups) plain (all-purpose) flour
125 g (4½ oz) salted butter
2 sachets (10 g/¼ oz each) baking powder
155 ml (5 fl oz) milk
CHICKEN
25 g (1 oz) soft brown sugar
2 boneless skinless chicken thighs
125 ml (4 fl oz/½ cup) olive oil
2 garlic cloves
1 pinch rosemary
BATTER
75 g (2½ oz/½ cup) plain (all-purpose) flour
60 g (2¼ oz/½ cup) cornflour (cornstarch)
½ chicken stock cube
135 ml (4½ fl oz) iced soda water (club soda)

For the strawberry jam: pour the sugar and juice and zest of the lemon over the halved strawberries. The next day, add the chillies, seeded and cut into strips of about 3 mm (⅛ inch). Bring to the boil, reduce the heat and cook for 20–25 minutes, stirring. Allow to cool. Repeat the process to obtain a jammy consistency. For the buns: gently mix together the flour, the cubed butter at room temperature and the baking powder. Add the milk, little by little, until you get a slightly sticky ball, then roll it out on a work surface to a thickness of 2 cm (¾ inch). Cut out eight biscuits with a cookie cutter (8 cm/3¼ inch diameter). Cook for 10 minutes in a 200°C (400°F) oven. For the chicken: dissolve the brown sugar and 30 g (1 oz) salt in 2 litres (70 fl oz/8 cups) water, then submerge the chicken thighs. Rinse well the next day. Mix together the olive oil, crushed garlic, rosemary and a pinch of salt and freshly ground black pepper. Coat the thighs with this marinade, cover and set aside in the refrigerator for at least 1 hour (up to 12 hours). Take the chicken out at least 30 minutes before cooking. Batter: Mix the flours with the crushed ½ chicken stock cube. Gradually pour the iced soda water into the middle and blend in. Mix until you have the consistency of a fritter batter. Dip the thighs into the batter, then fry them in the oil for 5–7 minutes in a deep-fryer at 180°C (350°F); the coating should be golden. Alternatively, heat 4 cm (1½ inches) of oil in a frying pan on a high heat and cook the thighs for 15 minutes, turning every 2 minutes. Drain off the excess oil on a rack. To assemble: open up the biscuit buns, spread both sides with the spicy jam, top with the fried chicken, a fried egg and a cheddar cheese slice. Top with the other half of the buns.

The food truck where all the film companies and studios go to grab food to feed their actors, proposed this exclusive recipe for Mother's Day. It brought back childhood memories for me, when my mother woke us up on Sunday with the smell of hot scones coming out of the oven.

PEANUT BUTTER & JELLY SANDWICH

MAKES 1 SANDWICH
2 large slices sandwich bread
40 g (1½ oz) peanut butter
40 g (1½ oz) seedless raspberry jam

Toast the bread. Spread one slice with peanut butter, the other with jam. Put the sandwich together and trim the crusts. Cut the sandwich on the diagonal.

It is a great honour to have the privilege of presenting Joan's recipes in this book, knowing that she does not like to write them down. It depends on the vegetables, the seasons, what's in the refrigerator but, most of all, what she feels like: it's a living thing! As a result, there are no written recipes at Joan's. I also had the privilege of meeting her daughters, Susie and Carol. Joan's on Third is above all a family institution.

HOLLYWOOD RECREATION CENTER. 122 COLE AVE

JOAN'S ON THIRD

BACON CHILLI DOG

MAKES 1 HOT DOG

1½ rashers bacon
1 pure beef sausage
15 g (½ oz) salted butter
1 hot dog bun
80 g (2¾ oz) Chilli (see page 261)
30 g (1 oz) cheddar cheese
½ onion

Wrap the bacon around the sausage (make a cut near one end of the sausage and insert the end of the half-slice to hold it). Brush the bacon-wrapped sausage with melted butter, then pan-fry on a medium heat, rolling it so the bacon browns evenly. Place the sausage in the hot dog bun, that has been lightly warmed in the oven. Top with chilli and grated cheddar cheese and place under the grill (broiler). Once the cheese has melted, serve with diced onion.

GRILLED CHEESE WITH TOMATO

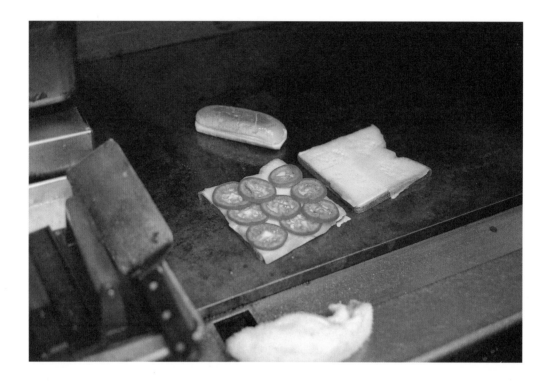

SERVES 1
50 g (1¾ oz) salted butter
2 slices sandwich bread
8 cheddar cheese slices
6–9 slices roma (plum) tomato

Lay the buttered slices of bread, butter side down, in a frying pan on a medium heat. While the bread browns, top each with four slices of the cheddar cheese. When the cheese starts to melt, arrange the tomato slices on top. After about 4 minutes, tip one slice onto the other and press down firmly with a spatula. Cut the sandwich on the diagonal when the cheese has finished melting.

GUACAMOLE & CHEDDAR FRIES HOT DOG

MAKES 4 HOT DOGS

1 kg (2 lb 4 oz) potatoes (bintje)

Peanut or other frying oil

8 cheddar cheese slices

Guacamole (page 260)

4 all beef sausages

4 hot dog buns

Pickled white onions (page 260)

4 large pickles (gherkins)

60 ml (2 fl oz/¼ cup) Honey mustard sauce (page 258)

Cut the unpeeled potatoes into sticks about 5 mm (¼ inch) wide. Rinse the potato sticks until the water runs clear and leave the potatoes in the water for at least 6 hours. Drain well. Deep-fry the potatoes for 5 minutes in 140°C (285°F) oil in a deep-fryer or in 5 cm (2 inches) oil in a frying pan on a medium heat. Shake them well to drain. Cool and place in the refrigerator. At serving time, deep-fry the potatoes in 180°C (350°F) oil in a deep-fryer or in a frying pan on a high heat for 3 minutes; they should be golden brown. Drain on paper towel to remove any excess oil. Immediately add the slices of cheddar cheese and guacamole. Cook the sausage according to the instructions on the packet, or the advice of the butcher. Heat the buns in the oven at 180°C (350°F) for 3 minutes. To assemble: place the sausages in the buns, scatter with pickled white onions, diced pickles and honey mustard sauce.

Until there is a photo of you eating a hot dog at Pink's, you aren't officially a Hollywood star. This legendary restaurant, with its infinitely customisable hot dogs, has just celebrated its 77th birthday.

STRAWBERRY LEMONADE

MAKES 5 GLASSES
600 g (1 lb 5 oz) strawberries
30 g (1 oz) caster (superfine) sugar
100 g (3½ oz) honey
3 organic lemons

Set a few strawberries aside and cook the rest in a 180°C (350°F) oven for 10 minutes, halved and sprinkled with sugar. Once they have cooled, blend them in a food processor with the honey and 250 ml (9 fl oz/1 cup) of water for 30 seconds. Pour the mixture into a jug. Blend two unpeeled lemons with 1.25 litres (44 fl oz/5 cups) water in a food processor. (If you prefer the lemonade to be less sour, you can remove the lemon peel before blending.) Pour into the jug and add water as needed to adjust the acidity. Add a few lemon slices and strawberries to decorate and enhance the flavour of the lemonade.

When you accidentally open your analog camera thinking you have rewound your film spool, but you haven't, there is nothing like a large Mexican strawberry lemonade to lift your spirits.

HOT FUDGE SUNDAE

SERVES 4

12 scoops vanilla ice cream
1 handful peanuts
4 preserved cherries
HOT FUDGE SAUCE
200 ml (7 fl oz) thin (pouring/whipping) cream
1 vanilla bean, seeds scraped
1 tablespoon icing (confectioners') sugar
160 g (5½ oz) crème fraîche
200 g (7 oz) dark chocolate
30 g (1 oz/¼ cup) unsweetened cocoa powder
100 ml (3½ fl oz) agave syrup
50 g (1¾ oz) soft brown sugar
30 g (1 oz) salted butter

For the hot fudge sauce: whip the cream and add the vanilla bean seeds and icing sugar. Stop when the cream starts to form peaks. Bring the crème fraîche gently to the boil with the chocolate, cocoa powder, agave syrup, brown sugar, butter and a pinch of salt, stirring continuously. Turn off the heat and continue stirring for 5 minutes. Place one scoop of ice cream in the bottom of a deep glass, then a little whipped cream, a little hot fudge sauce and some roughly crushed peanuts. Repeat twice and place a preserved cherry on top.

Not least because it is made from corn, hoecake (see page 154) is now one of my five favourite dishes. Even though it is impossible for your hoecake to be as good as the one made by Michael, the chef at Barrel & Ashes, which Angelenos can't get enough of, this recipe (my interpretation) should already convince you that hoecake is not just a 'savoury pancake'.

BARREL & ASHES

HOECAKE

MAKES 3 OR 4 HOECAKES
110 g (3¾ oz/¾ cup) plain (all-purpose) flour
100 g (3½ oz) polenta (cornmeal)
25 g (1 oz) caster (superfine) sugar
7 g (¼ oz) baking powder
5 g (⅛ oz) salt
1 egg, plus 1 extra egg white
265 ml (9½ fl oz) milk
90 g (3 oz) butter
Maple syrup
Onion rings (page 131), to serve
1 spring onion (scallion), sliced, to serve

Preheat the oven to 230°C (450°F). Mix together the dry ingredients. Mix together one egg, one whisked egg white and the milk. Tip the dry mixture into the wet mixture, then add 85 g (3 oz) melted butter. Blend in a food processor; the batter should be smooth. In a hot wide ovenproof frying pan on a medium heat, add the remaining butter in small pieces and tilt the frying pan to spread. When it starts to foam, pour in about a third of the batter; it must reach the edge. Cook for 2 minutes or until bubbles form around the edges. Place the frying pan in the oven and cook for 2–3 minutes; the centre must remain soft. Return the frying pan to the stove on a medium heat, flip the hoecake and cook for another 1–2 minutes; a small crust should have formed on the underside. Pour over some maple syrup, sprinkle with a pinch of salt and garnish with onion rings and sliced spring onion. Serve hot.

CHILI JOHN'S
CHILLI SPAGHETTI BOWL

SERVES 8

800 g (1 lb 12 oz) thick spaghetti
480 g (1 lb 1 oz/2½ cups) dried red kidney
beans
1 white onion, a few pickled green chillies
(page 259) and 1 small handful soup crackers,
to serve
OIL FOR THE CHILLI
2 garlic cloves
125 ml (4 fl oz/½ cup) extra-virgin olive oil
1 tablespoon chilli powder
½ teaspoon ground cumin
½ teaspoon ground coriander
½ teaspoon oregano
½ teaspoon cayenne pepper
CHILLI
1 onion
2 tablespoons canola oil
900 (2 lb) minced (ground) beef
1 teaspoon Worcestershire sauce
½ teaspoon Tabasco sauce
320 g (11¼ oz) Barbecue sauce (page 257)
1 teaspoon cayenne pepper

For the oil: sauté the chopped garlic in 1 tablespoon of the olive oil on a medium heat in a small saucepan. Stir for 2 minutes. Add the remaining olive oil and the dried spices and herbs. Heat until the oil comes to a bare simmer. Stir for about 3 minutes. For the chilli: sauté the chopped onion in the canola oil on a medium heat in a large saucepan, stirring for about 4 minutes. Add the beef and cook for about 6 minutes, stirring, or until the meat is just cooked. Add 1½ teaspoons salt, ½ teaspoon freshly ground black pepper, the Worcestershire sauce and the Tabasco sauce. Reduce the heat and add the barbecue sauce, mixing it in well. Pour all of the chilli oil into the meat, mix well. Bring to the boil on a medium heat. Reduce the heat to low and add the cayenne pepper. Cook, covered, for 15 minutes. Marinate for 3 days in a glass jar (keeps for 1 week). Cook the spaghetti according to the instructions on the packet and drain well. Reheat the beans or cook the dried beans as for chilaquiles (page 236). Serve the spaghetti, a ladleful of the chilli – having removed the excess oil – the kidney beans, some diced white onion, a few chillies in vinegar and some crackers.

Alec, Debbie and Anthony put their heart and soul into their food to keep the success of Chili John's going. It is the oldest operating restaurant in Burbank. Their recipe is hidden in a safe but, as a hint, Debbie doesn't hesitate to explain that it is a chilli in the truest Texas tradition, the recipe dating back to 1830. She adds: 'No water, no tomato, lots of salt, it's a pretty neat place'.

AVOCADO CHEESEBURGER

SERVES 4

3 tablespoons tomato sauce (ketchup)
½ teaspoon Tabasco sauce
4 rashers bacon
500 g (1 lb 2 oz) minced (ground) beef
8 cheddar cheese slices
4 buns
1 avocado
A few leaves of cos (romaine) lettuce
1 onion
1 tomato
1 large pickle (gherkin)

Combine the tomato and Tabasco sauces. Pan-fry the bacon on a medium heat for 5 minutes per side and drain on some paper towel. Shape the minced beef into four beef patties. Cook them on a high heat for 3 minutes on the first side. Season with salt and freshly ground black pepper. Turn them over, then lay two slices of cheddar in a star shape on each one. For a rare burger, leave it on the heat for another 3 minutes; for medium, 4 minutes; for well done, 5 minutes. Cut the buns in half horizontally and toast them. To assemble: place the cheese-topped burger on the bottom half of the bun, then two rashers of bacon, avocado slices, shredded cos lettuce, a little of the tomato-Tabasco sauce mixture, some diced onion, a round of tomato and a round of pickle. Top with the other half of the bun.

John and Veronica run one of the most respected restaurants in Burbank. No burger comes out of their kitchen without a flame over 50 cm (20 inches) high leaping up from the hotplate to give it the smoky flavour that's a signature of their restaurant.

PACIFIC COAST HIGHWAY, MALIBU

MELROSE TRADING POST

Chap. 5

VENICE

MAR VISTA

ABBOT'S PIZZA COMPANY

SALAD PIZZA

MAKES 1 PIZZA

Pizza dough for 1 base (recipe page 262,
or from your local pizzeria)

2 eggs

1 small handful poppy seeds

1 small handful sesame seeds

3 or 4 garlic cloves

100 g (3½ oz) grated mozzarella cheese

½ red onion

75 g (2½ oz) light crème fraîche (or light
sour cream)

1 big handful mixed salad leaves

1 tomato

½ white onion

60 g (2¼ oz) feta cheese

Lemon vinaigrette (page 259)

¼ avocado

Spread out the pizza dough to about 30 cm (12 inches) in diameter. Lightly whisk the eggs in a bowl. In another bowl, mix together the seeds and diced garlic. Brush the inside and outside edges of the pizza with the whisked eggs. Do the same with the mixed seeds – they need to stick to the egg. Sprinkle with the mozzarella and finely chopped red onion. In an oven heated to its highest temperature (ideally on a pizza stone), bake the pizza for 12–15 minutes; the edges should be golden brown. Spread a layer of light crème fraîche on the cooled pizza. Mix the salad leaves with the tomato, cut into eight wedges, the sliced half white onion and diced feta. Dress with the lemon vinaigrette. Spread the salad over the pizza. Add the avocado slices.

Whatever day of the week it is, if I go past Abbot's Pizza Company, I look at what they have ready by the slice. There is something addictive about their pizzas. I don't know if it is a secret ingredient, but it certainly has something to do with their know-how. When was I late for my classes, I appreciated their pizzas, which have the huge advantage of being able to be eaten at the wheel.

VENICE BEACH

PRAWN TACOS

MAKES 3 TACOS
3 large raw prawns (shrimp)
3 small corn tortillas
Olive oil
Baja sauce (page 257)
A few white cabbage leaves
1 sprig coriander (cilantro)
1 tomato
Tabasco sauce
3 pinches paprika
3 pinches chilli spice mix
BATTER
¼ fish stock cube
130 g (4½ oz) plain (all-purpose) flour
150 ml (5 fl oz) iced pale beer

For the batter: crush the fish stock cube in a bowl and add the flour and ½ teaspoon pepper. Gradually mix in the iced beer. Season the three peeled prawns with a pinch of salt and some freshly ground black pepper, dip them in the batter and deep-fry at 180°C (350°F) for 4 minutes. They should be crisp and golden. Drain on paper towel. Toast the tortillas for about 2 minutes on each side in a hot frying pan brushed with olive oil. For the taco, pour a little baja sauce in the middle of the tortilla, add some finely shredded cabbage, a battered prawn, some chopped coriander leaves, seedless diced tomato, some more baja sauce, some drops of Tabasco sauce, the paprika and chilli spice mix. Fold and serve.

KOMODO

BANH-MI CHICKEN TACO

SERVES 4

4 boneless skinless chicken thighs
1 tablespoon sugar
1½ tablespoons teriyaki sauce
250 ml (9 fl oz/1 cup) orange juice
2 garlic cloves
1 piece fresh ginger
4 tortillas

THE RADISH-CARROT PICKLE
125 ml (4 fl oz/½ cup) white vinegar
40 g (1½ oz) sugar
350 g (12 oz) radishes
220 g (7¾ oz) carrots
1 jalapeño

THE AIOLI
2 tablespoons Kewpie (Japanese)
mayonnaise
2 tablespoons hoisin sauce
2 tablespoons oyster sauce

For the pickle: bring 185 ml (5½ fl oz) water, the vinegar and sugar to the boil, mixing vigorously. Turn off the heat. Sprinkle 1 teaspoon salt over the julienned radishes and let it stand for 10 minutes. Combine the rinsed radishes with the julienned carrots and sliced jalapeño in a jar. Pour the warm pickling liquid over the vegetables and chill overnight. Clean the chicken thighs and dry them with paper towel. Mix together the sugar and 1 teaspoon each salt and freshly ground black pepper and, in a separate bowl, the teriyaki sauce, orange juice, crushed garlic and finely chopped ginger. Combine the two mixtures and add the chicken thighs. Marinate for 30 minutes to 2 hours. Cook the thighs on a low heat in a covered saucepan for 30–40 minutes, turning every 5 minutes. Turn the heat to high and cook for 3 minutes, stirring constantly. For the aïoli: whisk the Kewpie mayonnaise, hoisin sauce and oyster sauce for 2 minutes. Assemble the taco, in this order: tortilla, diced chicken topped with aïoli and pickled vegetables.

Their Vietnamese tacos are known beyond the borders. At Komodo, you can pretty much do what you like. The same goes for the staff, who don't hesitate to come to the other side of the counter to advise you or discuss. Perfect technique and understanding of the produce are shown in this brilliant concept.

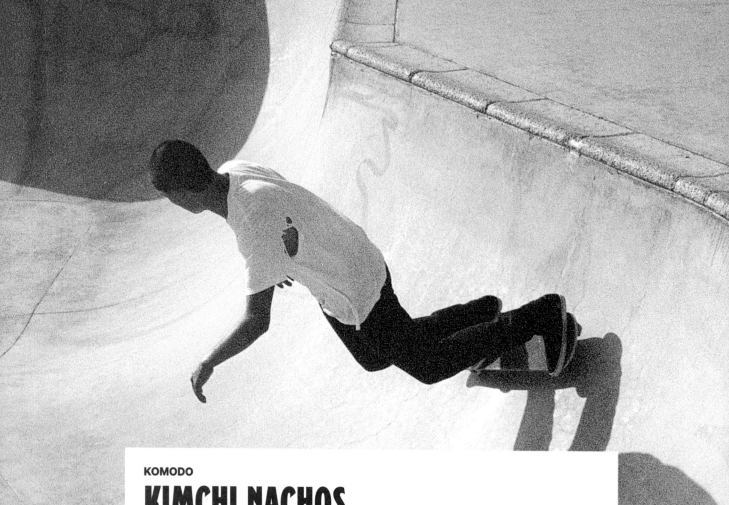

KOMODO

KIMCHI NACHOS

SERVES 2
8 corn tortillas
Peanut oil
2 tablespoons canola oil
1 tablespoon garlic
30 g (1 oz) crispy bacon
100 g (3½ oz) skinless chicken breast fillet
225 g (8 oz) kimchi (Asian food stores)
100 g (3½ oz) tomatoes
2 tablespoons jalapeños
50 g (1¾ oz) cheddar cheese
50 g (1¾ oz) mozzarella cheese
120 g (4¼ oz) sour cream
1 spring onion (scallion)
SRIRACHA AIOLI
100 g (3½ oz) garlic cloves
85 g (3 oz) sriracha (Thai chilli sauce)
55 g (2 oz) mayonnaise

Cut the tortillas into four and deep-fry in 170°C (325°F) peanut oil until crisp and golden, or about 30 seconds. Place the corn (tortilla) chips on paper towel and season with salt and freshly ground black pepper. For the sriracha aïoli: sauté the garlic cloves on a medium heat in a frying pan for 5 minutes, stirring regularly. Blend the garlic in a food processor with the sriracha sauce and mayonnaise until the mixture is smooth. Heat the canola oil in a frying pan on the hottest heat, and add the finely chopped garlic, finely chopped bacon and diced chicken for 30 seconds. The chicken should brown. Add the chopped kimchi and the seeded and diced tomatoes and jalapeños. Cook for 30 seconds, stirring well. Season. Cook for another 30 seconds. To assemble the nachos: make a layer of corn chips, kimchi mixture and grated cheese (cheddar and mozzarella). Repeat this process three times. Sprinkle with grated cheese and bake at 190°C (375°F) until the cheese melts. Top the nachos with the sriracha aïoli, a drizzle of sour cream and a little chopped spring onion.

CHRISTIAN. BELVEDERE SKATEPARK

GREEN SMOOTHIE

MAKES 1 GLASS
150 g (5½ oz) kale
1 apple
1 banana
500 ml (17 fl oz/2 cups) almond milk

Thinly slice the kale. Cut the apple into four and remove the core. Blend all the ingredients together in a food processor and serve immediately.

I was intrigued by this pioneering company of natural detox cures, which very hotly advertises its expertise in cold-pressed juices. I discovered a team with over 12 years of expertise in the quest for wellness through food, without compromising on flavour, and their recipes are addictive. Their Downtown production facility is ultra-secure and only supplied by local farmers' markets. Thank you, Kristen!

KALE JUNGLE BOWL

SERVES 1

2 kale leaves
1 small handful baby English spinach
125 ml (4 fl oz/½ cup) coconut milk
20 g (¾ oz) almond butter (organic food stores)
A few strawberries
½ banana
2 tablespoons Granola (page 196)
½ mango
80 g (2¾ oz) pineapple
A few mint leaves
Pollen (organic food stores)

Blend the kale, spinach, coconut milk and almond butter together in a food processor for about 30 seconds; the texture should be smooth and even. Pour into a large bowl and add pieces of strawberry and banana, the granola, pieces of mango and pineapple and a few mint leaves. Sprinkle with pollen.

PORCHETTA SANDWICH

MAKES 2 SANDWICHES
120 g (4¼ oz) rapini (broccoli rabe)
2 pinches chilli flakes
2 teaspoons Confit garlic (page 259)
Olive oil
200 g (7 oz) porchetta (stuffed roast pig)
1 baguette
60 g (2¼ oz) fontina cheese

Cut the rapini into pieces and mix with 3 pinches of salt, the chilli flakes, confit garlic and a tablespoon of olive oil. Let this mixture rest for 10 minutes, then spread it out on a baking tray and place under the grill (broiler) for about 3 minutes. Turn and cook for another 3 minutes. Sauté with the thinly sliced porchetta in a frying pan with a little olive oil on a high heat, stirring constantly. Cut the baguette in half and fill it with this mixture and pieces of fontina.

The fact that Travis and Kelly opened their doors to me is my greatest source of pride in this book. I had never seen such a place: Gjusta is home to one of the most well-stocked kitchens I have ever had the chance to visit. And everything is in its place. On their menu, absolutely everything is home-made under the unerring eye of Greg, a French chef who has settled in LA. In his free time, he escapes into the desert on a motorbike.

GUANCIALE PIZZA

MAKES 1 PIZZA

Pizza dough for 1 base (recipe page 262
or buy from your local pizzeria)
50 g (1¾ oz) grated mozzarella cheese
40 g (1½ oz) parmesan cheese
1 or 2 small green chillies
1 large handful green olives
3 thin slices guanciale (Italian food stores)
Olive oil
1 tablespoon rosemary
POMODORO SAUCE
250 g (9 oz) whole peeled tomatoes
Olive oil
½ onion
Roasted tomatoes (page 260)
½ teaspoon mixed dried herbs
½ teaspoon oregano

For the pomodoro sauce: purée the tomatoes in a blender or food processor and add a drizzle of olive oil. Add the chopped half onion and the roasted tomatoes and process. Bring to the boil in a saucepan, reduce the heat to low and cook for 1 hour, stirring regularly. Add the mixed herbs and oregano. Flatten the pizza dough: starting from the middle, leave a thick edge around the outside and stretch the base to the size you want (about 30 cm/ 12 inches in diameter). Spread the pomodoro sauce over the base with the bottom of a ladle, starting from the middle and tracing a spiral outwards. Top with the mozzarella, shavings of parmesan, round slices of chilli, the pitted and halved green olives and slices of guanciale. Cook the pizza for 12–15 minutes in an oven heated to its highest temperature (ideally on a pizza stone); the edges should start to blacken. Drizzle with olive oil and sprinkle with rosemary.

G.T.A. (GJELINA TAKE AWAY)
SALMON OPEN SANDWICH

SERVES 4
250 g (9 oz) cream cheese
1 bunch chives
1 lemon
4 eggs
4 slices of artisan-style olive bread
Pickled cucumbers (page 260)
4 slices smoked salmon
1 small handful capers

Mix the cream cheese with the chopped chives (setting a few aside), the juice of the lemon and a quarter of the grated zest. Hard-boil the eggs. Spread each toasted slice of bread with the chive cream cheese, then add the pickled cucumbers, a slice of smoked salmon, and a halved hard-boiled egg. Sprinkle with a little lemon juice and half a pinch of salt and freshly ground black pepper. Sprinkle with the remaining chives and the capers.

G.T.A. (GJELINA TAKE AWAY)
EGG-KALE OPEN SANDWICH

SERVES 4
40 g (1½ oz) anchovies in olive oil
1 tablespoon wine vinegar
100 g (3½ oz) Roasted tomatoes (page 260)
Grated zest of ¼ lemon
4 handfuls kale
4 eggs
4 slices artisan-style bread
80 g (2¾ oz) provolone cheese (Italian food stores)
Olive oil

Sauté the anchovies in oil in a frying pan for 2 minutes on a medium heat, mashing them with a spatula. Deglaze the pan with the vinegar. Add the roasted tomatoes, grated zest and the well rinsed and massaged kale leaves. Cook for another 2 minutes, mixing with the spatula. Season with salt and freshly ground black pepper. Poach four eggs (see page 262). To assemble: toast the bread, place some pieces of provolone, some kale and an egg cut in half on top. Finish with a drizzle of olive oil and half a pinch of pepper.

At G.T.A. (Gjelina Take Away) the art of the open sandwich is something akin to clockmaking. That's the feeling you get when you watch the cooks preparing take-away dishes and meals.

GJUSTA
SALMON PLATE

MAKES 4 PLATES

4 eggs
8 slices smoked salmon
2 handfuls baby salad leaves and a
mixture of herbs
100 g (3½ oz) Pickled red onions (page
260)
100 g (3½ oz) Cucumber and radish
pickles (page 259)
1 handful capers
Juice of 1 lemon
Olive oil
LABNEH (YOGHURT CHEESE)
300 g (10½ oz) yoghurt

For the labneh: place the yoghurt in the middle of a piece of
muslin (cheesecloth) with a pinch of salt. Fold in the edges
and sit the wrapped yoghurt in a sieve over a bowl. Place in
the refrigerator overnight. Hard-boil the eggs, cooking them for
6 minutes and 45 seconds. Allow to cool. To assemble: arrange
all the ingredients, except the lemon juice, oil and eggs, on a
plate. Top with the halved, hard-boiled eggs, dress with lemon
juice, drizzle some olive oil on the labneh and season with salt
and freshly ground black pepper.

G.T.A. (GJELINA TAKE AWAY)

ASPARAGUS & MUSHROOM FOCACCIA

MAKES 10 FOCACCIA
FOCACCIA
1 kg (2 lb 4 oz) plain (all-purpose) flour
30 g (1 oz) fresh yeast (from bakery)
20 g (¾ oz) salt
200 ml (7 fl oz) olive oil
Coarse salt
TOPPING
170 g (6 oz) oyster mushrooms
225 g (8 oz) asparagus
Olive oil
Coarse salt
55 g (2 oz) Confit garlic (page 259)
170 g (6 oz) truffle cheese (brie, pecorino or
Brillat-Savarin)
140 g (5 oz) fontina (Italian cheese)
10 eggs
50 g (1¾ oz) thyme
Zest of 1 lemon

For the focaccia: knead together the flour, yeast, salt and 600 ml (21 fl oz) water until you have a smooth dough, about 10 minutes. Incorporate 50 g (1¾ oz) of the olive oil and another 50 g (1¾ oz) water. Knead for another 5 minutes. Shape into a ball. Leave the dough to prove for 1 hour at room temperature on a floured work surface. Divide the dough into 10 focaccia, and spread the dough on baking trays lined with baking paper. Brush with a mixture of 150 ml (5 fl oz) water and the remaining olive oil. Let the dough prove again for 1½ hours at room temperature. Scatter with coarse salt. For the topping: sauté the mushrooms and asparagus, brushed with olive oil and sprinkled with coarse salt, in an oiled frying pan on a medium heat. Mix together and cook for 5 minutes. Scatter the focaccia with the mushrooms and asparagus, confit garlic and thin slices of the cheeses. Break an egg on top of each focaccia and spread it out. Sprinkle with thyme and lemon zest and bake in the oven for 15 minutes at the hottest temperature setting (ideally on a pizza stone).

GJUSTA

MULTIGRAIN PORRIDGE

MAKES 2 BOWLS
50 g (1¾ oz) millet
50 g (1¾ oz/¼ cup) red quinoa
50 g (1¾ oz) farro
½ vanilla bean
½ teaspoon cinnamon
50 g (1¾ oz) steel-cut oats
160 ml (5¼ fl oz) non-dairy milk
2 apricots
A few cherries

Cook the millet, red quinoa on a low heat in about 720 ml (24½ fl oz) water. Cook the farro according to the packet directions, then add to the millet and quinoa. Add the half vanilla bean, split in two, the cinnamon and ½ pinch of salt. Cook for another 10 minutes, stirring. Add the steel-cut oats and 250 ml (9 fl oz/1 cup) water. Cook until the grains soften, about 7 minutes. Serve with milk and the fruit.

MOTOR CYCLE SWAP MEET, VETERAN'S STADIUM, LONG BEACH

VILLAGE CAR WASH, 12415 VENICE BLVD LOS ANGELES

MUSHROOM BOWL

MAKES 3 BOWLS

100 g (3½ oz) brown rice
Olive oil
1 small onion
1 garlic clove
1 tomato
80 g (2¾ oz) broccoli or kale leaves
1 teaspoon Confit garlic (page 259)
1 tablespoon white wine vinegar
250 g (9 oz) mushrooms (porcini,
chanterelles or black trumpet
mushrooms)
Rosemary and fresh thyme
3 eggs
HOT SAUCE
1 tomato, peeled
30 ml (1 fl oz) hot water
1 small onion, chopped
45 ml (1½ fl oz) sriracha sauce (Thai hot
sauce)

Wash the rice three times and drain well. Lightly brown the rice in an oiled saucepan on a medium heat for about 4 minutes, stirring regularly. Blend together the onion, garlic and tomato with some salt in a food processor. Add this purée to the rice and simmer with 350 ml (12 fl oz) water. When the liquid has reduced down to the level of the rice, cover with a lid and cook for another 2 minutes. Let it rest for at least 20 minutes. Cook the chopped broccoli or kale leaves in simmering water, drain and add the confit garlic and mix. Season well with a mixture of 2 teaspoons olive oil, the vinegar, a pinch of freshly ground black pepper and pinch of salt. Sauté the mushrooms in a frying pan brushed with olive oil on a high heat for about 3 minutes, stirring. Reduce the heat to medium and add the rosemary and thyme. Cook for 5 minutes, stirring once a minute. Remove the mushrooms and, in the same frying pan, fry the eggs. Heat some olive oil, first add the white, then the yolk when the white just starts to simmer. Using a spatula, cover the yolk with the white, rotating the frying pan, to make a ball. Place the eggs on paper towel. For the hot sauce: blend the tomato with the hot water, onion, 2 pinches of salt and the sriracha sauce in a food processor. Assemble, in order: rice, mushrooms, kale and fried egg with a drizzle of hot sauce on top.

GJUSTA
GRANOLA

MAKES 1 KG (2 LB 4 OZ)
300 ml (10½ fl oz) maple syrup
75 g (2½ oz/⅓ cup) soft brown sugar
½ teaspoon cinnamon
A few drops natural vanilla extract
120 g (4¼ oz) chopped almonds
400 g (14 oz/4 cups) rolled (porridge) oats
100 g (3½ oz) pepitas (pumpkin seeds)
50 g (1¾ oz) black sesame seeds
100 g (3½ oz) sunflower seeds
2 tablespoons grapeseed oil
Almond milk, to serve
Berries, to serve

Heat the maple syrup and sugar in a pan until the sugar dissolves. When the mixture reaches about 40°C (105°F), add the cinnamon, ½ teaspoon salt and the vanilla extract. Pour over the almonds, oats and seeds and stir to coat. Spread the mixture over a baking tray brushed with grapeseed oil and cover with a sheet of baking paper. Bake at 160°C (315°F) for about 1 hour, stirring every 15 minutes. The granola should be golden brown when ready. Serve with almond milk and berries.

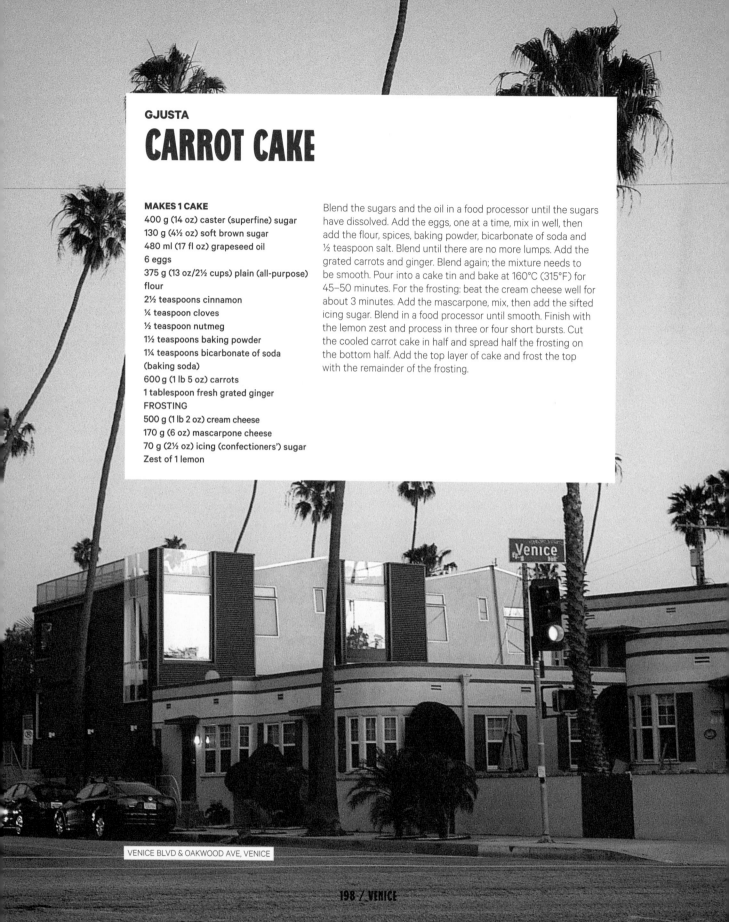

GJUSTA

CARROT CAKE

MAKES 1 CAKE
400 g (14 oz) caster (superfine) sugar
130 g (4½ oz) soft brown sugar
480 ml (17 fl oz) grapeseed oil
6 eggs
375 g (13 oz/2½ cups) plain (all-purpose) flour
2½ teaspoons cinnamon
¼ teaspoon cloves
½ teaspoon nutmeg
1½ teaspoons baking powder
1¼ teaspoons bicarbonate of soda (baking soda)
600 g (1 lb 5 oz) carrots
1 tablespoon fresh grated ginger
FROSTING
500 g (1 lb 2 oz) cream cheese
170 g (6 oz) mascarpone cheese
70 g (2½ oz) icing (confectioners') sugar
Zest of 1 lemon

Blend the sugars and the oil in a food processor until the sugars have dissolved. Add the eggs, one at a time, mix in well, then add the flour, spices, baking powder, bicarbonate of soda and ½ teaspoon salt. Blend until there are no more lumps. Add the grated carrots and ginger. Blend again; the mixture needs to be smooth. Pour into a cake tin and bake at 160°C (315°F) for 45–50 minutes. For the frosting: beat the cream cheese well for about 3 minutes. Add the mascarpone, mix, then add the sifted icing sugar. Blend in a food processor until smooth. Finish with the lemon zest and process in three or four short bursts. Cut the cooled carrot cake in half and spread half the frosting on the bottom half. Add the top layer of cake and frost the top with the remainder of the frosting.

VENICE BLVD & OAKWOOD AVE, VENICE

POKE-POKE

HAWAIIAN TUNA POKE

SERVES 1

120 g (4¼ oz) tuna fillet (sashimi quality)
3 tablespoons soy sauce
1 tablespoon sesame oil
2 pinches sesame seeds
1 green chilli
A few macadamia nuts
1 small white onion
1 spring onion (scallion)
80 g (2¾ oz) Vinegared sushi rice (page 261)

Cut the tuna into 2 cm (¾ inch) dice and mix with the soy sauce and sesame oil. Marinate in the refrigerator for 2 hours. Add the sesame seeds, the chilli sliced into rounds, the roughly crushed macadamia nuts, and the sliced white and spring onions. Place the cooled rice and tuna mixture in a bowl. This dish goes very well with diced ripe avocado, pickled ginger and wasabi.

These are the hands of Jason, a photographer, who often comes to Poke-Poke. This restaurant is located on the waterfront in Venice Beach. They were the first to offer these Hawaiian-style bowls of Ahi Tuna, and they remain the best. Jason is not the only one who thinks so!

STEVE RICHARDS. BELVEDERE SKATEPARK. EAST CESAR E CHAVEZ AVE, EAST LOS ANGELES

VEGAN LASAGNE

SERVES 2

MACADAMIA CREAM
150 g (5½ oz) macadamia nuts
240 ml (8 fl oz) water
2 teaspoons nutritional yeast
½ teaspoon lemon juice
¼ teaspoon salt
PISTACHIO PESTO
60 g (2¼ oz) pistachio nut kernels
15 g (½ oz) English spinach leaves
40 g (1½ oz) basil leaves
4 tablespoons extra-virgin olive oil
1 teaspoon lemon juice
RED CAPSICUM MARINARA
1 tomato
½ red capsicum (pepper)
30 g (1 oz) sun-dried tomatoes
1 tablespoon French shallot
1 teaspoon lemon juice
¼ teaspoon chilli flakes
2 teaspoons olive oil
HERB-INFUSED OIL
10 g (¼ oz) English spinach leaves
5 g (⅛ oz) basil
240 ml (8 fl oz) olive oil
ZUCCHINI NOODLES AND HEIRLOOM
TOMATOES
2 medium zucchini (courgettes)
Olive oil
2 oxheart tomatoes
GARNISH
Cherry tomatoes
Fresh basil

For the macadamia cream: soak the macadamia nuts in 500 ml (17 fl oz/2 cups) water for 7 hours and drain. Blend all the remaining macadamia cream ingredients together in a food processor. The final texture should be like ricotta cheese. For the pistachio pesto: process the pistachio nut kernels in short bursts, add the spinach, herbs and half a teaspoon salt and process again in short bursts. Mix in the lemon juice and olive oil. Don't overprocess, keep it the texture of a pesto. For the red capsicum marinara: seed the tomato and the half capsicum and blend with the sun-dried tomatoes (soaked beforehand in water for 4 hours and squeezed out), the shallot, lemon, ¼ teaspoon salt and the chilli flakes in a food processor, adding the olive oil, little by little, with the processor still running. For the herb-infused oil: gently process the spinach, basil, oil and a pinch of salt together in a food processor. Strain and put in a bottle. For the zucchini noodles: using a mandoline, cut 18 slices of zucchini, about 7 cm (2¾ inches) long and 2 mm (⅛ inch) thick, and lay them on baking paper with a little oil. Season with salt and dab the zucchini with paper towel to absorb any excess moisture. Slice the tomatoes to the same shape. To assemble: brush a plate with herb-infused olive oil and make a layer of zucchini, a layer of sauces (pesto, marinara, cream), three overlapping zucchini slices, a layer of sauces, a layer of tomatoes, three zucchini slices and finish with some pesto and macadamia cream. Garnish with cherry tomatoes and basil.

It was Nadja and Karen, whom I met the day before in Gjusta, who opened the doors of this vegan temple to me, which has an international vegan cooking school on the first floor above the restaurant. Thank you, Leigh, for your hospitality!

N CAHUENGA BLVD & LEXINGTON AVE

MOTOR CYCLE SWAP MEET, VETERAN'S STADIUM, LONG BEACH

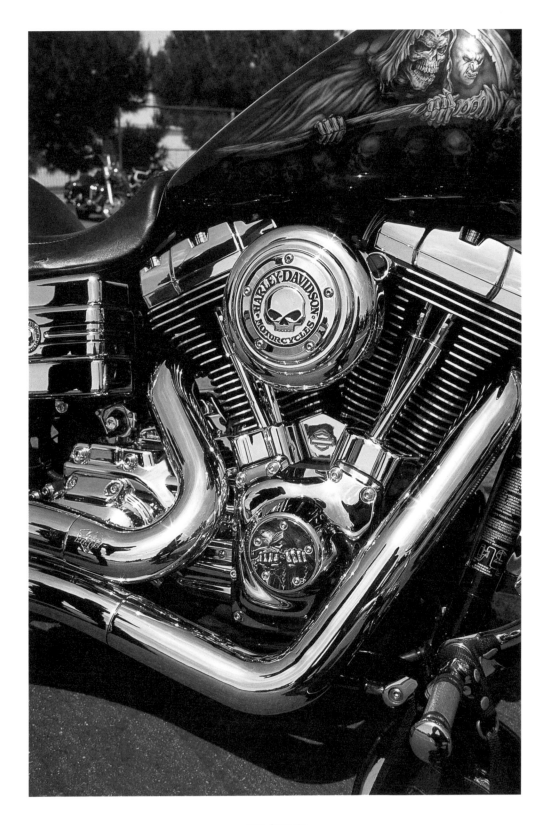

SANTOUKA (MITSUWA MARKET)

PORK RAMEN

MAKES 4 BOWLS RAMEN
Vegetable oil
300 g (10½ oz) wheat noodles, thin
2 spring onions (scallions)
A few sheets nori seaweed (dried or fresh)
THE TONKOTSU BROTH
750 g–1 kg (1 lb 10 oz–2 lb 4 oz) pork bones
(trotters or leg bones)
Spring onions (scallions) or salad onions
THE BRAISED PORK
500 g (1 lb 2 oz) pork belly
150 ml (5 fl oz) soy sauce
125 ml (4 fl oz/½ cup) sake
15 ml (½ fl oz) mirin (very mild sake)
30 ml (1 fl oz) oyster sauce
50 g (1¾ oz) sugar
3 garlic cloves, 1 French shallot, 1 onion,
1 carrot
DEGLAZING LIQUID
2 tablespoons soy sauce, 2 tablespoons mirin

For the broth: submerge the pork bones in a large quantity of water, bring to the boil and cook for 15 minutes. Take the bones out and clean the pot. Bring the same quantity of fresh water to the boil. Meanwhile, rinse the bones and remove any remaining impurities. Simmer the bones again for 20 minutes, removing any scum or solids that rise to the top. Cover and cook for at least 3 hours, ideally 10–12. Strain. For the braised pork: tie the pork into a compact shape, with the meat on the inside. Bring a saucepan of water to the boil with all the braised pork ingredients, leaving the garlic, shallot and onion unpeeled·and slicing the carrot into rounds. Pour this mixture over the pork belly and bake in a 135°C (275°F) oven for at least 3 hours, turning it over every hour. The pork needs to be half-submerged in the liquid at all times. Cool the braised pork in its juices, then slice. Sauté the slices in vegetable oil on a high heat. For the deglazing liquid: mix together the soy sauce and mirin and deglaze the meat. To assemble: in a large bowl, pour in some boiling broth, the noodles, cooked according to the instructions on the packet, the deglazed pork, one or two pinches of chopped spring onion, and the nori seaweed prepared as per the instructions on the packet.

SANUKI (MITSUWA MARKET)
BEEF UDON

MAKES 4 BOWLS UDON
300 g (10½ oz) udon noodles
400 g (14 oz) beef, thinly sliced
1 tablespoon grapeseed oil
60 ml (2 fl oz/¼ cup) soy sauce
60 ml (2 fl oz/¼ cup) mirin (very mild sake)
2 spring onions (scallions)
60 g (2¼ oz) wakame seaweed
THE DASHI
30 g (1 oz) kombu seaweed
1 litre (35 fl oz/4 cups) mineral water
20 g (¾ oz) dried bonito flakes

For the dashi: cook the kombu in the mineral water for 2 hours (don't let the temperature rise above 70°C/158°F). Add the dried bonito and let it infuse for 3 minutes, then strain the dashi. Cook the udon noodles as per the instructions on the packet. Sauté the beef slices in oil on a very high heat until coloured. Mix together a tablespoon of the soy sauce and a tablespoon of the mirin and deglaze the pan. Add the rest of the soy sauce and mirin to the dashi, bring to the boil and reduce the heat to low. Season with salt and freshly ground black pepper. Serve the dashi soup, udon, spring onions and beef scalding hot in a bowl. Garnish with the wakame seaweed.

Each of my visits to the Mitsuwa Market Place has been unforgettable, from every mouthful of ramen or scalding hot udon that I've eaten, to just wandering through the Japanese supermarket, where you can find everything you want (fresh and in the grocery aisles). These two dishes require patience to be successful. On that front, no one can match Santouka for ramen and Sanuki for udons. Their reputation is international, and their secrets are as well kept as the formula for Coca-Cola.

Chap. 6
VENTURA
MALIBU
PACIFIC PALISADES

MULLIGATAWNY SOUP
ROOTY FRUITY JUICE

ANOO CHANDRASHAKER'S RECIPE

MAKES 1 SOUP TO SERVE 5

115 g (4 oz) butter
5 carrots
120 g (4¼ oz) onions
4 celery stalks
2 garlic cloves
1 teaspoon turmeric
1 tablespoon curry powder
1 bay leaf
180 g (6½ oz) basmati rice
210 g (7½ oz) red lentils
2 apples
1 large potato
1 sweet potato
240 ml (8 fl oz) coconut milk

MAKES 1 JUICE

200 g (7 oz) beetroot (beet), 200 g (7 oz) apple, 200 g (7 oz) carrot,
1 piece fresh ginger

SOUP

Heat the butter in a large saucepan on a medium heat and add
the diced carrots and onions, sliced celery and crushed garlic.
Cook, stirring, for 6 minutes, until everything softens. Add the
spices, bay leaf and ½ teaspoon freshly ground black pepper, cook
for another 3 minutes. Add 2 litres (70 fl oz/8 cups) water and let
the mixture simmer for 30 minutes. Add the rice, lentils, diced
apples and potatoes. Cook for another 20 minutes, covered. Add
the coconut milk and cook, stirring, for 5 minutes. Season with
1 teaspoon salt.

JUICE

Juice all of the ingredients, alternating with pieces of ginger.

Every Wednesday morning, Steve's farm opens its doors to keen volunteers. Each day, the harvest makes it way to The Farmer and the Cook restaurant, which he runs with his wife, Olivia, in Ojai, Ventura. The whole menu of the restaurant is organised around what the farm produces. Although it is located on the site of a former prison, it is the intense feeling of freedom enjoyed by Nicolas and Johnny, Steve's employees, that I will remember. They go surfing almost every day before or after the harvest and wouldn't change their job for anything in the world.

RANCHO DEL PUEBLO FARM. RICE ROAD & BALDIUM ROAD, OJAI

STEVE'S PICK-UP TRUCK, W EL ROBLAR DR & N LA LUNA AVE, OJAI

NEPTUNE'S NET SEAFOOD RESTAURANT

FISH & CHIPS
SANGRIA

FISH AND CHIPS
SERVES 4

110 g (3¾ oz/¾ cup) plain (all-purpose) flour
1 teaspoon garlic powder
1 egg
1 fish stock cube
300 ml (10½ fl oz) cold beer
4 long cod fillets
200 g (7 oz) Japanese (panko) breadcrumbs
French fries, to serve
Tartare sauce (page 258), to serve

SANGRIA
MAKES 1 LITRE (35 FL OZ/4 CUPS)

1 apple
1 orange
A few mint leaves
30 g (1 oz) soft brown sugar, plus extra
150 ml (5 fl oz) Sprite
100 ml (3½ fl oz) Coca-Cola
750 ml (26 fl oz) red Burgundy wine
30 ml (1 fl oz) orange juice

FISH AND CHIPS

Mix together the flour, garlic powder, 1 teaspoon salt and ½ teaspoon freshly ground black pepper. Add the egg. Dissolve the fish stock cube in the cold beer and mix with the egg and flour mixture. Cut the fish fillets in half on the diagonal, dip them in the flour, then dip them in the batter and finally in the breadcrumbs, pressing them on well. Deep-fry the fillets at 180°C (350°F) for 4 minutes in a deep-fryer or for 3 minutes each side in 1 cm (½ inch) oil in a frying pan on a medium heat. Serve with French fries and the tartare sauce.

SANGRIA

Core the apple, cut it into wedges and thinly slice the wedges across. Seed and cut the orange into wedges, without peeling. Place the apple and orange into a carafe with the mint and brown sugar. Mash with a wooden spoon for about 1 minute. Add the soft drinks and mash again. Pour in the wine, mixing at the same time. Adjust the taste with more or less orange juice and brown sugar.

This is a legendary place for all bikers around the world. Located at the intersection of the famous Mulholland and Pacific Coast Highways, two major thoroughfares for Californian road trips, you enjoy some of the best fish and chips in the country under the deafening roar of Harley Davidsons – all opposite one of Malibu's most beautiful surf spots.

CAFFE' DELFINI

ZUCCHINI SPAGHETTI BOLOGNESE

SERVES 4

6 zucchini (courgettes)
Basil, to serve
BOLOGNESE SAUCE
2 garlic cloves
2 onions
1 tablespoon olive oil
1 bay leaf
200 g (7 oz) minced (ground) veal
2 tomatoes
400 ml (14 fl oz) tomato passata (puréed tomatoes)
30 g (1 oz) butter
2 tablespoons fish sauce

For the bolognese: sauté the roughly chopped garlic and thinly sliced onions in the olive oil in a saucepan on a high heat until the onions are translucent and starting to brown. Add the bay leaf. Gradually add the minced meat on a medium heat. Season with salt and freshly ground black pepper. Add the roughly chopped tomatoes and passata on a low heat. Simmer for at least 10 minutes. At the end of the cooking time, add the butter and fish sauce. Remove the bay leaf. Julienne the zucchini and draw out the liquid with some salt. Add the zucchini to boiling water for 1 minute, drain and pat dry while still hot. Mix the zucchini with the sauce and serve with basil.

The day before I visited Caffe' Delfini, Cindy Crawford confessed to Alex and Gianpetro that they ran the most romantic restaurant in the world! When they were getting established, they accepted the challenge that California seemed to be posing them, using their Italian know-how: 'Make food that is delicious, but not fattening'. One day, by chance, at the market, Alex discovered zucchini that was cut and cooked like spaghetti. With a veal-based bolognese sauce, it became the legendary 'zinguine' of Caffe' Delfini.

W CHANNEL ROAD & PACIFIC COAST HIGHWAY

CAFFE' DELFINI

ALCOHOL-FREE DECAF TIRAMISU

SERVES 6
5 eggs, separated
150 g (5½ oz/⅔ cup) caster (superfine) sugar
500 g (1 lb 2 oz) mascarpone cheese
Mug of prepared decaffeinated coffee
2 packets ladyfinger biscuits (savoiardi)
30 g (1 oz) dark chocolate, finely grated

Whisk the egg yolks with the sugar, add the mascarpone and mix together. Beat the egg whites to soft peaks and add to the mascarpone mixture. Pour the cooled mug of decaffeinated coffee into a deep plate and roll the ladyfingers quickly in the liquid so they don't become too soggy. In a rectangular dish, arrange a layer of biscuits, then a layer of cream. Repeat the process. Dust with the grated chocolate, cover with plastic wrap and set aside in the refrigerator for 24 hours.

VENTURA PIER, VENTURA

CALIFORNIA ST MALL & VENTURA PROMENADE

Chap. 7
SILVER LAKE
WESTLAKE
HIGHLAND PARK
LOS FELIZ

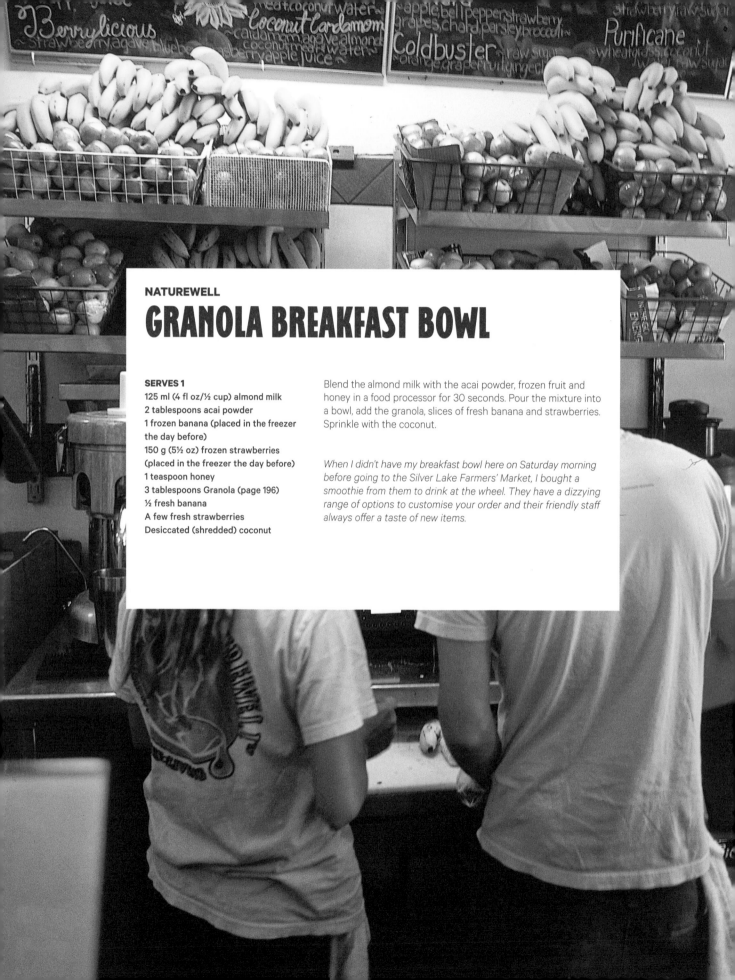

NATUREWELL

GRANOLA BREAKFAST BOWL

SERVES 1

125 ml (4 fl oz/½ cup) almond milk

2 tablespoons acai powder

1 frozen banana (placed in the freezer the day before)

150 g (5½ oz) frozen strawberries (placed in the freezer the day before)

1 teaspoon honey

3 tablespoons Granola (page 196)

½ fresh banana

A few fresh strawberries

Desiccated (shredded) coconut

Blend the almond milk with the acai powder, frozen fruit and honey in a food processor for 30 seconds. Pour the mixture into a bowl, add the granola, slices of fresh banana and strawberries. Sprinkle with the coconut.

When I didn't have my breakfast bowl here on Saturday morning before going to the Silver Lake Farmers' Market, I bought a smoothie from them to drink at the wheel. They have a dizzying range of options to customise your order and their friendly staff always offer a taste of new items.

NATUREWELL

DATE-COCONUT SMOOTHIE

MAKES 1 SMOOTHIE

3 or 4 dates

250 ml (9 fl oz/1 cup) coconut milk

60 g (2¼ oz) fresh coconut meat

1 small handful almonds

1 frozen banana

1½ tablespoons Granola (page 196)

1 teaspoon maca powder (organic food stores)

1 tablespoon hemp protein powder (organic food stores)

Pit the dates and place them with the rest of the ingredients in a blender. Blend for approximately 30 seconds or until smooth.

TACOS AL PASTOR HORCHATA

SERVES 6 TO 8

TACOS AL PASTOR

1 kg (2 lb 4 oz) pork fillet
6–8 corn tortillas
1 tablespoon olive oil
Tabasco sauce
1 large onion
½ bunch coriander (cilantro)
4 limes
Tabasco sauce, to serve
MARINADE
1 pineapple
3 garlic cloves
½ bunch coriander (cilantro)
125 ml (4 fl oz/½ cup) orange juice
60 ml (2 fl oz/¼ cup) white vinegar
25 g (1 oz) chilli powder
1 teaspoon oregano
1 teaspoon cumin
1 teaspoon white pepper
2 small chipotle chillies in adobo sauce (sold in tins at specialty stores)
2 teaspoons adobo sauce (sold in tins at specialty stores)
2 teaspoons salt

HORCHATA

200 g (7 oz) rice
20 g (¾ oz) cinnamon, plus extra for sprinkling
400 ml (14 fl oz) sweetened condensed milk
400 ml (14 fl oz) evaporated milk
30 g (1 oz) blanched almonds
50 g (1¾ oz) caster (superfine) sugar
Ice cubes

TACOS AL PASTOR

Flatten out the pork well. For the marinade: dice half of the pineapple (put some aside) and juice the rest. Mix together the halved garlic, half a bunch of coriander and the remaining marinade ingredients in a bowl. Transfer to a bag, add the pork and make sure it is well impregnated with the marinade. Place in the refrigerator on a plate overnight. Remove the pork from the plastic bag and cook the pork and its marinade in the oven for 30 minutes at 220°C (425°F), or until it starts to brown. Take the fillet out of the oven and turn it over. Lower the oven to 180°C (350°F) and cook for 1½ hours. Cut the pork into slices or small cubes and return it to the dish with the rest of the marinade. Toast the tortillas for about 2 minutes on each side in a hot frying pan brushed with olive oil. To assemble the taco: place some marinated pork with a little Tabasco sauce on the tortilla, add some diced onion, chopped coriander and a few pieces of diced pineapple. Serve with a wedge of lime and some Tabasco sauce.

HORCHATA

Submerge the well-rinsed rice and 15 g (½ oz) of the cinnamon in about 250 ml (9 fl oz/1 cup) water in a bowl. Mix together with your fingers. Let the rice soften for at least 3 hours. Blend in a food processor at maximum speed with the condensed and evaporated milks, blanched almonds and sugar for at least 3 minutes. Transfer to large jug with 2.25 litres (70¾ fl oz) water and a little more cinnamon. Mix together. Serve with ice cubes and sprinkle with more cinnamon.

The bright colours, the sign lettering, the atmosphere, the aromas: I love everything about Tacos Delta. This is where I went to eat the best breakfast in the world: chilaquiles (see page 236). The recipe has been passed down over generations and is a well- guarded secret. So even if you try your hardest with this recipe, which is my interpretation, their original version will transport you to Mexico City, where I tasted them for the first time a few years earlier.

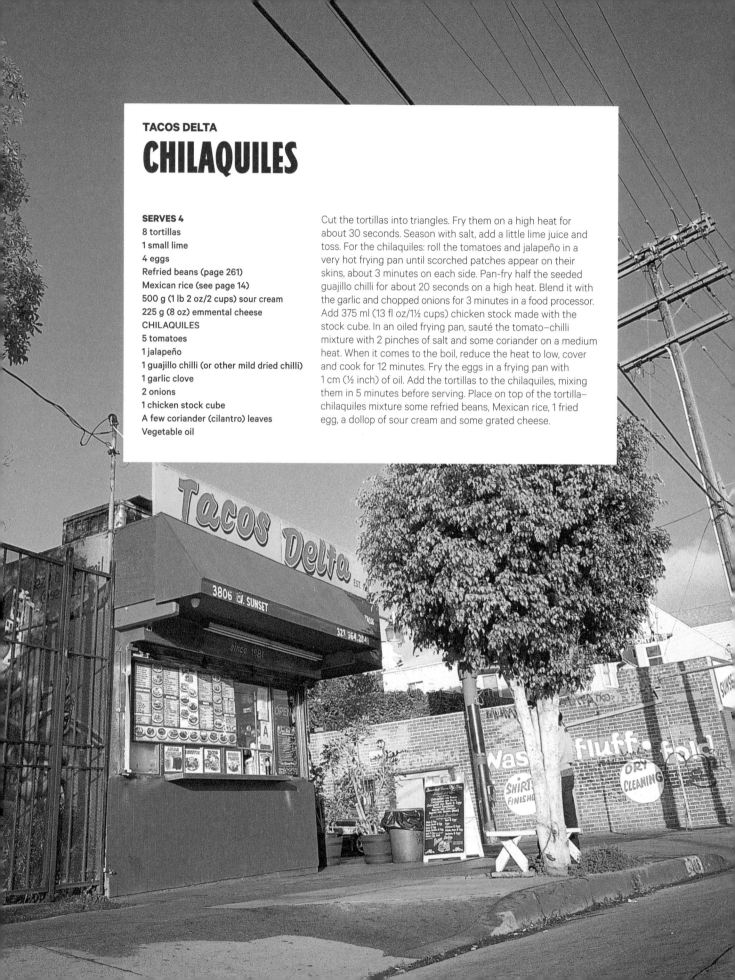

TACOS DELTA
CHILAQUILES

SERVES 4
8 tortillas
1 small lime
4 eggs
Refried beans (page 261)
Mexican rice (see page 14)
500 g (1 lb 2 oz/2 cups) sour cream
225 g (8 oz) emmental cheese
CHILAQUILES
5 tomatoes
1 jalapeño
1 guajillo chilli (or other mild dried chilli)
1 garlic clove
2 onions
1 chicken stock cube
A few coriander (cilantro) leaves
Vegetable oil

Cut the tortillas into triangles. Fry them on a high heat for about 30 seconds. Season with salt, add a little lime juice and toss. For the chilaquiles: roll the tomatoes and jalapeño in a very hot frying pan until scorched patches appear on their skins, about 3 minutes on each side. Pan-fry half the seeded guajillo chilli for about 20 seconds on a high heat. Blend it with the garlic and chopped onions for 3 minutes in a food processor. Add 375 ml (13 fl oz/1½ cups) chicken stock made with the stock cube. In an oiled frying pan, sauté the tomato–chilli mixture with 2 pinches of salt and some coriander on a medium heat. When it comes to the boil, reduce the heat to low, cover and cook for 12 minutes. Fry the eggs in a frying pan with 1 cm (½ inch) of oil. Add the tortillas to the chilaquiles, mixing them in 5 minutes before serving. Place on top of the tortilla–chilaquiles mixture some refried beans, Mexican rice, 1 fried egg, a dollop of sour cream and some grated cheese.

GLUTEN-FREE LEMON CAKE VIETNAMESE COFFEE

MAKES 1 CAKE

110 g (3¾ oz) butter, 150 g (5½ oz/⅔ cup) caster (superfine) sugar, 2 eggs, 2 lemons, 90 g (3 oz) superfine brown rice flour (organic food stores), 10 g (½ oz) tapioca flour, 35 g (1¼ oz) potato starch, 35 g (1¼ oz/⅓ cup) almond meal, ½ teaspoon xanthan gum, ½ teaspoon bicarbonate of soda (baking soda), 85 ml (2¾ fl oz) lemon juice, 85 ml (2¾ fl oz) fermented milk, ½ teaspoon natural vanilla extract

GLAZE

2 tablespoons hot water, 1 tablespoon milk, 150 g (5½ oz) icing (confectioners') sugar, 15 g (½ oz) butter, 1 small lime, 1 or 2 drops natural vanilla extract

VIETNAMESE COFFEE

SERVES 1

3 espresso coffees (25 ml/¾ fl oz each), 25 ml (¾ fl oz) sweetened condensed milk, 150 g (5½ oz) ice cubes

THE CAKE

Beat the butter and sugar in a cold bowl for 5 minutes. Add the eggs and zest of the lemons and blend in a food processor for 5 minutes; the texture should be smooth and uniform. In another bowl, mix together the flours, potato starch, almond meal, xanthan gum, bicarbonate of soda and ½ teaspoon salt. Mix the lemon juice with the fermented milk and vanilla in a glass. Combine the three mixtures. Pour the batter into a greased tin and bake at 180°C (350°C) for 45 minutes to 1 hour; the blade of a knife inserted into the cake should come out clean. For the glaze: mix the hot water and milk with the icing sugar, melted butter, lime juice and vanilla until well blended. Pour over the warm cake.

THE VIETNAMESE COFFEE

Mix the espressos and condensed milk together well. Pour over ice cubes in a glass. Serve with a straw.

Although sadly now closed, on the edge of the Silver Lake Farmers' Market, Mornings Nights Cafe was the neighbourhood café where all the locals liked to meet. As well as their delicious gluten-free cakes, you could find your caffeine fix here to get your day off to a good start.

ORIGINAL TOMMY'S
CHILLI CHEESEBURGER

MAKES 4 CHEESEBURGERS
THE CHILLI
450 g (1 lb) minced (ground) beef
1 carrot
1 beef stock cube
1 tablespoon olive oil
2 tablespoons chilli spices
½ teaspoon salt
½ teaspoon paprika
½ teaspoon garlic powder
½ teaspoon onion powder
½ teaspoon pepper
1 tablespoons cornflour (cornstarch)
1 tablespoon white vinegar
4 tablespoons plain (all-purpose) flour
1 pinch cayenne pepper

THE CHEESEBURGER
500 g (1 lb 2 oz) minced (ground) beef
Fine sea salt
8 cheddar cheese slices
4 hamburger buns (or white English muffins)
A little butter
1 onion
2 tablespoons honey mustard
1 large gherkin (pickle)
1 large oxheart tomato

For the chilli: bring the beef to the boil with 750 ml (26 fl oz/3 cups) water, the carrot and stock cube. When the water has evaporated, add the rest of the chilli ingredients. Cook on a low heat for about 2 hours. For the cheeseburger: shape the beef for the burger into four patties, season with the sea salt and cook in a hot frying pan on a high heat, 3 minutes per side for rare. Flip the burgers and lay two slices of cheddar in a star shape on each one. Halve the buns and toast for 2 minutes in a hot frying pan with a little butter. Assemble, in order: bottom half of bun, patty with melted cheese, chilli, diced onion, honey mustard, gherkin slices, slice of tomato, top half of bun.

In seventy years, few businesses can claim to
have had as many imitators. At Tommy's,
Angelenos eat in their car in the central parking
lot or at one of the stand-up tables all around.
Faithful to the wish of its founder, Tommy
Koulax, they still add 1–2 ladlefuls of chilli to
every item on the menu.

S WESTLAKE AVE & S ALVARADO ST

CHRISTINA. MELROSE TRADING POST

W OLYMPIC BLVD & S ALVARADO ST, LOS ANGELES

KITCHEN MOUSE
PARFAIT

MAKES 10 BOWLS GRANOLA

300 g (10½ oz/3 cups) rolled (porridge) oats
40 g (1½ oz) linseeds (flax seeds)
35 g (1¼ oz) pepitas (pumpkin seeds)
35 g (1¼ oz) sesame seeds
30 g (1 oz) sunflower seeds
40 g (1½ oz) chia seeds
½ teaspoon salt
60 ml (2 fl oz/¼ cup) brown rice syrup (organic food stores)
555 ml (19 fl oz) maple syrup
60 ml (2 fl oz/¼ cup) coconut oil
475 ml (16¾ fl oz) hot water
1 vanilla beans, seeds scraped
2 teaspoons natural vanilla extract
Yoghurt
Fresh fruit

Mix all of the dry ingredients together. Mix the rice syrup with 80 ml (2½ fl oz/⅓ cup) of the maple syrup. Mix the wet and dry mixtures together and place on a baking tray lined with baking paper and brushed with coconut oil. Bake in a 160°C (315°F) oven for about 30 minutes, stirring every 10 minutes. Pour 250 ml (9 fl oz/1 cup) of the hot water over the split vanilla bean and extract in a bowl. Stir. Pour in the rest of the water and the remaining maple syrup. Mix well and let the syrup cool. Discard pod. To make a parfait: pour about 80 g (2¾ oz) yoghurt into the bottom of the bowl, then the same volume of granola and fresh fruit. Top with 2–3 tablespoons of the vanilla–maple syrup.

Erika, the founder of Kitchen Mouse, fell in love with the space. She set up her café in because of its high ceilings that were reminiscent of New York, where she has spent half her life. What makes her huevos rancheros (see page 250) delicious is her recipe for enchilada sauce. Despite the crowds of customers on the day I visited, I was very touched by Erika's patience and generosity, while running one of the greatest restaurants in Los Angeles. It's somewhere I could easily eat every day, all year long.

GOMASIO BROWN RICE CAKES

SERVES 2
200 g (7 oz) cooked brown rice
1½ tablespoon sesame seeds
2 tablespoons Ponzu sauce (page 258)
2 tablespoons agave syrup
1 spring onion (scallion)
3 tablespoons coconut oil
80 g (2¾ oz) oyster mushrooms
Coriander chutney (page 260)
Lemon chilli sauce (page 258)
4 pinches gomasio
CHILLI AND PURPLE MIZUNA SALAD
A few small shishito or green chillies
1 tablespoon olive oil
1 large handful of purple mizuna

Process half the cooked rice in a food processor until a ball forms. Mix this ball with the rest of the cooked rice, along with the sesame seeds, ponzu sauce, agave syrup and finely chopped spring onion. Shape the mixture into small round pucks, about 2 cm (¾ inch) thick and 6 cm (2½ inches) wide. Cook these rice cakes in a frying pan with 2 tablespoons of the coconut oil for about 3 minutes on each side. Sauté the mushrooms in a frying pan on a high heat with the remaining coconut oil, stirring constantly. For the salad: brush the shishito chillies with olive oil and season with 2 pinches of salt. Cook them in a frying pan on a very high heat stirring regularly for about 5 minutes, or until they soften and their skin starts to bubble. Let them cool, then mix with the mizuna. Place two rice cakes and some coriander chutney on a plate, and top with the chilli and mizuna salad dressed with the lemon chilli sauce. Sprinkle each plate with gomasio.

HUEVOS RANCHEROS

SERVES 2

8 small corn tortillas
80 g (2¾ oz) Refried beans (page 261)
4 Fried eggs (page 262)
100 g (3½ oz/1 cup) grated cheddar cheese
A few green cabbage leaves
1 bunch coriander (cilantro)
A few pepitas (pumpkin seeds)
1 bulb spring onion (scallion)
1 avocado
1 small lime
ENCHILADA SAUCE
1 onion
60 ml (2 fl oz/¼ cup) olive oil
120 g (4¼ oz) crushed tomatoes
55 g (2 oz) tomato paste (concentrated purée)
30 g (1 oz) rice flour
35 g (1¼ oz) chilli powder
½ teaspoon garlic powder
1 teaspoon salt
½ teaspoon ground cumin
½ teaspoon oregano
1 pinch ground cloves
300 ml (10½ fl oz) orange juice
300 ml (10½ fl oz) vegetable stock
1 red chilli

For the enchilada sauce: sauté the diced onion with 1 tablespoon of the olive oil in a frying pan on a high heat, stirring, for 2 minutes. Reduce the heat to medium, then add the tomatoes, tomato paste, remaining olive oil and the rice flour. Cook for about 1 minute. Add the spices, orange juice and vegetable stock and cook for 5 minutes, until the mixture thickens. Sauté the chilli on a very high heat in a frying pan until scorched patches appear on the skin, about 3 minutes. Add the amount of chilli you like to the sauce and blend in a food processor. To assemble: cover a plate with enchilada sauce, place four hot tortillas on top, top with sauce, then add refried beans and two fried eggs. Add some more sauce, top with grated cheese and place the dish in the oven to melt the cheese. Add the chopped green cabbage, some coriander leaves, pepitas, sliced spring onion and half an avocado. Squeeze over a little lime juice.

ALCOVE CAFÉ & BAKERY

COBB SALAD

SERVES 2

3 tablespoons olive oil
2 tablespoons mustard
1 garlic clove
1 pinch dill
1 skinless chicken breast fillet (about 120 g/4¼ oz)
2 eggs
6 rashers smoked bacon
½ cos (romaine) lettuce
½ iceberg lettuce
2 tomatoes
80 g (2¾ oz) Bleu d'Auvergne blue cheese
1 ripe avocado
1 pretzel or half a baguette
Vinaigrette (page 259)

Whisk 2 tablespoons of the olive oil with the mustard for 2 minutes, then add the crushed garlic, dill, and a pinch each of salt and freshly ground black pepper; whisk for another 3 minutes. Place the chicken, cut into strips, in this marinade, cover and set aside in the refrigerator for at least 1 hour (or up to 12 hours). Cook the chicken in a hot frying pan on a medium heat with the remaining olive oil for 4 minutes on each side. Cook two hard-boiled eggs. Lay the bacon on a baking tray between two sheets of baking paper. Bake at 130°C (250°F) for 25 minutes. Place a mixture of the shredded lettuces in a deep plate, then arrange the diced seeded tomatoes, cooled diced marinated chicken, small squares of cooled bacon, cubes of blue cheese, a boiled egg and a sliced half avocado. Serve the pretzel and vinaigrette on the side.

The Cobb Salad is one of Los Angeles' most iconic dishes. With its vinaigrette and pretzel, the version at Alcove, which I always order with a chai tea, is my favourite.

ABBOT KINNEY BLVD & BROOKS AVE, VENICE

DANNY. BELVEDERE SKATEPARK

THE BASICS

SAUCES
BARBECUE SAUCE

½ onion
240 g (8¾ oz) tomato sauce (ketchup)
115 g (4 oz) soft brown sugar
5 g (⅛ oz) butter
240 ml (8 fl oz) water
50 ml (1½ fl oz) vinegar
1 tablespoon Worcestershire sauce
1 teaspoon salt
¼ teaspoon freshly ground black pepper
¼ teaspoon celery seeds

Chop the onion, mix with the rest of the ingredients in a saucepan and cook on a medium heat for 15 minutes, stirring regularly.

BAJA SAUCE

1 teaspoon coriander (cilantro)
60 g (2¼ oz/¼ cup) mayonnaise
60 g (2¼ oz) light crème fraîche or light sour cream
1 teaspoon lime juice
½ teaspoon mustard
1 pinch celery salt
½ pinch freshly ground black pepper
½ pinch cayenne pepper

Chop the coriander and mix with the rest of the ingredients. Place in the refrigerator for 1 hour.

SPREADING SAUCE

110 g (3¾ oz) mayonnaise
110 g (3¾ oz) tomato sauce (ketchup)
1 teaspoon Savora mustard sauce
2 tablespoons cornichons (baby gherkins)
½ teaspoon salt
½ teaspoon freshly ground black pepper
½ teaspoon sugar
1 teaspoon cider vinegar

Whisk together the mayonnaise, tomato sauce and Savora. Mix in the finely diced cornichons and the other ingredients. Mix vigorously for 2 minutes. The sauce should be smooth and thick.

RANCH HOUSE SAUCE

10 g (¼ oz) parsley
15 g (½ oz) parmesan cheese
1 garlic clove
180 g (6½ oz) mayonnaise
120 g (4¼ oz) buttermilk
1 pinch tarragon
1 pinch dill
1 pinch chives
1 teaspoon mustard
1 teaspoon onion powder
½ teaspoon salt
½ teaspoon freshly ground black pepper

Mix together the chopped parsley, grated parmesan cheese, crushed garlic and the rest of the ingredients. Set aside in the refrigerator for at least 30 minutes.

PEANUT SAUCE

1 garlic clove
120 g (4¼ oz) peanut butter
2 tablespoons soy sauce
1 tablespoon sesame oil
1 teaspoon soft brown sugar
1 teaspoon lemon juice
125 ml (4 fl oz/½ cup) water

Crush the garlic and blend with the rest of the ingredients in a food processor for 1 minute.

THAI SAUCE

4 garlic cloves
200 g (7 oz) peanut butter
230 ml (7¾ fl oz) hoisin sauce
60 ml (2 fl oz/¼ cup) water
4 tablespoons sesame oil
2 tablespoons wine vinegar
2 tablespoons oyster sauce (Asian food stores)
2 tablespoons honey
2 teaspoons ground ginger
2 teaspoons soy sauce
2 pinches cayenne pepper

Chop and crush the garlic and mix with the rest of the ingredients in a saucepan. Bring to the boil on a medium heat, stirring. Cook for 1 minute, then remove from the heat.

BUFFALO SAUCE

150 ml (5 fl oz) Tabasco sauce
100 g (3½ oz) butter
20 ml (½ fl oz) white vinegar
½ teaspoon Worcestershire sauce
½ teaspoon cayenne pepper
½ teaspoon garlic powder
½ teaspoon celery salt
½ teaspoon white pepper

Mix everything together and bring to the boil, stirring constantly. When the sauce comes to the boil, take off the heat but keep stirring well.

HOLLANDAISE SAUCE

200 g (7 oz) butter
4 egg yolks
15 ml (½ fl oz) lemon juice
1 teaspoon mustard
1 pinch salt
1 pinch freshly ground black pepper

Melt the butter on a low heat, without stirring. Place the egg yolks in a heavy-based saucepan. On a very low heat, whisk the eggs for at least 5 minutes; the volume must at least double without the eggs cooking. Gently incorporate the melted butter, continuing to whisk. When the sauce has doubled in volume, add the lemon and mix it in. Add the mustard, salt and pepper.

RUSSIAN SAUCE

40 g (1½ oz) mayonnaise
30 g (1 oz) light crème fraîche (or light sour cream)
25 g (1 oz) tomato sauce (ketchup)
15 ml (½ fl oz) cornichons (baby gherkins)
15 ml (½ fl oz) lemon juice
1 teaspoon horseradish
1 pinch salt
1 pinch freshly ground black pepper

Mix the mayonnaise, crème fraîche and tomato sauce together well for 3 minutes. Add the diced cornichons and the other ingredients, mix together for 3 minutes.

CAESAR SALAD SAUCE

MAKES 500 ML (17 FL OZ/2 CUPS)

45 g (1½ oz) parmesan cheese
25 ml (¾ fl oz) wine vinegar
25 ml (¾ fl oz) balsamic vinegar
¾ teaspoon Tabasco sauce
1 teaspoon Worcestershire sauce
1 tinned anchovy in oil
25 g (1 oz) mustard
25 ml (¾ fl oz) lemon juice
1 teaspoon salt
1 teaspoon freshly ground black pepper
400 g (14 oz) mayonnaise

Blend the grated parmesan cheese and the rest of the ingredients, except the mayonnaise, in a food processor. The texture should be smooth and creamy. Add the mayonnaise, whisk, and add some water if necessary.

TARTARE SAUCE

2 large gherkins (pickles)
1 tablespoon capers
120 g (4¼ oz/½ cup) mayonnaise
1 tablespoon wine vinegar
1 teaspoon mustard
1 pinch freshly ground black pepper
1 pinch salt

Mix the diced gherkins, chopped capers and the remaining ingredients in short bursts in a food processor until well mixed but not puréed.

SMOKY TOMATO SAUCE

200 g (7 oz) tomato sauce (ketchup)
130 g (4½ oz) tomato paste (concentrated purée)
15 g (½ oz) soft brown sugar
80 ml (2½ fl oz/⅓ cup) water
2 teaspoons chilli spice mix
1 teaspoon liquid smoke (American food stores)
2 tablespoons grapeseed oil

Mix all the ingredients together in a saucepan, bring to the boil and cook for 1 hour.

TAHINI SAUCE

240 g (8¾ oz) tahini (Middle Eastern or organic food stores)
470 ml (16½ fl oz) water
60 ml (2 fl oz/¼ cup) lemon juice
1 pinch salt
1 pinch freshly ground black pepper
½ pinch cayenne pepper

Mix all of the ingredients together in a blender on minimum speed for 20 seconds.

SPICY MAYONNAISE

20 g (¾ oz) parmesan cheese
120 g (4¼ oz) Kewpie (Japanese) mayonnaise (Asian food stores)
30 g (1 oz) sriracha sauce
1 teaspoon lime juice
1 teaspoon sambal oelek (Asian food stores)

Finely grate the parmesan and mix vigorously with the rest of the ingredients.

SOY-MUSTARD SAUCE

50 g (1¾ oz) soy sauce
50 g (1¾ oz) mustard

Gradually whisk the soy sauce into the mustard.

SOY-GINGER SAUCE

470 ml (16½ fl oz) water
50 g (1¾ oz) fresh ginger
235 ml (8 fl oz) organic soy sauce

Bring the water to the boil with the ginger, peeled and sliced into rounds. Reduce the heat to a low simmer. Cover and cook for 20 minutes. Add the soy sauce and cook for another 5 minutes.

HONEY MUSTARD SAUCE

65 g (2¼ oz) mustard
100 g (3½ oz) honey
1 teaspoon thyme
30 g (1 oz) mustard seeds

Vigorously mix all the ingredients together. Place in the refrigerator.

LEMON CHILLI SAUCE

1 tablespoon freshly chopped ginger
2 tablespoons sriracha sauce (Asian food stores)
1 teaspoon salt
125 ml (4 fl oz/½ cup) lemon juice
125 ml (4 fl oz/½ cup) olive oil
1 teaspoon chives

Blend the sliced ginger, sriracha sauce and salt in a food processor, with enough lemon juice so they mix together. Pour in the olive oil, the rest of the lemon juice and the chives. Mix.

PONZU SAUCE

2 tablespoons soy sauce
1½ tablespoons dashi (home-made or from a cube, from Japanese food stores)
1 tablespoon lime juice
2 teaspoons rice vinegar
1 tablespoon mirin (Asian food stores)
1 tablespoon soft brown sugar

Mix together all of the ingredients and let it sit for at least 1 hour.

CHIPOTLE AIOLI

20 g (¾ oz) chipotle chillies in adobo sauce (in tins from specialty food stores)
1 garlic clove
40 g (1½ oz) tomato sauce (ketchup)
80 g (2¾ oz) mayonnaise

Mixed together the chopped chipotle chillies, the very finely chopped garlic, tomato sauce and mayonnaise until smooth.

TOMATO PIZZA SAUCE

500 g (1 lb 2 oz) whole peeled tomatoes (tinned)
½ onion
1 anchovy in oil (tinned)
2 tablespoons olive oil
1 tablespoon mixed dried herbs

Purée the tomatoes in a food processor, then bring to the boil with the chopped half onion and anchovy with a drizzle of olive oil. Reduce the heat to the lowest setting and cook for 1 hour, stirring regularly. Add the mixed herbs.

HARISSA

6 red capsicums (peppers)
480 ml (16½ fl oz) olive oil
2 tablespoons salt
3 tablespoons cumin seeds
1 tablespoon fennel seeds
1 tablespoon caraway seeds
1 tablespoon freshly ground black pepper
5 medium garlic cloves
2 tablespoons smoked paprika

Brush the capsicums with olive oil, sprinkle with 1 tablespoon salt, and cook in a 220°C (425°F) oven for 6 minutes. Place the whole spices on another baking tray and cook for another 6 minutes. Blend the cooled chopped roasted capsicums with the garlic in a food processor. Grind the toasted spices and add them to the capsicum purée with some paprika. Blend in a food processor until smooth. Add the remaining salt and the pepper and mix in slowly. Stir in the olive oil gradually until the colour lightens and the mixture is creamy.

HARISSA HOLLANDAISE

200 g (7 oz) butter
4 egg yolks
15 ml (½ fl oz) lemon juice
1 teaspoon mustard
1½ tablespoons harissa paste (tube)
1 pinch salt
1 pinch freshly ground black pepper

Melt the butter on a low heat, without stirring. Place the egg yolks in a saucepan. Place the saucepan on a very low heat (or over simmering water). Whisk the eggs for at least 5 minutes. The volume should at least double, without the eggs cooking, so no steam or smoke should appear. Incorporate the melted butter very gently, continuing to whisk. When the sauce has doubled in volume, add the lemon juice and mix it in. Add the mustard, harissa, salt and pepper, then mix.

VINAIGRETTE

2 tablespoons olive oil
1 tablespoon balsamic vinegar
1 teaspoon mustard
1 teaspoon honey
1 pinch salt
1 pinch freshly ground black pepper

Whisk the olive oil with the vinegar, add the mustard and mix, then add the honey and mix again. Season with salt and pepper.

LEMON VINAIGRETTE

125 ml (4 fl oz/½ cup) olive oil
60 ml (2 fl oz/¼ cup) wine vinegar
1 small bunch curly-leaf parsley
1 garlic clove
45 ml (1½ fl oz) lemon juice
30 g (1 oz) mustard
1 teaspoon oregano
½ teaspoon salt
½ teaspoon freshly ground black pepper

Emulsify the olive oil with the wine vinegar. Mix with the chopped parsley, crushed garlic and the rest of the ingredients, then transfer to a resealable container that can be used as a shaker. Shake vigorously before pouring over a salad.

CONDIMENTS

CONFIT GARLIC

Olive oil
24 garlic cloves

Pour enough olive oil into a saucepan to cover the peeled garlic cloves. Cook the cloves in the oil, kept at a bare simmer but under boiling point, for between 45 minutes and 1 hour. The cloves should be tender but not falling apart. Pour into a jar with a lid.

PICKLED GREEN CHILLIES

MAKES 1 JAR

1 garlic clove
400 ml (14 fl oz) white vinegar
200 g (7 oz) sugar
400 ml (14 fl oz) water
½ teaspoon salt
1 pinch cinnamon
1 pinch turmeric
3 bay leaves
200 g (7 oz) small green chillies

Crush the garlic and bring all the ingredients, except the chillies, to the boil in a saucepan on a medium heat. Add the chillies and cook, covered, on a low heat for 15 minutes. Pour into a glass jar. Cool at room temperature. It will be ready after 3 days and keeps for up to 1 week.

CUCUMBER & RADISH PICKLES

340 g (11¾ oz) cucumbers
200 g (7 oz) radishes
1 teaspoon salt
40 g (1½ oz) sugar
130 ml (4¼ fl oz) white vinegar
200 ml (7 fl oz) water

Slice the cucumbers and radishes into rounds, toss with the salt and let them drain for at least 1 hour, stirring after 30 minutes. Dissolve the sugar in the vinegar and water in a bowl. Put the drained vegetables into a jar, pour over the liquid and refrigerate for at least 24 hours.

PICKLED RED ONIONS

1 litre (35 fl oz/4 cups) red wine vinegar
3 garlic cloves
5 red onions

Pour the vinegar and garlic into a large saucepan on a medium heat, bring to the boil and cook for 5 minutes. Add the onions and bring back to the boil. Cook on a low heat, covered, for 10 minutes. Drain the onions, keeping the liquid. Place the onions in a bowl with the garlic, pour the liquid over and cool. Place in the refrigerator for at least 24 hours.

PICKLED CUCUMBERS

900 g (2 lb) small cucumbers
145 g (5 oz) kosher salt (American food stores)
480 ml (17 fl oz) white vinegar
480 ml (17 fl oz) cider vinegar
240 ml (8 fl oz) water
130 g (4½ oz) sugar
1 tablespoon cumin
1 tablespoon mustard seeds
1 teaspoon chilli powder

Slice the cucumbers into rounds. Combine all the other ingredients in a saucepan on a medium heat and bring to the boil. Continue stirring until the sugar has completely dissolved. Turn off the heat and allow to cool for 15 minutes. Pour the liquid over the cucumbers placed in a container or resealable jar. Let them stand for at least 4 hours and keep up to 2 days.

PICKLED WHITE ONIONS

70 ml (2¼ fl oz) white vinegar
70 ml (2¼ fl oz) water
160 g (5½ oz) onions
1 sprig thyme
1 pinch fennel seeds

Bring the vinegar, water, chopped onions, thyme and fennel seeds to the boil. Turn off the heat and allow to cool. Place the onions and liquid in a jar, consume within 2 days.

CORIANDER CHUTNEY

1 bunch coriander (cilantro)
1 handful cashews
1 small cube fresh ginger
1 red chilli
2 teaspoons salt
Juice of 1 lime

Blend all the ingredients together in a food processor.

ROASTED TOMATOES

5 tomatoes
2 tablespoons olive oil
2 garlic cloves
1 teaspoon oregano
½ teaspoon paprika
1 teaspoon thyme
2 bay leaves
1 tablespoon salt
¼ teaspoon freshly ground black pepper
½ teaspoon sugar

Preheat the oven to 160°C (315°F), then cut the tomatoes into quarters and remove the pulp and seeds and reserve. Pour over the olive oil and add the diced garlic and all the herbs, spices and sugar to the tomatoes. Make sure the tomatoes, skin and flesh, are well coated with the oil and seasonings. Transfer the tomatoes to a baking tray lined with baking paper. Pour over the reserved tomato pulp. Bake for about 45 minutes – stop cooking before the tomatoes start to collapse. When cool, transfer to a plastic container with a lid, and use within 3–4 days.

PEPPERCORN MIX

100 g (3½ oz/⅔ cup) black peppercorns
50 g (1¾ oz/⅔ cup) white peppercorns
25 g (1 oz) long pepper (gourmet delicatessens)
15 g (½ oz) pink peppercorns
10 g (¼ oz) sichuan peppercorns
Vegetable oil

Toast all of the peppercorns separately in a hot frying pan lightly brushed with vegetable oil for 2 minutes. Once they have cooled, mix them together and crush using a mortar and pestle.

SIDES
KALE SIDE

MAKES 1 SERVE

1 French shallot
1 garlic clove
2 tablespoons vegetable oil
135 g (4¾ oz) kale
500 ml (17 fl oz/2 cups) water
60 ml (2 fl oz/¼ cup) soy sauce
1 small piece fresh ginger
2 tablespoons sesame oil
1 handful pomegranate seeds

Sauté the finely chopped shallot and crushed garlic in the vegetable oil on a high heat for 3 minutes. Reduce the heat to medium, add the roughly chopped kale and cook for 3 minutes, stirring. Mix together the water, soy sauce, finely chopped ginger and sesame oil and pour into the frying pan. Cook for about 5 minutes, stirring, until the kale softens. Serve cold with the pomegranate seeds.

GUACAMOLE

4 avocados
1 lime
200 g (7 oz) tomatoes
40 g (1½ oz) onion
1 teaspoon cumin
1 teaspoon paprika
Tabasco sauce (or 1 green chilli)
½ bunch coriander (cilantro)
10 g (¼ oz) salt
½ teaspoon freshly ground black pepper
25 ml (¾ fl oz) olive oil

Mix together the mashed avocados, lime juice, diced tomatoes, chopped onion, cumin and paprika, 2–3 drops of Tabasco sauce (or the green chilli, seeded and very finely chopped) and the chopped coriander leaves. Season and pour in the olive oil.

REFRIED BEANS

450 g (1 lb) dried red kidney beans
2.8 litres (98 fl oz) water
2 teaspoons salt
1 bay leaf
2 onions
1 chicken stock cube
3 tablespoons lard or 30 ml (1 fl oz)
vegetable oil
3 garlic cloves
1 jalapeño

Soak the dried beans overnight in the water with the salt. The next day, rinse thoroughly to remove any small stones. Bring the water to the boil with the bay leaf, 1 chopped onion and the crumbled chicken stock cube. Reduce the heat and simmer very gently, covered, for about 2½ hours, or until the beans are tender and lose their skin. Remove the onion and bay leaf, drain the beans and keep the cooking liquid. Heat the lard on a high heat in a deep frying pan, add the crushed garlic, the other chopped onion and seeded and sliced jalapeño. Cook for about 3 minutes, stirring, until softened not browned. On a medium heat, add some of the cooked beans and 250 ml (9 fl oz/1 cup) of the cooking liquid. Mix together well. Mash the beans to the consistency of a dry purée. Cook for about 5 minutes longer. Repeat the process and season with salt and freshly ground black pepper.

RECIPES
CHILLI

50 ml (1½ fl oz) canola oil
900 g (2 lb) minced (ground) beef
180 g (6½ oz) onions
1 generous tablespoon finely chopped garlic
3 tablespoons chilli powder
¾ teaspoon ground cumin
¼ teaspoon red chilli flakes
1 teaspoon oregano
120 g (4¼ oz) tomato paste (concentrated purée)
2 beef stock cubes
550 g (1 lb 4 oz) drained red kidney beans

Heat the canola oil on a medium heat in a large frying pan. Cook the minced beef, stirring, for 6 minutes, or until browned. Drain off the fat and transfer the cooked beef to a wide rondeau-style pan (a wide shallow saucepan). In the same frying pan you cooked the beef in, fry the diced onions and finely chopped garlic for 5 minutes. Take off the heat. Add the chilli powder, cumin, chilli flakes and oregano. Stir to mix through the garlic and onions well. Add the tomato paste. Return to the heat on a low temperature and stir for 5 minutes. Add 850 ml (29½ fl oz) beef stock, made up with the stock cubes, according to the instructions on the packet. Stir for another 2 minutes until well mixed. Transfer everything to the rondeau pan with the drained beef and season with salt and freshly ground black pepper. Bring everything to the boil on a medium heat. Reduce the heat to low, half-cover the pan and let it simmer for 1¼ hours. Add the drained beans, stir and cook for another 15 minutes.

TEMPURA PRAWNS
SERVES 1

40 g (1½ oz) plain (all-purpose) flour
40 g (1½ oz) cornflour (cornstarch)
1 egg yolk
½ teaspoon salt
½ teaspoon sugar
75 ml (2¼ fl oz) iced soda water (club soda)
2 litres (70 fl oz/8 cups) peanut oil
200 g (7 oz) prawns (shrimp)

Mix together the flours, egg yolk, salt and sugar. Gradually mix in the iced soda water and stir vigorously. Heat the peanut oil in a deep-fryer or frying pan on a medium heat. Dip the prawns in the batter, then deep-fry each prawn for about 1½ minutes until golden brown. Drain each prawn on paper towel.

VINEGARED SUSHI RICE

6 sushi = 150 g (5½ oz); 1 maki = 25 g (1 oz) rice ; 1 tango roll = between 4 and 6 maki
300 g (10½ oz) white rice
35 ml (1 fl oz) white rice vinegar (Asian food stores)
1½ tablespoons sugar
1 pinch salt

Wash the rice three times in fresh water in a perforated pan. Let the rice rest for 40 minutes in cold water. Drain and let the rice dry for 10 minutes. Cook, covered, for 10 minutes on a high heat or until steam appears, then for 10 minutes on a low heat. In a small saucepan on a low heat, whisk together the vinegar, sugar and salt for 5 minutes, the sugar must be dissolved. Mix this liquid into the rice, stirring constantly, until the rice reaches room temperature.

FRIED EGGS

Heat some olive oil in a frying pan, add the egg white first, then the yolk when the white starts to simmer. Using a spatula, cover the yolk with the white, rotating the frying pan so that you make a ball. Place on paper towel.

POACHED EGGS

Place some plastic wrap in a small bowl and pour in a few drops of olive oil. Break the egg into the bowl and tie the plastic wrap into a knot on top to enclose the egg. Repeat the process for each egg to make four 'bulbs'. Fill a large saucepan two-thirds full with water and bring to the boil. Turn off the heat and wait for the bubbles to disappear. Place the four eggs in the water and let them cook for 3½ minutes. Remove the eggs from the water, then cut off the knot to remove the eggs without piercing them.

PIZZA DOUGH

MAKES 4 BASES

10 g (¼ oz) sugar
1 tablespoon treacle or molasses
450 ml (16 fl oz) water
10 g (¼ oz) fresh yeast (from bakery)
10 ml (¼ fl oz) olive oil
750 g (1 lb 10 oz) soft (T45) flour or plain (all-purpose) flour
15 g (½ oz) coarse salt

Dissolve the sugar and treacle in the water heated to 40°C (104°F), add the yeast and mix with your fingers. Pour 90 per cent of the oil into the water and mix for 1 minute. Add the flour and salt. Put the mixture into an electric standmixer and knead on low speed for about 3 minutes. Add the rest of the oil and knead on medium speed for 4 minutes. Divide the dough into four portions, knead and form into balls. Place each oiled ball in an oiled bowl, cover with plastic wrap and place in the refrigerator for 3 days. The dough is ready when you can see small dark fermentation bubbles.

CORNED BEEF

SERVES 2

1 kg (2 lb 4 oz) chuck or blade beef
THE BRINE
2 litres (70 fl oz/8 cups) water
2 teaspoons paprika
½ cinnamon stick
2 teaspoons freshly ground black pepper
2 teaspoons mustard seeds
2 teaspoons ground ginger
2 teaspoons chilli
4 teaspoons quatre-épices (French spice mix)
1 teaspoon dried thyme
3 garlic cloves, bruised
200 g (7 oz) coarse sea salt
100 g (3½ oz) soft brown sugar

Rinse and dry the beef. Make a few holes in the meat with a thin meat fork or large needle. For the brine: bring the water to the boil, add all of the brining ingredients and mix. Once the sugar and salt have dissolved, or after about 3 minutes, remove from the heat. Place the liquid in the refrigerator. Pour the cold liquid over the meat in a suitable deep, clear container or in a large zip-lock bag. The meat needs to be kept completely submerged for the whole time it is in the refrigerator. Use a small plate to keep the meat submerged if needed. Check the meat is still submerged every day. Leave in the refrigerator for between 10 days and 6 weeks.

DRINKS
HOME-MADE LEMONADE

MAKES 1 LITRE (35 FL OZ/4 CUPS)

3 tablespoons honey
750 ml (26 fl oz/3 cups) mineral water
250 ml (9 fl oz/1 cup) fresh lemon juice
2 or 3 sprigs mint

Bring the honey and 250 ml (9 fl oz/1 cup) of the water to the boil. Mix together and cool at room temperature, cover and place in the refrigerator. Mix the lemon juice (seeds removed but not the pulp) with the remaining water, then combine the two mixtures. Add some bruised mint leaves. Serve well chilled.

PACIFIC COAST HIGHWAY AND GETTY VILLA DR, MALIBU

ADDRESS BOOK

WEST LOS ANGELES

THE APPLE PAN
10801 W Pico Blvd, Los Angeles, CA 90064, USA

SANTA MONICA

THAI DISHES
1910 Wilshire Blvd, Santa Monica, CA 90403, USA

SANTA MONICA SEAFOOD MARKET & CAFÉ
1000 Wilshire Blvd, Santa Monica, CA 90401, USA

PINKBERRY
1456 3rd St, Promenade, Santa Monica, CA 90401, USA

CORA'S COFFEE SHOPPE
1802 Ocean Ave, #B, Santa Monica, CA 90401, USA

LA URBAN FITNESS
3015 Main St, Santa Monica, CA 90405, USA

BRENTWOOD

A VOTRE SANTE
13016 San Vicente Blvd, Los Angeles, CA 90049, USA

FARMSHOP
Brentwood Country Mart, 225 26th St #25, Santa Monica, CA 90402, USA

SAWTELLE

HARA SUSHI INC
12222 Wilshire Blvd #101, Los Angeles, CA 90025, USA

DOWN TOWN LOS ANGELES

GRAND CENTRAL MARKET
317 S Broadway, Los Angeles, CA 90013, USA

SPRINKLES CUPCAKES
735 S Figueroa St, Los Angeles, CA 90017, USA

CALIFORNIA PIZZA KITCHEN
735 S Figueroa St #305, Los Angeles, CA 90017, USA

IMPRESSO CAFE
1115 S Hope St, Los Angeles, CA 90015, USA

INTELLIGENTSIA COFFEE COFFEEBAR
3922 W Sunset Blvd, Los Angeles, CA 90029, USA

CHINATOWN

PHILIPPE THE ORIGINAL
1001 N Alameda St, Los Angeles, CA 90012, USA

UNIVERSITY PARK

JACKS N JOE
2498 S Figueroa St, Los Angeles, CA 90007, USA

LOS ANGELES TRADE-TECHNICAL COLLEGE
400 W Washington Blvd, Los Angeles, CA 90015, USA

ART DISTRICT

ZINC CAFE & MARKET & BAR
580 Mateo St, Los Angeles, CA 90013, USA

PIZZANISTA!
2019 E 7th St, Los Angeles, CA 90021, USA

HERMOSA BEACH

PARADISE BOWLS
1246 Hermosa Ave, Hermosa Beach, CA 90254, USA

ABIGAILE
1301 Manhattan Ave, Hermosa Beach, CA 90254, USA

INGLEWOOD

PANN'S RESTAURANT
6710 La Tijera Blvd, Los Angeles, CA 90045, USA

RANDY'S DONUTS
805 W Manchester Blvd, Inglewood, CA 90301, USA

HUNTINGTON PARK

IN-N-OUT BURGER
6000 Pacific Blvd, Huntington Park, CA 90255, USA

HOLLYWOOD

BEACHWOOD CAFE
2695 N Beachwood Dr, Los Angeles, CA 90068, USA

HOLLYWOOD FARMERS' MARKET
DTLA CHEESE / PRESS BROTHERS
JUICERY / EGGSLUT
1600 Ivar Ave, Los Angeles, CA 90028, USA

THE OINKSTER HOLLYWOOD
776 Vine St, Los Angeles, CA 90038, USA

JOE'S PIZZA
6504 Hollywood Blvd, Los Angeles, CA 90028, USA

BEVERLY

CANTER'S DELI
419 N Fairfax Ave, Los Angeles, CA 90036, USA

FREE RANGE
8400 Melrose Pl, West Hollywood, CA 90069, USA

JOAN'S ON THIRD
8350 W 3rd St, Los Angeles, CA 90048, USA

FAIRFAX

PINK'S HOT DOGS
709 N La Brea Ave, Los Angeles, CA 90039, USA

MELROSE TRADING POST
7850 Melrose Ave, Los Angeles, CA 90046, USA

STUDIO CITY

BARREL AND ASHES
11801 Ventura Blvd, Studio City, CA 91604, USA

BURBANK

CHILI JOHN'S
2018 W Burbank Blvd, Burbank, CA 91506, USA

LARRY'S CHILI DOG
3122 W Burbank Blvd, Burbank, CA 91505, USA

VENICE

KREATION KAFE & JUICERY
1202 Abbot Kinney Blvd, Venice, CA 90291, USA

KOMODO
235 Main St, Venice, CA 90291, USA

ABBOT'S PIZZA COMPANY
1407 Abbot Kinney Blvd, Venice, CA 90291, USA

GJELINA TAKE AWAY
1427 Abbot Kinney Blvd, Venice, CA 90291, USA

GJUSTA
320 Sunset Ave, Venice, CA 90291, USA

POKE-POKE
2011 Ocean Front Walk, Venice, CA 90291, USA

PLANT FOOD AND WINE
1009 Abbot Kinney Blvd, Venice, CA 90291, USA

1701 OCEAN FRONT WALK
1701 Ocean Front Walk, Venice, CA 90291, USA

MAR VISTA

MITSUWA MARKETPLACE SANTOUKA/SANUKI
3760 S Centinela Ave, Los Angeles, CA 90066, USA

VENTURA

THE FARMER AND THE COOK
339 W El Roblar Dr, Ojai, CA 93023, USA

MALIBU

NEPTUNE'S NET SEAFOOD RESTAURANT
42505 Pacific Coast Hwy, Malibu, CA 90265, USA

PACIFIC PALISADES

CAFFE' DELFINI
147 W Channel Rd, Santa Monica, CA 90402, USA

SILVER LAKE

NATUREWELL
3824 Sunset Blvd, Los Angeles, CA 90026, USA

TACOS DELTA
3806 Sunset Blvd, Los Angeles, CA 90026, USA

MORNINGS NIGHTS CAFE
1523 Griffith Park Blvd, Los Angeles, CA 90026, USA
NOW CLOSED

WESTLAKE

ORIGINAL TOMMY'S
2575 W Beverly Blvd, Los Angeles, CA 90057, USA

HIGHLAND PARK

KITCHEN MOUSE
5904 N Figueroa St, Los Angeles, CA 90042, USA

LOS FELIZ

ALCOVE CAFE & BAKERY
1929 Hillhurst Ave, Los Angeles, CA 90027, USA

INDEX

PICKLE (GHERKIN)
Salmon plate · 186

PINEAPPLE
Kale jungle bowl · 178
Spinach & pineapple juice · 126
Vitality smoothie · 56

PISTACHIO NUT KERNEL
Vegan lasagne · 202

PIZZA
BBQ chicken pizza · 132
Guanciale pizza · 182
Kale pizza · 34
Mac & cheese pizza · 84
Pizza dough · 262
Salad pizza · 168
Thai chicken pizza · 52

PLANT MILK
Multigrain porridge · 190

PLANT PROTEIN POWDER
Muscle Beach Venice smoothie · 18

POLENTA (CORNMEAL)
Hoecake · 154

POMEGRANATE
Frozen yoghurt · 20

PORCHETTA
Porchetta sandwich · 180

PORK
Pork ramen · 208
Tacos al pastor · 234

POTATO
Chicken wings hash brown · 100
Eggs Benedict · 103
Guacamole & cheddar fries hot dog · 146
Mulligatawny soup · 212

PRAWN (SHRIMP)
Cioppino (fish and seafood stew) · 22
Corona maki roll · 42
Prawn pad thai · 30
Prawn tacos · 170
Tango maki roll · 40
Tempura prawns · 261

PROVOLONE CHEESE
Egg-kale open sandwich · 184

QUINOA
Fez bowl · 120
Multigrain porridge · 190

RADISH
Avocado & radish toast · 80
Banh-mi chicken taco · 172
Cucumber & radish pickles · 259

RAPINI (BROCCOLI RABE)
Porchetta sandwich · 180

RASPBERRY
Muscle Beach Venice smoothie · 18

RED KIDNEY BEANS
Chilaquiles · 236
Chilli spaghetti bowl · 156
Huevos rancheros · 250
Refried beans · 261

RED WINE
Sangria · 220

RICE
Chicken breakfast burrito · 14
Chilaquiles · 236
Corona maki roll · 42
Gomasio brown rice cakes · 248
Mulligatawny soup · 212
Mushroom bowl · 194

Sophia bowl · 116
Tacos al pastor · 234
Tango maki roll · 40
Vinegared sushi rice · 262
Veggie burger & kale side · 122
Veggie garden wrap · 32

RICE PAPER
Corona maki roll · 42

RICOTTA CHEESE
Avocado-pesto-ricotta toast · 62
Avocado toast · 54
Mac & cheese pizza · 84

ROLLED (PORRIDGE) OATS
Granola · 196
Multigrain porridge · 190
Parfait · 246
Porridge · 114

SAGE
Fried chicken sandwich · 98

SAKE
Sake bomb · 44

SAUERKRAUT
Corned beef Reuben sandwich · 136

SESAME SEED
Corona maki roll · 42
Gomasio brown rice cakes · 248
Granola · 196
Parfait · 246

SMOKED SALMON
Salmon open sandwich · 184
Salmon plate · 186

SOY SAUCE
Ponzu sauce · 258
Soy-ginger sauce · 258
Soy-mustard sauce · 258

SPAGHETTI
Chilli spaghetti bowl · 156

SPINACH (ENGLISH)
Eggs Benedict · 103
Kale jungle bowl · 178
Spinach & pineapple juice · 126
Vegan lasagne · 202
Veggie garden wrap · 32
Vitality smoothie · 56

SPRING ONION (SCALLION)
Beef udon · 209
Pork ramen · 208
Prawn pad thai · 30
Thai chicken pizza · 52

SRIRACHA
Lemon chilli sauce · 258
Spicy mayonnaise · 258

STRAWBERRY
Acai breakfast bowl · 90
Fried chicken sandwich & spicy strawberry jam · 138
Frozen yoghurt · 20
Granola breakfast bowl · 230
Strawberry lemonade · 150
Strawberry smoothie · 88

SUNFLOWER SEED
Granola · 196
Parfait · 246

SWEET POTATO
Mulligatawny soup · 212

SWORDFISH
Swordfish sliders · 26

TABASCO SAUCE
Buffalo sauce · 257

TAHINI
Tahini sauce · 258

TOFU
Sophia bowl · 116

TOMATO
Avocado cheeseburger · 160
BBQ chicken pizza · 132
Chicken breakfast burrito · 14
Chilaquiles · 236
Chilli cheeseburger · 240
Cioppino (fish and seafood stew) · 22
Double cheeseburger · 108
Egg-kale open sandwich · 184
Eggs Benedict · 103
Grilled cheese with tomato · 144
Guacamole · 260
Guanciale pizza · 182
Huevos rancheros · 250
Mushroom bowl · 194
Prawn tacos · 170
Roasted tomatoes · 260
Salad pizza · 168
Swordfish sliders · 26
Tomato pizza sauce · 258
Vegan lasagne · 202
Veggie burger & kale side · 122
Veggie garden wrap · 32
Zucchini spaghetti bolognese · 222

TOMATO SAUCE (KETCHUP)
Barbecue sauce · 257
Chipotle aïoli · 258
Russian sauce · 257
Smoky tomato sauce · 258
Spreading sauce · 257

TORTILLA
Banh-mi chicken taco · 172
Chicken breakfast burrito · 14
Chicken-cheese pitta · 126
Chilaquiles · 236
Huevos rancheros · 250
Kimchi nachos · 174
Prawn tacos · 170
Tacos al pastor · 234
Veggie garden wrap · 32

TRUFFLE CHEESE
Asparagus & mushroom focaccia · 188

TUNA
Hawaiian tuna poke · 200

VANILLA (EXTRACT AND BEAN)
Banana cream pie · 70
French toast · 102
Multigrain porridge · 190
Parfait · 246
Porridge · 114
Vanilla cupcakes · 50

VANILLA ICE CREAM
Hot fudge sundae · 152

VEAL
Zucchini spaghetti bolognese · 222

WAKAME
Beef udon · 209

WALNUTS
Avocado-pesto-ricotta toast · 62
Kale side · 122
Porridge · 114

WHITE FISH
Cioppino (fish and seafood stew) · 22

ZUCCHINI (COURGETTE)
Vegan lasagne · 202
Veggie garden wrap · 32
Zucchini spaghetti bolognese · 222

RECIPE INDEX

ROADWAY INN. VINE ST